'SECULAR CHRISTIANITY' AND GOD WHO ACTS

'Secular Christianity' and God Who Acts

by

Robert J. Blaikie

WILLIAM B. EERDMANS PUBLISHING COMPANY
GRAND RAPIDS, MICHIGAN

Printed in the United States of America

To

MOTHER

Contents

		page
Foreword by Professor Torrance		9
Preface		11
INTRODUCTORY		13

PART I

THE SHAPE OF THE PROBLEM:

The Secular and the Biblical

Chapter

1	The Secular Presupposition	37
2	The Biblical Presupposition	48
3	The Acts of God in 'Secular Christianity' and in Biblical Theology	63

PART II

THE SECULAR OUTLOOK AND ITS CONSEQUENCES

4	Science and Human Action	77
5	Existentialist Theology and Action	89
6	Linguistic Theology and Action	103
7	History and Action – On a Secular Base	122

PART III

TOWARDS A MODERN BIBLICAL THEOLOGY

8	History and Action – Towards a Better Foundation	139
9	The Supernatural and Action – 'Miracles'	162
10	Subject, Object, and Action	181
11	Time, Eternity, and God Who Acts – Some Modern Views	202

CONCLUSION: A CALL FOR INTEGRITY	215
Notes	233
Subject Index	249
Index of Names	254

Foreword

This is a book of remarkable candour, sound judgment and downright integrity, clearly written and well argued, which it is most refreshing and exciting to read. I would bespeak for it a warm welcome by Christians of all Communions as a work that really gets to grips with difficulties that have perplexed and confused so many people, and helpfully guides them into a saner and better-grounded understanding of the Christian message in the modern world.

In recent years many people, some of them very eminent, have been putting abroad a reinterpretation of the New Testament witness to Jesus Christ and His Gospel in which there is no miracle, no resurrection of the body, and no belief in a life after death. This is a thoroughly secularized version of Christianity in which the world is regarded in complete detachment from God and God is relegated to some realm of inertia from which any interaction on His part with nature or history is ruled out altogether. High claims are advanced for this 'secular Christianity', that it is forced upon us by a scientific understanding of the universe and an enlightened scholarly approach to the Bible. Mr Blaikie, however, is not intimidated by these claims, for he is convinced that they are bound up with an obsolete conception of the universe, deriving from the eighteenth and nineteenth centuries, as a closed mechanical system in which all things are to be explained naturalistically through unbreakable chains of cause and effect. He takes his own stand firmly in the twentieth century of Relativity Theory and Quantum Mechanics, and argues powerfully for a modern understanding of the Biblical account of God as the God who really acts, and succeeds in bringing sanity and honesty into the interpretation of the Scriptures in a way that men of common sense and sound science can readily appreciate.

The source of the difficulty in much modern thought, and of the muddled and self-contradictory thinking that characterizes 'secular Christianity', is traced back to the deep split between subject and object in European philosophy. This gave rise to an abstract, impersonal, and objectivist outlook upon the world, which has had a damaging and restrictive effect in man's knowledge of himself and the universe around him, as well as isolating his thought from God. But of course a God who is inert is soon recognized to be otiose, so that this line of thinking quickly ends up in 'the death of God'. Over against that whole approach, however, Mr Blaikie sets the notion of the human self as active agent, in which the self is not isolated from the world, for it is action that links together the self and the world in a dynamic unity that transcends the fatal split between subject and object. The whole range of modern thought requires to be re-formulated in this light, and in particular the theological question whether God has acted in history. Indeed, it is when we think in this deeper and fuller way of the basis of man's knowledge and life in the world opened out by modern science that we are able not only to reach a more adequate understanding of human activities in nature and history, but to appreciate the biblical message of the living God who is personal Agent, who acts in history as well as creation, and who establishes personal relations between us and Himself in space and time.

Mr Blaikie thinks out of an active parish ministry, deeply aware of people's religious needs and of the relevance of the Christian Gospel to them. He writes with a clarity and ability which many academic theologians will envy even if they are unable to follow him in some of his interpretations of philosophical and scientific ideas. Without committing myself to all he has to say, I would like to support him unhesitatingly in his main position and to commend *'Secular Christianity' and God who Acts* as one of those rare books that brings a great wind of fresh air to clear away the fog of confusion and leads Christians into an understanding of their faith that is rationally well grounded and intellectually reliable. The publication of this book early in 1970 surely signifies that the wild detour of the nineteen sixties is at an end.

THOMAS F. TORRANCE

Edinburgh

Preface

To ask the right questions, students are often told, is more important than to know the right answers : for the answers depend on the questions. I believe the really important question for today is : What is action? The sterility and frustration of much academic life in this age is probably largely due to the fact that so few have seriously asked or attempted to answer this question.[1]

The claim made in this study is that using the concept of action for axe, a clear path can be cut through the thickets of various 'disciplines' in the jungle of modern thought – scientific, historical, philosophical and theological. Looking out across the academic landscape from the viewing-point to which this leads us, it can be clearly seen that the secular world-view so dear to some 'modern men' is self-contradictory and absurd, and that the biblical Christian Faith, when expressed in modern terms, yields a world-view very much more rational and comprehensive, and therefore more adequate to the needs of the citizens of this New World into which scientific technology is leading us.

Although the writing of this book was triggered by the recent widely publicized theological controversy in New Zealand, yet it makes only the briefest reference to that debate. For the view of the 'New World' described by Principal Geering in his book *God in the New World* appears to be the one put forward by Copernicus (d. 1543) and Galileo (d. 1642) and given classical formulation by Sir Isaac Newton (d. 1727). He gives no hint of the fact, universally agreed amongst scientists, that the publication of Einstein's Theory of Relativity (1905), and the development later of quantum physics, replaced this 'old' world-view with one in many respects very different, which has presented quite different problems and possibilities. His theological references also are mainly pre-twentieth century. It is, however, with the modern problems of this twentieth century world-view that we are concerned in this book.

That a discussion of these 'new world' problems may seem sometimes strange and perhaps difficult to some who are more at home in the thought-world of the nineteenth and earlier centuries is only to be expected. But in theology, as in other aspects of life, we must try to keep abreast of the times.

There has recently been increasing agreement that thinking and learning usually proceed better through dialogue or discussion than through lecture or monologue. Except for the many silent theological 'discussions' I have had – made possible by many publishers –

with the books of uncounted authors, I could never have reached the views here expressed. I have tried, by means of many quotations, to present the argument in a somewhat dialogical form; and the degree of my indebtedness, especially to those most extensively quoted, will be obvious. Acknowledgment is therefore gratefully made for permission to use the following copyright material:

Alec Allenson, *Miracles and the Resurrection* by I. T. Ramsey et al.; Wm. B. Eerdmans, *Systematic Theology* by C. Hodge and *Theology in Reconstruction* by T. F. Torrance; Harper & Row, *Time and Free Will* by H. Bergson, *Salvation in History* by O. Cullmann, *An Existentialist Theology* by J. Macquarrie, *Theology of Hope* by J. Moltmann, *Theology as History*, ed. by J. M. Robinson, and *Secular Christianity* by R. Gregor Smith; Humanities Press, *The Self as Agent* and *Persons in Relation*, both by J. Macmurray; Judson Press, *God in the New World* by L. Geering; Lutterworth Press, *Guide to the Debate about God* by D. Jenkins; Macmillan, *The Secular Meaning of the Gospel* by P. van Buren; Oxford University Press, *Science and Christian Belief* by C. A. Coulson; Sheed and Ward, *Sense, Nonsense and Christianity* by H. Meynell; S.P.C.K., *Religion and Science—Conflict and Synthesis* by I. T. Ramsey; The Aristotelian Society, "What is Action?" by J. Macmurray; *Time* magazine, "Is Heresy Dead?"; University of Chicago Press, *Personal Knowledge* by M. Polanyi; Westminster Press, *Christ and Time* by O. Cullmann and *History Sacred and Profane* by A. Richardson; World Publishing, *Existence and Faith—Shorter Writings of Rudolf Bultman* ed. by S. M. Ogden.

I wish to acknowledge also my deep appreciation of Professor Torrance's gracious agreement to write the Foreword for this book. Though I have never had the privilege of studying under him, his personal interest in my attempts at theological writing and his encouragement have meant more to me than I can say; and without them this book could hardly have been started.

To my wife and children who have cheerfully endured considerable inconvenience through the preparation of this book, and to the members of my congregation who have uncomplainingly accepted less of their minister's time than they might have demanded, I express my sincere thanks. Also to my sister-in-law Mrs Anderson for considerable typing assistance, and to several people who have helped by reading and correcting the typescript and proofs, especially to my mother, Mr Ross Palmer and Miss C. Leckie.

R. J. BLAIKIE

Introductory

"The whole Bible and the Christian preaching which is its climax are concerned chiefly and indeed almost solely with the proclamation of God's action in history: and the New Testament is centred upon God's culminating action in the resurrection of Jesus Christ from the dead."

(Alan Richardson, The Bible in the Age of Science,
p. 127, S.C.M. Press, 1961)

A great stir has been caused in the Church – and in the world – by the report from some modern theologians that God is dead. People do not like to linger long beside a corpse: and therefore we may assume this announcement by the 'death of God' theologians to be an indication of the imminent disintegration of their own group within the Church. But unless their news is widely believed among Christians, the Church may be expected to survive. *Should* their message be believed? And if not, what comes next in theology after the scare about God's death?

" 'The resurrection of theism' after the death of God can be a live option," Carl Henry has written, "if the evangelical vanguard becomes theologically engaged at the frontiers of modern doubt ... A new prospect for systematic theology is at hand, and a growing demand exists for a comprehensive world-view that does full justice to the real world of truth and life and experience in which man must make his decisions."[1] This study on the theme of ACTION with its focus on questions raised by the biblical affirmation of the mighty acts of God is intended to constitute such a theological engagement at the frontiers of modern doubt.

God, according to the Psalmist, "made known his ways to Moses, his acts to the people of Israel." (Ps. 103:7) What are these 'acts of God'? They are, of course, the basic units in the story told by the Bible. But what, more precisely, is an 'act' – any act? And what sort of analogy is there between the acts of men and the acts of God, in terms that are readily intelligible to modern man in this revolutionary and scientific age? This sort of question about the acts of God expresses an urgent and widespread interest today.

In an article headed "How Do We Recognise God's Action?",[2] Roger L. Shinn reports on a Geneva Conference on the theme "Christians in the Technical and Social Revolution of our Time". "Repeatedly speakers called on the Church to recognise *God's activity* in the revolutions that are shaking the power structures of the world," he writes. " ... The theologians there sometimes pointed out that a long ecclesiastical tradition had exaggerated those notes of Scripture that tell of God's changeless eternity and had suppressed the faith in the living, active God who works his will in history." There was apparently a tendency among some of the activist theologians in this Conference to assume that virtually all the social revolutions of our day are instances of God's action: others, however, challenged this view. "Denys Munby, British economist, said: 'But we want to know from the theologians where is God at work in these dynamic forces and where is the devil at work?' ... In so bewildering a history as our own, can we distinguish with any clarity those acts and those revolutions that are of God? ... Christians believe in God's activity in history. How in our confusion do we recognise His activity and distinguish it from the activities of His enemies?"[3]

Such questions about social changes and how far they include God's action are among the most pressing problems in modern theology. Commenting on the "Uppsala Drafts" published in preparation for the 1968 Fourth Assembly of the World Council of Churches, an editorial in *Christianity Today* said:[4] "The undoubted truth that God providentially superintends all history is here given a new and sinister edge by the identification of God's purpose with the historical process. The specific work of God is confused with the general." It is against this tendency of activist theologians today, to apply the phrase 'what God is doing in the world' in support of whatever happens to be their own particular political or social prejudice, that Paul Ramsey has protested in his book *Who Speaks for the Church?* (1967). God, according to many of these theologians, is 'where the action is'. But examination often reveals that by 'the action' they seem to mean just human action – men's struggles and achievements through political and social activity – and not something done specifically by God conceived as a personal Agent.

Does God Himself really act? Has He acted in the past in history, and can He act in miracles today? Is not the concept of an 'act' inseparable from the concept of purpose in a personal Agent? And if so, does not the need for integrity with words require those who no longer believe that God is a living, personal Agent to stop using the terms 'acts of God', 'God in action' and the like, when they are referring to something other than purposeful and deliberate acts of such a God? Or is it reasonable that concepts like 'revolutionary social forces', or even 'the Church', should be hypostatised as a personal agent, and then be called 'God' in statements about 'the acts of God', without this unusual meaning being clearly indicated? Some such juggling with words would appear to be inevitable in any attempt to speak of God in a secular way or to translate the Gospel into secular terms. But does not this sort of juggling with 'God' really constitute a denial of the very foundation of the Christian Faith?

In biblical religion, as based on faith in 'God who acts', and on a view of man as *responsible* before God for his actions, the concept of 'action' is a peculiar mark – indeed the distinguishing mark – of *personal* reality, and is surely therefore of fundamental importance for Christian theology. That it has received so little systematic attention from theologians – as a glance at the index of most theological works will confirm – is therefore strange. Our thesis in this study is that this concept of 'action' is the key which can open for us not only a new understanding of the recent developments of theology through 'Secular Christianity' to the conclusion that God is dead, but also a new vision of the exciting world of tomorrow's Christian theology, after 'the death of God'.

SUBJECTIVITY AND ACTION

The God who has recently died is a God who cannot –

15

logically cannot possibly – *act*. He is the Subject-God of the philosophers and academic theologians, conceived in the context of the Critical Philosophy and developed on the basis of the subject/object distinction which (though present in earlier days also) has increasingly characterised all precise thinking about the world – philosophical, scientific, historical and religious – since the time of the great French philosopher, René Descartes.

Just before the middle of the seventeenth century Descartes announced that his rigorous exercise of systematically doubting everything that Reason could doubt had brought him at last to a solid foundation-principle upon which rational certainty and true knowledge could be built. His formula was 'I think, therefore I am'. This new formula changed the general pattern of philosophical thinking, which has built mainly on the same foundation ever since, with the Critical Philosophy of Immanuel Kant giving definitive form to the era and underlining, as essential and primary for all thinking, the distinction between the 'subjective' and 'objective' aspects of experience. Academic theology also, of course, has been dominated by the thought-patterns of this movement.

The general nature of the basic modern theological problem was correctly seen many years ago to be related to this distinction between subject and object in our understanding; and various inadequate suggestions (at some of which we shall be looking later) have been offered for solving it.

A new kind of certainty had become possible in 'knowledge' with the development of the experimental methods of objective science, and this accentuated the tendency for the wise and cultured people of the world to dismiss with scorn the claim made by Christians that in the Bible they have a special source of sure and certain knowledge – *revealed* knowledge of God and His acts – which however cannot be tested and verified at the crucial points by the methods of objective science. In 1799, in an effort to meet these critics, Friedrich Schleiermacher, who is often called the father of modern theology, published a book with the title *On Religion – Speeches to its Cultured Despisers*. In face of the challenge from the Secularist champions of science, who could support their knowledge of the objective, observable world with such authoritative evidence, Schleiermacher had come to the conclusion that it is necessary for religion to stop arguing with science about matters of fact

16

concerning this world. In this area of interest, it must be conceded that science had or could find the answers. Religion must
now confine itself to what Schleiermacher regarded as its own
proper sphere, that of *feeling* – in particular the feeling of
absolute dependence. When religion came into conflict with
science over some matter of fact, that ground must be yielded
to science, and an effort should be made to re-interpret the
religious statement in subjective terms. Thus the common-sense
unity of human thinking came to be divided up, at least for
those scholars who wished to continue the practice of religion
as well as accepting the truths of science. Here, at the beginning
of the modern tradition in theology, as David Jenkins remarks,
"Schleiermacher is locating the basis of religion in *pure
subjectivity*."[5] The alternative for 'cultured people' seemed to
be to abandon religion.

The writings of a young Danish philosopher some fifty years
later may be noted as another land-mark on the road towards
the predicament of theology today. Søren Kierkegaard (to
whose influence the modern Existentialist movement is often
traced back) reinforced the subjective/objective division in a
vehement protest against the fashionable deference offered to
scientific truth. He considered that "a preoccupation with
science and with objective thinking ('objectivity') betrayed a
desire to remain a mere spectator and to shirk the necessity of
choosing for oneself. It was in opposition to this attitude that
he proclaimed that 'truth is subjectivity'."[6]

Coming down to the present day, we find John Macquarrie,
in a discussion of Tillich's views on God, writing: "It may
well be the case that modern philosophy from Kant onward
has discredited the old-style rational metaphysics, but, as Nicolas
Berdyaev acutely observes: 'It is not true to say that Kant
makes an end of all metaphysics: he merely makes an end of
the metaphysics of the naturalistic rationalist type, metaphysics
which are derived from the *object*, from the world, and he
reveals the possibility of metaphysics based on the *subject*, of a
metaphysics of freedom.' "[7]

These brief historical references help to indicate the way in
which the thinking of many intellectually alert Christians was
and is split onto two levels: the 'objective' level for science
with its empirically attested 'facts', and the 'subjective' level
for religion with its emotionally confirmed convictions. The

development of nineteenth century theological Liberalism, especially in Germany, presupposed and used this division, isolating from each other the 'truth' of science and the 'truth' of religion. Some leading Conservative theologians of that day, however, protested against this trend, as full of error and fraught with danger for the Christian Faith. Thus the great Scottish theologian James Denney, writing in 1895, deplored the fact that Ritschl ("by far the most influential, most interesting and in some ways most inspiring of modern theologians") carefully separates religious and scientific thinking onto different levels. For him, Denney declared, "theology, instead of involving such a general view of the world and of life as I have spoken of – instead of standing in direct and vital connection with the whole framework of our knowledge – is shut up into itself, and doctrine of God though it be, neither affects nor is affected by, any independent scientific interpretation of God's world . . . Made avowedly, at least by theologians, in the interest of religion, it [i.e. this separation between the religious and scientific as subjective and objective respectively] ends, as a rule, in leaving religion without its essential supports."⁸ This, of course, is exactly what has now transpired; and the consequent conclusion is being openly declared by the more logical and courageous of the modern heirs of subjectivist Liberalism, the so-called 'Secular Christians', in the catch-word 'God is dead'.

This strange, self-contradictory expression of the secular outlook in the Church in our day, like some earlier episodes in the development of theology along these subject/object lines, has laid claim to the title 'The New Theology'. It could much more appropriately be described, however, as the death-throes of the old theology of the age of Critical Reason, based on the foundation of Descartes' thinking Subject. For the startling fact is that starting from this initial presupposition that man – or 'person' – is basically a 'thinking Subject' with the world as the 'object' of his thinking, *it is impossible without logical inconsistency to reach (or to agree with) the conclusion that man is also an 'Agent', free and able to act in the observable world, or to make in it purposeful changes.* The same impossibility applies, by analogy, to God conceived as personal in this way – as Subject for whom the world is Object. Thus either to insist (with common-sense) that men are 'Agents', free to act in the world; or to affirm (with the Bible) the existence of the Living God who acts in history, is to call into radical question the whole subject/object tradition of Western thought, which leads with irresistible logic to the conclusion that all real action in the observable world is impossible. This means that God cannot act – and therefore has not acted – in world history; and that consequently the Agent-God of biblical faith must be considered to be 'dead'. The same logic, consistently applied, leads to the conclusion that man (as Agent) is also dead! Is not this a *reductio ad absurdum* of the whole argument; and so, the death of the old subjective theology, rather than the death of the Biblical God, and of man?

WHAT IS THE PROBLEM OF ACTION?

To the man of common-sense it will seem absurd that anyone should consider it logically impossible – or even a problem – to acknowledge that men are 'Agents', people who are free to change the world through action. And if he reads on through the pages of our discussion, we may appear to him to be suggesting that hitherto men have always been regarded essentially as Thinking Subjects – as minds or souls able to *think* – and that it has been left for Professor John Macmurray to tell us in his book *The Self as Agent*[9] that in reality we are not mere thinking Subjects but also, and primarily, acting Agents. This of course is nonsense, for the truth is that sensible people have always known that men can and do act in the world, and that God also, if He is personal, must be able to act in the world. So what's the problem?

The answer is – there is *no* problem about the possibility of human action, for the man of simple common-sense; and no problem about the possibility of God's acting in history and through miracles for the common-sense Christian believer. The problem arises for the man who aspires to exact logical thinking, especially in the scientific style (which conforms with or gives form to, modern philosophy); because the methodological presuppositions of this whole style of thinking oblige him to think dualistically, to regard the world 'objectively' as what is observed, and himself as thinking Subject who is the observer. Since the basic presupposition of this 'objectivity' is that the world is wholly 'determined' in a closed system of natural causes and effects, there can be no personal freedom possible in it, and the concept of purposeful, world-changing action becomes irrational!

As applied to theology and to God, this situation means that for many a theologian who in the integrity of his respect for truth wants to think with scientific rigour and objectivity, the possibility of miracles – of God really acting in history to achieve His purpose – has seemed to be fenced around with insuperable intellectual barriers. So intent have theologians been on their own special problem, as to how the possibility of God's actions can be rationally acknowledged, and what consequences follow if they cannot be acknowledged, that they have failed to notice the parallel problem with regard to the acts of men. Recently, however, as we shall see, thinkers in other academic fields – especially science, history and philosophy – have been noticing and expressing their concern about the absurd conclusion which follows necessarily from assuming initially (with Descartes, Kant and the Critical Philosophy) that man is essentially a 'mind' or 'subject' who thinks *about* the objective world, from which he distinguishes himself. The alternative is to presuppose (as we advocate with Macmurray) that man is a united psycho-somatic (or body-mind) agent living and acting *in* the world, in which he properly belongs; and that the correct foundation-formula on which to build rational knowledge is 'I *act*, therefore I am', instead of 'I think, therefore I am'.

It is difficult for common-sense to appreciate that the making of this simple change, and the adoption as the foundation for rational thought of this 'new' formula which any simpleton could have told us is true, constitutes a radical and revolutionary step for 'exact' thinkers; and that the systematic development of the consequences of this change may be expected to solve (by dissolving) many of the problems that have tortured the minds of philosophers and historians, scientists and theologians for centuries. But such is the case: and it is largely with this matter that we shall be concerned in what follows.

A helpful illustration of the importance of this change of ultimate presuppositions may be given in terms of an analogy from the way we use our eyes. By using both eyes together in the normal manner we see things easily and unthinkingly as 'whole' in a four-dimensional way (including time as a dimension). If we close one eye and look at things with only one eye we see them rather differently, in a flat, three-dimensional way (including time). Now when you look at the world through a microscope or telescope you can see things which are invisible to ordinary vision : and you can make much better sense of them if you keep one eye closed and take a one-eyed view of the world. In rifle-shooting, again, you can score better marks by closing one eye and relying on the one-eyed view. It would be easy – and would seem sensible in some ways – to conclude that because you can hit the target more often with a rifle and see microscopic and telescopic wonders better with one eye than with two, therefore the one-eyed view, with a dimension less than the two-eyed view gives, shows us how things truly are : and that the common-sense assumption of the normal two-eyed viewer – that he is seeing the world more accurately as four-dimensional – is just a popular and 'uncritical' misconception!

Transpose this now to apply to the way in which we see things with our 'mind's eye'. When we are conscious of the world and ourselves in a simple and unsophisticated, common-sense sort of way, we 'know' reality as whole and (so to speak) as four-dimensional, with ourselves living and *acting in* the world. The 'subjective' and 'objective' aspects are bound together – indeed they are not even critically separated so that they need to be *bound* together. We know ourselves to be free agents, able to *act* in the world and to execute in it changes which we have planned and intended – and there is no problem of action. We are aware that 'thinking' is one special sort of activity among others – though it is also an aspect of all action, in the form of purpose or intention. Now if we close (as it were) one eye of our total awareness in living, acting experience, and try to eliminate everything 'subjective' that comes from our 'selves' and to look at the world in a purely 'objective' way, we find that this one-eyed view of the world, using scientific methods and technology, helps us to hit the 'target of achieve-ment' in a way that gives a power over nature and a new range of knowledge which would be quite impossible apart from this separation of subject and object in our thinking.

In some measure this distinguishing of the self as thinking subject from everything else as 'object of thought' – the adopting of the 'spectator attitude' – must have pre-dated the birth of human language and of all discursive thinking by men : but in a way that did not fracture man's thought-world into a sharp subject/object dualism. Just such a dualistic splitting of the wholeness of man's life, however, is precisely what the deliberate 'objectivity' of modern scientific thinking demands. And some philosophers (or scientists thinking philosophically and not scientifically), being greatly impressed by the splendid achievements made possible by this one-eyed view adopted by the scientific method, have declared that the objective view is the 'true' view of the world, and that science is the only reliable source of truth, the whole truth, about the nature of the real world. The objective view affirms universal determinism of natural causes and effects, and has no place for personal freedom (or 'freedom of the will' as it is sometimes called in the context of the subject/object dualism). Therefore of course it follows that the common-sense, 'two-eyed' conviction that men are free and can act to change the observable world in accordance with personal purposes – the 'I act, therefore I am' conviction – must be rejected as a popular misconception due to simplistic, un-Critical thinking!

The philosophical point of view from which this 'one-eyed' declaration is made is that of *the secular outlook*.

Calling the scientific point of view a 'one-eyed view' is not intended to derogate from the value of the immense achievements of science: to try to do that today would be both foolish and futile. But it is to claim that the scientific picture of the world – all the various scientific pictures of the world – however important they may be, cannot add up to a *complete* picture of the world, and cannot give the whole truth about it. Indeed science yields an essentially limited and distorted picture. When this 'objective' picture of reality as painted by science is affirmed by the 'secular outlook' as giving the whole truth or as including all real 'knowledge' (and this, we repeat, is not a scientific conclusion but a philosophical judgement – indeed really an affirmation of 'faith') then we are in intellectual trouble: for we thus create for rational thought insoluble problems in connection with the possibility of action in the world, leaving open no other logical conclusion than that action is impossible: the Creator-God who acts in the Bible's story is therefore a 'myth', or 'dead', and men as free agents are merely imaginative figments. The only way out is to go back – to Descartes and Kant in the world of Western thought – and find what was wrongly done in the setting out of the problem.

"We live," wrote H. H. Rex, "on this side of a rupture which divides the whole history of mankind into two sections; the one extending from the cavemen to the men of the Renaissance, and the other covering this post-Cartesian world of ours. On the surface it may seem preposterous to lump the cavemen, Plato and Michelangelo into one class, and the rest of us into another. And yet, so long as we fail to appreciate the full magnitude of this fact, we have understood very little about the nature of the modern secular world."[10] This passage is quoted with approval (as true) by L. G. Geering in the Preface to his *God in the New World*[11] and with critical disapproval (as false) among the opening words of the first chapter in E. M. Blaiklock's reply, *Layman's Answer*.[12] In a strange way both, I believe, are right – and therefore both also wrong!

With Descartes there was indeed established a radically new foundation for critical thought, which has dominated the academic world since, and upon which the 'objectivist' views of science and of 'secular man' are built. These presuppositions, consistently applied (as we shall show) indicate as 'irrational' the recognition of 'persons as agents' and of their 'actions': and in this absurdity our post-Cartesian age is genuinely different from all other ages of human life, including those of Plato and the cavemen. The question is whether we are right in our difference.

After the remark quoted above, Rex goes on to say that, "while before this divide the natural universe itself had a soul, it is now soulless, like a machine. It is this recognition of the true nature of the universe in the post-Cartesian world which has changed our condition radically and completely." Taken literally, it is of course nonsense to say that in pre-Cartesian Christendom it was believed that the universe 'had a soul'. What was believed was that in and yet 'beyond' or 'above' and before the 'appearances' of the universe there is a living and personal Creator-God whose purposes give meaning to the observable world and show that it is *not* merely a machine: as it was also believed that in and yet beyond the appearance of observable man – man's organic structure etc. – there is a *personal* reality which gives a special meaning to some 'human events', as purposeful *acts*. The inevitable conclusion, logically, from the premises of Descartes and his followers, is that the universe *is* a mere machine and that 'God is dead': but equally that men are mere machines, and that 'persons are dead'.

The important question, therefore, which this study is concerned to examine, is whether the time has now arrived for us to acknowledge that in the basic presuppositions of their world-view, as recognising the reality of persons and of action, the cavemen and Plato were much closer to the heart of the truth than the secular 'objectivist' thinkers of the post-Cartesian age of Critical Reason. I believe that without rejecting the insights of science, but rather enhancing them, we must now acknowledge the absurdity of the secular world-view, and join hands again with the other ages of humanity in acknowledging – or at least in not absurdly denying – the reality of action and of freedom for persons in the observable world.

The use of the illustration about binocular and monocular vision should help us to see how it can happen that the discussion of some problems, which to the man of common-sense may seem to be just a lot of unnecessary big words about something that is quite straightforward, can be of the greatest importance, and altogether unavoidable, for those who must think through a situation with precision and in a comprehensive way. To write a book about how we can acknowledge without rational inconsistency that action is possible, and that the concept of the acts of God in our world is not irrational, may seem to many ordinary Christian believers to be a waste of time and a lot of nonsense. *Of course* action is possible, and *of course* God can act in our world if He wants to! I am sure that those who think this way are quite right. But there *is* a vital problem here for precise and systematic thought. And indeed those in our 'secular age' who look to the criterion of science as the sole and adequate guide to truth, if they are logically consistent (which most of them are not), must face this problem. Anyone also who wants to understand what modern theology, and the general turmoil in the academic world today, are all about will have to take the trouble to understand the structure of this problem.

To some people this no doubt sounds very complicated and strange – and so it is! The thinking that is necessary to sort out these problems is not easy: but it must be done, and done now in this time when God's death has been announced, so that we may see how this conclusion about the death of the God of philosophical and theological thought is logically inevitable and must be accepted as true; while realising also that it need not upset unduly those whose theological position is 'biblical'. For the God of the Bible is not an abstract Subject-God : He is and always has been the *God-who-acts*, the Agent God who is Creator and Redeemer of men-who-act; men whom He has made in His own image as responsible agents. This God, the Living God of the Christian faith mightily acting in history to raise up Jesus Christ (who had died on the cross for sinners) to life continued and renewed as eternal life in which others may share – *this* God is still very much alive !

A NEW THEOLOGY?

From the theology of the Death of God we must turn to a theology of God alive, God at work in the world today. This phrase itself almost constitutes the basic definition commonly given of God the Holy Spirit. "If the Holy Spirit means the living action of God in the world (and we can accept this as a provisional definition)," G. S. Hendry has written,[13] "our formulations cannot hope to catch up with the reality." From the unbalanced emphasis on Christology in the period now ending, an emphasis which has for so many degenerated into a sort of secular Jesusology, the Christian Church must return to a fully biblical acknowledgement of the living God in Trinity, God who as Holy Spirit unceasingly comes to His people in the here and now, breaking forth ever new dimensions of truth which are always found to focus on, and to derive from the revelation in, Jesus Christ as the altogether unique One, the only Mediator between God and man, who by the miraculous act of God became true man while also remaining true God.

The startling news announced by the 'death of God' theologians has frequently been counter-balanced in recent years by news of claims, often apparently extravagant and irrational, that God is demonstrating His vitality in the Church again today in strange and spectacular ways – that God the Holy Spirit is very much alive and at work in the world, answering prayers, healing the sick, raising up the spiritually dead, and blessing His People with joy and assurance. Must it not seem likely then that if the Church can blow the froth of irrational superstition, sub-personal doctrine and an unbiblical emphasis on

25

'tongues' and the like, off the top of the overflowing cup of Christian exuberance now held by the modern 'Pentecostalists', from which so many in the various denominations are sipping during these days, we shall find in the fresh knowledge of God's active presence with us in the Holy Spirit the refreshing draught of 'new' theological truth so much needed in our day?

A NEW PRIESTHOOD?

One of the blessings of a time of new beginnings, such as has been opened to us after the death of the God of the academic 'Critical' theologians, is the opportunity it may offer the Church to escape from the control of the specialised theological 'priesthood' which has increasingly asserted its claims in the Protestant Churches in recent decades. For example, one Church recently received with approval as "the definition of the aims and methods of theological education" a Statement which referred to our understanding of the Bible itself and how its message is to be received in our Church today. "It may be painful to acknowledge the fact," it declared with general reference, "but we can no longer assume that what seems to be the plain meaning of the Biblical passage is indeed what its author intended to convey."[14] In fact, the Statement held, it is necessary in these days first of all to understand a vast store of information amassed by "the devout labours of Biblical scholars since Reformation times", before one can properly understand and use the Bible. "The understanding of this complex fund of material calls for technical skills of an increasingly specialist order: but it cannot be neglected."[15]

In other words – and this view would find wide support in many denominations today – the Word of God as conveyed to men through the Bible cannot today be properly received and understood by the simple layman, even though he may be a man of deep faith and spiritual insight. It is apparently only "the wise according to worldly standards" – educated in literary and historical criticism as based on the presuppositions of the Critical Philosophy – who are thought to hold the key to the understanding of God's truth today; and it would seem that this is held to be so, irrespective of whether they believe in the living, acting God of the Bible and have a vital faith-relationship with the living, Risen Christ, or not. How strikingly this contrasts with

St. Paul's view as expressed in I Corinthians 1:18 – 2:16. The ordinary layman on this 'modern' view, it would seem, cannot receive a real understanding of God's Word directly through the Bible with the help of the Holy Spirit alone; nor even with the additional help of the scholarship of the Church through the ages: for only the 'critical' scholarship of the post-Reformation period and "especially during the last century"[16] can make it possible for him to hear and understand aright! Only as mediated through the scholarly priesthood of the modern 'Biblical Critics' can ordinary people receive the truth of God's Word from the Bible!

This is surely a strange position for Churches to reach which claim to be Reformed Churches and to be true to the spirit of the Reformation! "Grace and truth came through Jesus Christ," (John 1:17) the only Mediator between God and man – so the Gospel proclaims, and the Reformers held this to be essential. No mediating sacerdotal priesthood is needed (as the pre-Reformation clergy claimed) to convey God's *grace* to the common man: nor (contrary to the claims of these modern theologians) is any academic priesthood necessary to convey the *truth* of God to the common man. "Puncturing what they regarded as the pretensions of the professional clergy came as close as anything to being what the whole Reformation was about," writes T. A. Gill.[17] "The direct access of each man to the only mediator demanded the down-grading of all those officers of the Church who had long been interposed between the believer and God." Today, therefore, when exalted claims are made for the critically trained academic clergy as the essential mediators of the truth of God to men, then talk about the need for a New Reformation seems extremely apt. But what is required is certainly not the sort of thing advocated by J. A. T. Robinson in his book *The New Reformation?*, involving capitulation to the claims of this academic theological priesthood with its increasingly secular theology. The Church today, if it is faithful to the principles of the Reformation and to the guidance of the Living God, the Holy Spirit, will not continue to tolerate or approve a self-exalting hierarchy of would-be essential mediators-to-men of the truth of God; especially if they deny that the God of truth is the living, personal, biblical God who acts.

As seen from a point of view which accepts the primary and

essential presupposition of the whole Bible – the belief that the true God is a God who really acts in our world and communicates personally with men – the fact of the matter would seem to be that the Critical Theologians, after all their brilliant dualistic excursions into the subject/object world in which a God who really acts in the world cannot be tolerated, must now return and learn the elements of Christian truth again from simple believers, to whom God has revealed them through the Bible and by His Spirit.

James Barr's brilliant semantic studies have (perhaps not always justly) lashed the academic backs of many learned theologians, whose cherished learning, he claims, had led them into error instead of truth. We would do well to ponder today the closing paragraphs of his *Biblical Words for Time*.[18]

"The considerable armoury of linguistic material which has been assembled in this book," he writes, "is not intended to impress people, or to suggest that biblical interpretation cannot be undertaken without Syriac and Coptic and the like. On the contrary, since biblical interpretation in theology must work from the things said in the Bible, and not from the lexical resources used in saying them, the fundamental points of biblical assertion will normally be visible to those who do not know the original languages. Those who do know them will be able to understand the text with very much greater accuracy, provided that their knowledge of the original language is in fact sound, careful and accurate in detail; but it is unlikely that in more than a few special cases this knowledge will lead to a recognition of some biblical conception which is vital to the understanding of the Bible, but which is quite invisible to the reader of the English Bible, because it is tied to the layout of the Greek or Hebrew lexical stock. If such cases were both numerous or important, one need hardly remark, it would be a poor prospect for the average layman – and indeed, one may add, for the average minister, whose Greek and Hebrew are not always excessively fluent."

The prospect for the average layman today in the area of Christian theology is not a poor one, however; it is bright indeed, compared with the way in which it has recently been painted by secular theologians. For after the Holy Spirit – God who acts in the world – has given us the New Reformation which is again urgently needed in the Church, our new priest-

28

hood must be the Priesthood of all Believers – of the many with common-sense and simple faith, and not of an esoteric clique trained in the patterns of Critical thought, whose members become experts in word-games and ambiguity.

A NEW WORLD-VIEW?

The younger generation today is convinced – and with good reason – that we are entering a New Age of technological advance and achievement, a New World of opportunity. Professor Margaret Mead emphasised the truth in this conviction when she pointed out to the Uppsala meeting of the World Council of Churches that already today – reversing the age-old structure of human society – the 'experienced' members in our Western Community are not the 'elders' of our social groups, but the younger adults, those under forty years of age. These people understand and take for granted things which to their seniors are still astonishing mysteries; and many of them have had a range of experience – with space capsules, piloting jets, programming computers and all sorts of other things – of which the older members of our world neither know now nor are ever likely to learn anything at first hand.

Speaking recently with a University student who is a committed Conservative Christian, in the New Zealand context which had just received L. G. Geering's book *God in the New World*, the present writer remarked that it would not be long before E. M. Blaiklock's reply to it, *Layman's Answer*, became available. "Yes!" the student replied. "But I don't like some of his chapter headings," he added, having seen these advertised, "for example, 'No New World'. We young people believe that we *are* entering a new world in these days."

Only a new world-view of some sort is likely to be considered adequate, by this new generation, to include all the wonders of their experience. Scientific technology is providing them with their new world: but how are they to understand and evaluate it all? If many in this generation are to become or remain Christian in their outlook, a new Christian world-view as part of a new Christian theology is likely to be required. They are asking for 'bread': will the Church give them 'a stone'? They seek (to use again words of Carl Henry already quoted) "a comprehensive world-view that does full justice to the real world of truth and life and experience in which man must make his decisions." Must they accept a narrow-minded and exclusive 'secular world-view', based on the ultimate 'Thinking Subject' presupposition of objective science, which by logical necessity excludes all rational recognition of *action* in the observable world; which has no room for the living, transcendent Creator-God of Christian faith; and in which man is only a machine, an automaton responding automatically to stimuli in deterministic patterns of behaviour? Or shall we offer them a new world-view that presupposes *action* as the primary reality of life and experience, and sees man as a responsible agent in a world given unity and purpose as the act of the Creator Agent-God whom we know through the Holy Spirit and in Jesus Christ who is the centre of the new creative act of God? These are the alternatives open today: the secular world-view or the Christian one.

'Secular Christianity', of course, claims to be a bridge between these two: but it is a hollow, false claim. If it is Christian, it cannot be secular: and if it is secular, then it is not Christian, for it cannot consistently include even the most fundamental and essential presupposition of all biblical theology – the conviction that God is One who acts with purpose in a personal way in this world.

Any appearance that 'Secular Christianity' may have of being effectively both secular and Christian at the same time is based on muddled thinking or on a deliberate ambiguity in the use of words. The deliberate ambiguity, seen at sharp focus in relation to the concept of 'action', and especially the Resurrection, seems to be characteristic of most of the committed promoters of 'Secular Christianity': and the muddled thinking – influenced no doubt by the knowledge that already so many in the Church are or think they are supporters of this movement – seems to characterise those still-non-secular theologians who today write in sympathetic exposition of 'what the Secular Christians mean', and who urge us to accept and indeed welcome their views as proper expressions of the Christian Faith, even if we would not ourselves express it in the same way.

Pausing here for a moment to consider what may be the real meaning of 'Secular Christianity' we seem to be faced with two major alternatives: one trivial and true, the other fundamental but false. The one generally followed by the peace-making or compromising theologians is to assume that the champions of Secular Christianity do not really *mean* what they *say,* but are deliberately using words in a very ambiguous way to try to shock people into recognising an important truth within the traditional structure of the Faith – that it is wrong for Christians to over-emphasise God, heaven, life after death, and so on, and allow a serious reduction of interest in man, this world, this life, etc. This alternative indicates 'Secular Christianity' (or 'religion-less Christianity' with its 'holy world-liness' etc.) as true but relatively trivial. For the important message it conveys could be communicated much more intelligibly in other ways. Any possible extra benefit that might conceivably be gained by using this way instead of expressing the same truths in more conventional ways, could not possibly compensate for the enormous confusion and damage caused in the Church by this con-joining of concepts which the dictionary defines as mutually exclusive, this redefining of basic theological terms. Genuine Christianity has *always* included a deep concern for this world of men whom God so loved that He gave His only Son to die for them. All attempts in the Church to reject the proper Christian emphasis on the importance of man's life in this world, as being in polar relation with the life beyond death, heaven and God, have always sooner or later been rejected by the Church as error and heresy. There is certainly no need for any 'secular' help to introduce this dual or 'polar' emphasis to the Church in a 'New Theology'. It has been at the heart of the Christian faith from the start, and a call back to the biblical heritage is what is needed, not something called 'Secular Christianity'.

Is this really what all the fuss over 'Secular Christianity' is about in modern theology? – is it really just a call back to biblical Christianity? – for this, in effect, is what seems to be the interpretation given by many of those theologians who now urge us to accept and welcome 'Secular Christianity' within the Church. But if this is indeed all that is meant, then surely the whole movement of 'Secular Christianity' should be de-plored and rejected, for quite unnecessarily causing great confusion and strife within the Church; everyone who cherishes integrity with words and straightforward dealing should oppose it.

The other alternative is to assume that the theological promoters of 'Secular Christianity' are not merely playing with words nor lightly changing the definitions of Christian terms; but that they have, as they claim, something of fundamental importance to communicate, and that they mean much more fully what their words have said than most of their sympathetic interpreters will allow. 'Secular Christianity', in this case, may be understood to mean by the word 'secular' an outlook which is incompatible with belief in the living, personal God who acts, the God of biblical faith; an attitude which cannot acknowledge the possibility that men may know (through revelation) of a reality beyond the reach of natural science, which we may call 'heaven, God's dwelling place': and so on. If this is so – and this is the way in which their position is understood in this study – what is offered by 'Secular Christianity' is fundamentally important, but false. It involves a radical inversion of the whole structure and form of biblical Christianity, conceiving 'God' as contained within or as an aspect of the natural world, instead of (with the Bible) as active Creator and Lord 'over' the natural world. It therefore offers a world-view which is incompatible with, and an alternative to, the world-view of any Bible-based Christianity: and it must be rejected as false by the standards of the Christian Faith.

A good example of the sort of confused argument used in commending a sympathetic tolerance of Secular Christianity within the Church is to be found in John Macquarrie's new book, *God and Secularity*. Already in the title can be seen the fundamental mis-relation of concepts which largely vitiates his argument. Here he yokes together an ontological concept (God) and an attitude concept (Secularity) as being in 'polar' relationship with each other. Contrary to some who deny that 'God' is essentially related to 'being' and who understand 'God' simply as an attitude concept (a 'blik' sign), Macquarrie insists throughout this book that in Christian usage the word 'God' must be understood ontologically: and in this he is surely correct.[19] He is equally clear that by the word 'secularity' he means an attitude: "Secularity is taken to mean the outlook characterised by the attitudes of modern science and, more generally, of this-worldly concerns."[20]

We are of course familiar with the polar relationship within the Christian Faith between God and the world, on the ontological plane. And on the level of attitudes we know of the polar contrast between the *exclusively* this-worldly interests of the secular outlook, and the outlook of bible-based Christian faith which must always retain *both* God and the world in polar tension.[21] But what kind of logic must one use to see in polar tension God Himself and a this-worldly human attitude? Must it not be granted that eagerness to find common ground, to compromise with meanings and definitions so that we may all accept each other (and accept especially 'Secular Christianity') as having important Christian insights, has here played havoc with logic, and produced nonsense?

The truth is that secularity and Christian Faith are alternative and incompatible ways of looking at reality, one capable of seeing nothing beyond this 'natural' world, whereas the other sees this world as the creation of God who is beyond, before, and other than the world, the supernatural Creator. Secularity has nothing to offer man today except a 'one-eyed' view of realities which (despite certain advantages of the 'one-eyed' view) can be much more adequately seen and much more truly understood from the 'two-eyed' point of view of Christian Faith.

This is not, however, just a call back to traditional forms of theology, and to well-worn ecclesiastical clichés which fail to grip men's minds in this new and exciting age. For there is now dawning a new day for Western thought-structures in general as well as for Christian theology. From the spring of an action-accepting presupposition there are now beginning to flow streams of thought – philosophical, historical and theological – which are new and profound but also genuine and concordant with common-sense in a way that has not been true of academic thought for many years: streams which set the whole enterprise of the sciences and their world-views in a wide rational context, as important but limited aspects of knowledge and as products of human action: and which open up also for theology new channels that run into the great river of biblical and historical theology, as based on faith in the Living God who acts.

The new action-based theology for the late twentieth century turns out in the providence of God to have the same basic presupposition as the whole Bible and the faith of the Christian Church through the centuries – that *action* is the primary reality of our world, as revealed in God who acts, the Creator-God. We discover – and why should it be with astonishment? – that man's most careful systematic thinking today looks as though it may be catching up again with the living, acting reality of God who goes ahead and calls us to follow, who has been waiting for us and inviting us to return from our broken wanderings of mind to Him who is the Truth, and who makes all things new.

The following chapters constitute an attempt to expound and examine these convictions in a more systematic way.

PART I

THE SHAPE OF THE PROBLEM:
The Secular and the Biblical

CHAPTER 1

The Secular Presupposition

What is secular man's deepest and most unquestioned assumption about the nature of knowledge and of reality? Though less a formulated belief than an attitude, it is that science, ultimately, is the only source of true knowledge, and that anything which cannot be investigated by the empirical methods of science is probably not real.

"Today," David Jenkins suggests, "anyone who counts as a scientist . . . counts also, without having to establish his claim, as an authority . . . And if what you want to know is the sort of thing about which he cannot tell you, then it becomes very doubtful whether that sort of thing is a real sort of thing at all. Facts are facts and everything else is mere matter of belief, opinion, attitude, taste . . ."[1] And Alan Richardson remarks that "one of the genuinely ideological assumptions of Western society today is that truth as such is that which has been established by scientific method of the type which has been so successful in natural science : everything else, such as religious truth, artistic standards, ethical norms, is a matter of 'opinion' and will remain so until 'science' (especially psychology and the social sciences) is in a position to settle questions about religion and human destiny definitively. The temper of our times is in this sense positivistic."[2] This is what we speak of as 'the secular attitude'.

That ours is an increasingly secular age is accepted today without question by almost everyone; and this has momentous significance for the future of religion. In his book *Honest Religion for Secular Man*, Lesslie Newbigin takes 'secularism' to refer to "a system of belief, or an attitude, which in principle denies the existence or the significance of realities other than those

37

which can be measured by the methods of natural science."
He quotes the definition of the word given by the Jerusalem
meeting in 1928 of the International Missionary Council: "a
way of life and an interpretation of life that include only the
natural order of things and that do not find God, or a realm
of spiritual reality, necessary for life and thought."[3]

The secular attitude, secularisation, secularity, secularism –
each theologian makes his own special emphasis in defining these
terms; but their general import is clear. These are not, of course,
new terms in our Western society. The strange new thing about
our day is that the radical empiricism of the secular attitude
has now been embraced, on the level of presuppositions, by some
within the Church. For the 'secular Christian' shares this presupposition with other secular men; his 'Christianity' is built
on the foundation of this secular attitude towards truth and
reality. An American Episcopal clergyman, Paul van Buren,
for example, who claims to be a 'secular man', in his book
The Secular Meaning of the Gospel wrote: "We set out on this
study with certain acknowledged commitments to what we
called 'secular thought' and we said that secularism, as we are
using the term, is grounded in empirical attitudes . . ."[4] His clari-
fication of the modern meaning of the Gospel, he says, "has been
accomplished by a frankly empirical method which reflects the
thinking of an industrialised, scientific age. It has taken certain
empirical attitudes characteristic of modern thought seriously
and accepted them *without qualification*."[5]

The basic secular presupposition, then, is not primarily ontological, or metaphysical (i.e. not concerned with the nature of
reality); it is primarily epistemological, or concerned with the nature of *knowledge,* for it defines the only method of investigating
reality that will be recognised as yielding 'knowledge' or 'truth'.

Like the presuppositions of the metaphysical systems (often
religious) which the secular man seeks to discredit, this methodological presupposition is *accepted without any proof* that it is
true. "The basic presuppositions we have about the world,"
van Buren remarks, "are not verifiable, and yet everything we
do depends on them, as Hume taught us."[6] The secular presupposition is accepted 'by faith alone'! This, then, is the
fundamental faith affirmation of the consistent Secular
Christian: that whatever cannot be examined and tested by the
methods of empirical science is not in the deepest sense 'real' and

cannot become an object of 'knowledge' or a source of 'truth'.

What sort of world-view emerges on the foundation of this basic secular presupposition? Harvey Cox, in *The Secular City* insists repeatedly that a proper use of the secular presupposition – or a proper expression of the secular attitude – does not and cannot yield any single closed world-view. For this reason he deplores 'secularism' as he understands it. "Secularisation," he writes, "implies a historical process... in which society and culture are delivered from ... closed metaphysical world-views ... Secularism, on the other hand, is the name of an ideology, a new closed world-view which functions very much like a new religion."[7] Cox considers it highly unlikely that we shall ever again be able to subsume the various departments of knowledge within any one unifying world-view. The proliferation of world-views and their progressive relativisation is the hallmark of our time, he believes. It is part of what we mean by secularisation.

These comments accord with the obvious fact that the scientific view of the world is in constant flux today. Apparently incompatible theories about the nature of reality, each finding some empirical confirmation, co-exist side by side as respectable scientific theories. Is light, for instance, best understood in terms of 'waves' or 'corpuscles'? Is the basic constituent of the natural universe better described as 'matter' or as 'energy'? Science answers "both at once, and therefore neither in an exclusive or absolute sense". Again we ask today, "Did the universe have a true beginning? Did it start with a great primeval bang, and has it always been expanding, or has it existed forever essentially the same – its galaxies drifting apart while others are born to fill the space between, so that the words 'eternity' and 'infinity' maintain their literal meaning in an unending past and future?"[8] Or does the universe 'oscillate', so that it "expands after a big bang, contracts to an extremely dense state, and then explodes outwards again in an 80-billion year never-ending cycle" – being thus conceivable as finite rather than infinite, at least in a spatial sense?[9]

All three views have their supporters today among eminent scientists, and they are all sufficiently definite world-views to permit visual, diagrammatic representation for the assistance of popular understanding.

All could be called 'scientific world-views'; but none could be called exclusively '*the* scientific world-view'.

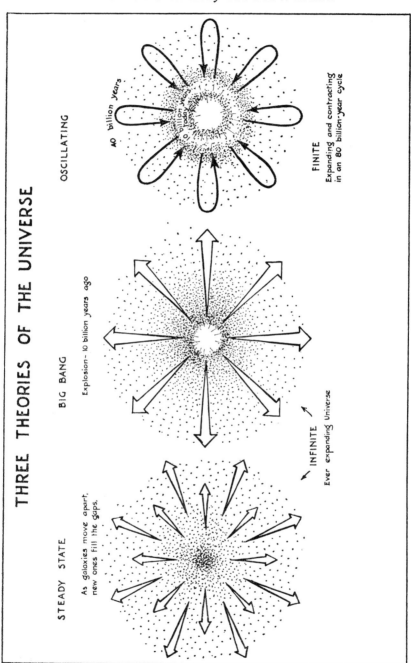

THREE THEORIES OF THE UNIVERSE

STEADY STATE

As galaxies move apart, new ones fill the gaps.

INFINITE
Ever expanding Universe

BIG BANG

Explosion – 10 billion years ago

OSCILLATING

40 billion years

FINITE
Expanding and contracting in an 80 billion-year cycle

Whichever view finds the strongest support from empirical evidence at any time will at that time be favoured by the unprejudiced scientist. He is indifferent as to which one is true, wanting only to find out the truth. The tide of evidence ebbs and flows; and, so far as science is concerned, all these scientific views may conceivably be rejected, in due course, in favour of some new one that accounts better for the empirical facts. Proliferation and relativisation of world-views are indeed currently acceptable, and inevitable, on the basis of this secular presupposition, which accords the place of supreme authority in the world not to any particular system of reality nor to God, but to the experimental verification methods of empirical science.

What then is the meaning today of the term 'the scientific world-view'? "The modern scientific world-view," writes David Jenkins, "takes it for granted that the universe is a *closed system* with its own independent laws and patterns which are or can be open to discovery by observation and investigation."[10] This is not really (as it might appear to be) a contradiction of Harvey Cox's insistence that the secular attitude is incompatible with devotion to any *one* closed world-view. What Jenkins is really affirming is that to accord exclusive authority to the experimental methods of science means that every one of the various alternative systems of 'knowledge' which these methods may yield is necessarily 'closed' against anything else which might be claimed as knowledge – for example 'revelation'. L. G. Geering's book *God in the New World* exemplifies this 'Secular Christian' outlook. Having set forth empirical science as 'the new source of knowledge', he then declares roundly: "Theology cannot be defined as the study of the revealed knowledge of God, for there is none."[11] Based on the sole authority of science, the uni-verse, in this scientific view, is bound to be seen as 'uni' – as one – a closed and unified system. But it is only the 'form' that is closed. The 'contents' of the scientific world-view – the theories which are held as to the nature of its constituent realities and the details of its scientific 'laws' – are wide open, and subject to unlimited variation as more and different 'facts' are noted.

CONCEPTS AND IMAGES – THOUGHT AND IMAGINATION

If we wish now to represent diagrammatically the constant *form* of this 'scientific world-view' so that we can imagine or picture to ourselves what the world-as-we-know-it is like, and not just think of it, the 'base' of our representation must obviously be 'The Empirical Methods of Science'. For this is the epistemological foundation upon which the whole secular world-view rests. And, for the 'superstructure' of truth or reality which we set up on this base, what shape could be more appropriate to represent our four-dimensional space-time continuum which is said to curve back upon itself, than the sphere (for a model) or the circle (for a picture).

It is, as we have seen, of no consequence to the secular scientist whether we fill this circle-image with a "big-bang", 'steady-state', 'oscillating', or some other general view of the universe; whether we imagine the light in it to be like 'waves' or 'corpuscles', and so on – provided only that these contents are filtered into the universe of knowledge through the empirical methods of science, and that they are regarded as entirely 'relative' and subject to replacement by later theories under the empirical criterion.

This distinction which we have suggested between concepts and images, between thought and imagination, is very important. That is notoriously true in connection with theology (which we shall discuss later); but it is true also of science. Much of our discussion of the scientific world-view has already been concerned with various mental images or pictures of reality; but the scientist does not take them to be literal representations of the true nature of reality: they are 'mere images', and they can lead to absurdity if their logical implications are pursued consistently to the end. Thus the image of 'curvature', which seems to be implied in the mathematical equations of the theory of relativity, if pressed (spatially) to the full-circle image, seems to mean (in terms of the time factor), that if you travel far and fast enough into the future, you will finally arrive in the remote past! Even in science, this is surely absurd! It is mathematical equations, which scientists *think*, and not mental images which they *imagine*, that are generally acknowledged as offering the most accurate description the scientist can give of reality, of the 'facts'.

But, despite the dangers and inaccuracies inherent in their use, the scientist cannot dispense with symbolic and pictorial images and models in his thinking – for, as C. A. Coulson has said, "greatness in science is associated not with facts, but with *imagination*".[12] "The story of physics," Coulson elaborates, "is simply full of changed models for space. At one period space is a plenum, full of vortices or their equivalent: at a later time it is empty: then it is the seat of electric and magnetic forces: next it is an aether: under Einstein's influence it becomes curved: the quantum theoreticians now load it full with zero-point vibrations and imaginary oscillators..."[13]

R. E. D. Clark speaks of a "tendency which is characteristic of investigations in nearly every field of science at the present time. It has been found repeatedly that no progress is possible until the scientists let their minds jump right out of one discipline into another. How is an atom constructed? The *analogy* of the solar system at once suggested itself and was developed mathematically in the early days. What is the atomic nucleus like? Two analogies are used, both successful as far as they go – it may resemble a drop of liquid (with the particles in close contact) or a small ball of gas (in which particles collide only occasionally)... What about living organisms?... Nerves are compared to wires carrying electric currents, the brain to a computer... Boldly we use ideas and images that are logically quite out of place... So we are learning slowly that knowledge cannot exist without symbols. The old idea, so beloved of the sceptic, that science would bring us down to some sort of bedrock truth, quite literal and symbol-free, has gone for good."[14] C. S. Lewis, referring to Mr. Edwyn Bevan's *Symbolism and Belief* in the course of a discussion of this subject, concludes: "To think, then, is one thing, and to imagine another. What we think or say can be, and usually is, quite different from what we imagine or picture; and what we mean may be true when the mental images that accompany it are entirely false."[15] In spite of the dangers of using mental images, however, creative thinking even in science cannot work without them.

Having defended the propriety of employing 'images' to depict the scientific world-view (the word 'view' here, indeed, seems to demand pictorial representation) in respect both of its formal outline and of its factual contents, we must consider further what the nature of these contents should be.

Reference has been made to the 'empirical attitudes' of secular man, and to what we defined as his fundamental presuppositions, "that science is the only source of true knowledge, and that anything that cannot be investigated by the empirical methods of science is not real." But it must be strongly affirmed that not all scientists are, in this sense of the word, 'secular' men. This narrowly exclusive presupposition, which not only declares the importance of empirically verified knowledge, but goes on to deny the possibility of any other sort of knowledge or reality, probably *must* be accepted by every scientist *as scientist* and for the purposes of his scientific work. But *as a man,* the scientist may well have a broader vision of reality, so that he can see his experimental scientific work as but one aspect of his life, and realise that the truth it yields is but one aspect of his knowledge. He may indeed see – as many scientists of course have seen – that to accept without qualification the secular view, that all human knowledge can be adequately accounted for in terms of the empirical methods of science alone, is excessively narrow-minded and leads to absurdity.

Thus M. Polanyi, a distinguished physical chemist, declares in a monumental work on scientific method, that "the prevailing conception of science, based on the disjunction of subjectivity and objectivity, seeks – and must seek at all costs – to eliminate from science ... passionate, personal, human appraisals of theories ... For modern man has set up as the ideal of knowledge the conception of natural science as a set of statements which is 'objective' in the sense that its substance is entirely determined by *observation*." Such scientific knowledge cannot consistently include, on its own presuppositions, a recognition of the scientist's own "passionate participation in the act of knowing".[16]

This means, in effect, that for empirical science, and for the secular man who accepts its presuppositions as adequate and absolute, everything without exception must be seen or interpreted ultimately in terms of objective observable 'events' or 'occurrences' in a closed, causally determined world-view. Even human actions, in so far as they achieve changes in the observable world, must be viewed through the spectacles of empirical objectivity, so that they cannot be regarded as deliberate, *intentional acts,* which consciously aim at the achievement of a personal purpose, but only as objective *events* in a chain of natural causality. These events are the basic units with which science works, objective units which can be systematically observed and recorded as 'facts'. And the task of scientific theory is to discover and chart the patterns of invariable connection or of causal relation between these events, and to embody these patterns in the simplest possible formulation, as 'laws of nature'. Such scientific laws are regarded, (since Kant's time), as regulating our thinking rather than reality itself, and so as "rules by which one may come to make a true statement of unknown fact on the basis of facts that are already known";[17] and their value is entirely dependent on the assumption of invariable and unchanging basic patterns of regularity throughout the whole universe – on the uniformity or constancy of nature.

This, then, is what the secular man means by 'nature' – and nature comprises the *whole* contents of his world-view. It is a closed system containing 'causally related events' in which the patterns of regular connection can, in principle at least, be fully discovered and described by empirical science. On this view, of course, to conceive or imagine any reality (such as a Creator-God) before, beyond or above the empirical realities open to investigation and description by science must be regarded as intolerable and irrational dualistic nonsense. For secular man, the supreme authority, the object of his most fundamental faith and trust, is the empirical verification principle of science. For him, this empirical principle stands in the place given by the Christian to God, and excludes the possibility of any 'revelation' other than that from scientific 'discovery'. He accepts without question, with dogmatic, fundamentalist certainty, the complete adequacy of this principle as the sole source of knowledge and the only adequate test of reality.

For those who accept the empirical, secular presupposition, as the 'Secular Christians' do, it seems clear that if concepts such as 'God', 'revelation', 'resurrection', 'heaven', 'life-beyond-death' and the like are to be accorded any meaning at all, as referring to some sort of reality, they must somehow be reinterpreted in terms of empirical realities or of natural occurrences, understood as wholly contained within the natural world.

Thus the living Creator-God of biblical theology who is before and beyond nature (supernatural) is declared to be 'dead': and for those theologians who wish to continue using the word 'God' it comes to mean not a transcendent Person but an immanent principle within nature – an impersonal 'ground of being' or 'the constancy of nature' or 'Love' without a Lover,

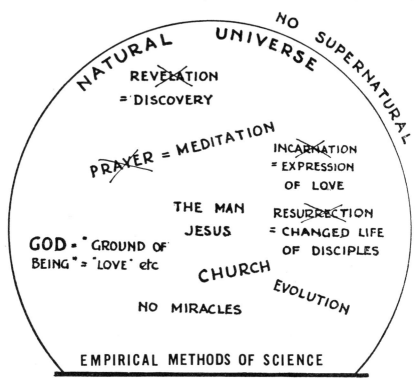

THE 'SECULAR CHRISTIAN' WORLD-VIEW

or 'the depth of human existence', or some such thing. 'Revelation' becomes an aspect of human discovery, since communication from such a 'God' is absurd. Nor, of course, can this sort of 'God' *act*, in nature and history: and so 'miracles' become 'unusual events whose cause is not (yet) understood and which therefore cause astonishment', or something of the kind. The 'Incarnation' cannot here mean that from beyond nature God sent His Son into the world to become man, for 'God' is within and not beyond nature. It is therefore 're-interpreted' to the effect that since, in the life of the Galilean peasant Jesus of Nazareth, love found uniquely perfect expression – and 'Love' is 'God' – this constituted the incarnation of 'God' in Jesus, and was at the same time the most perfect fulfilment of Man, whose true nature it is to love. In the secular world-view there is, of course, no 'heaven' above or beyond nature, and no life for man beyond natural death. The Resurrection of Jesus therefore receives re-interpretation by the 'Secular Christians' as a transforming psychological experience which the disciples had after their Master's death, as they reverently remembered Him, by which they were enabled to share something of His loving outlook and attitude towards men. For them, in this way, He 'came alive'; though for Him personally, as for all men, death was the end. In the same 'empirical' way 'prayer' and all other basic Christian concepts are 're-interpreted' by the 'Secular Christians'.

Such, then, is the shape and theological content of the world-view of 'Secular Christianity', based on the primary secular presupposition, with its exaltation of the empirical methods of science. It is, of course, very different from the world-view of Biblical Christianity, to which we now turn.

CHAPTER 2

The Biblical Presupposition

"In the beginning God created the heavens and the earth." This very first affirmation in the Bible presupposes the living Creator-God, God before and beyond all things, *God in action* as Creator of all else that is. It is this which is the basic and constant presupposition of the whole Bible, Old Testament and New. There is no attempt in the Bible to prove or defend this presupposition. It is simply assumed, as what is basically 'given', to be accepted 'by faith alone'. God is the creative primary Agent: living, personal, and able to act in fulfilment of His purposes.

"What pervades the Bible is the unmistakable presence of the *living* God," one theologian has recently written. "The Scriptures from Genesis to Revelation make it insistently clear that God is alive and active. He creates, he moves, he speaks, he divides, he calls, he sees, he blesses. (Gen. 1) He is Alpha and Omega, the first and the last, the Beginning and the End. (Rev. 22:13) ... St. Paul's 'good news' is that men should turn to the living God. (Acts 14:15) ... The Church is 'The Church of the living God' ..."[1] The God of the Bible is the living God, and He is known to be living because He is a God who *acts*.

The basic presupposition of biblical theology therefore is ontological, affirming the existence of God who acts. The immediate epistemological consequence of this must be the recognition of 'revelation' as a source of knowledge alongside the knowledge yielded by science. Revelation comes to men through the acts of God together with a 'word' – a conceptual interpretation of these particular acts as *God's* acts.

"Biblical theology," G. E. Wright has written in his book

48

God Who Acts, "is a theology of recital or proclamation of the acts of God, together with the inferences drawn therefrom."[2] Alan Richardson declares that the backbone of the Old Testament faith, like that of the New, is a *kerugma* – a proclamation of "the mighty acts of God".[3] Referring to what he calls "the central features of the biblical truth of revelation", G. E. Ladd writes: "God has revealed himself to men not only in words but first of all in acts, in deeds, in historical events."[4] K. S. Kantzer states: "According to most contemporary theologians the method of divine revelation consists of the 'mighty acts' of God in nature, in history, in conscience, in the human soul, and above all, in Jesus Christ."[5] He goes on to quote John Baillie who wrote: ". . . one of the points in which there appears a remarkable breadth of agreement in recent discussion . . . is this: that God reveals himself *in action* – in the gracious activity by which he invades the field of human experience and human history . . . The Bible is essentially the story of the acts of God."[6] The same emphasis finds expression in the theology of Wolfhart Pannenberg and his increasingly influential circle in Germany today. ". . . I have related none of the other traditionally-asserted forms of divine self-manifestation to the modern problem of revelation," Pannenberg wrote in his recent dialogue with American theologians, "but rather precisely this idea of the self-confirmation of God through his action."[7] T. F. Torrance maintains that the very heart of the Reformation was that mediaeval Roman theology was "subjected to searching criticism in an effort to purge it of alien conceptions of deity and nature and to restore in its fulness the biblical notion of the living God who freely and actively intervenes in history."[8]

Names and quotations could be multiplied, but the point is sufficiently made. For those whose starting point is *biblical* rather than *secular*, the basic presupposition is the reality, power and over-all authority of God as Agent, God who acts. This is the fundamental faith-affirmation of the biblical Christian: God is real and active, and all other reality and activity originates from Him. It is in terms of this fact, for the Christian, that every claim to truth must ultimately be assessed.

Only this presupposition (we maintain), affirming the primacy not only of God but also of action, can bind into a coherent unity the kaleidoscopic diffractions of human knowledge, including those aspects distinguished as objective and subjective, discovered and revealed, natural and supernatural.

GOD AND THE WORLD

These divisions in knowledge, it has been said with some truth by R. Bultmann and others, are products of thinking which is more 'advanced' and less 'primitive' than that found in the Bible. Of Hebrew thought, as contrasted with Greek thought, Bultmann writes: "There is no conception of the 'cosmos', of 'nature', of the law of nature. The world is never objectified as a natural order whose eternal laws are open to intellectual apprehension. There is no natural science or physics ... God's revelation in nature is not seen in the ordered course of natural history, but in unusual and terrifying occurrences like storm and earthquake."[9]

There is both truth and confusion in Bultmann's contention. It is true that "the world is never *objectified* as a natural order" in biblical theology; but far from viewing this as a primitive disadvantage for thought, we would claim that many of the troubles into which modern theology has fallen originate from its initial acceptance, as 'given' and unavoidable, of science's useful but unsatisfactory and ultimately untenable divorce of the objective from the subjective aspects of reality. (The efforts of Bultmann and his Existentialist colleague, F. Gogarten, to re-marry subjective and objective in the chapel of Existentialism, [though unsuccessful as we shall later show] indicate an awareness of the acute problems which this division creates.) To accord to 'objective knowledge' a unique status as the only true or real knowledge (which is what the 'scientism' of secular man does) is to make the division absolute and irreparable. Only by challenging and qualifying this distinction at the beginning, at the level of presuppositions, (as we shall do later) can that unity of thought be preserved which allows an adequate account of reality and of life to be given.

However, if biblical theology – especially in the Old Testament – has no objectified and impersonal view of nature and natural law, so that it regards everything that happens as the dynamic, personal activity of God, how can it also be true, as Bultmann claims, that "God's revelation in nature is *not* seen in the ordered course of natural history"? Many passages could be quoted to the contrary, but perhaps Psalm 19 is sufficient: "The heavens are telling the glory of God; and the firmament proclaims his handiwork. Day to day pours forth speech, and night to night declares knowledge." (v. 1, 2) What we must say, surely, is that for the Hebrews in Old Testament times, everything in nature was seen as ultimately 'act of God': but some special, 'unusual' occurrences – storm, earthquake and the like – were seen as God's *mighty acts*, as miracles. These were understood to be the result of His immediate purpose and direct personal intervention, and to constitute *special* revelation, as interpreted by the Prophets.

It must be noted, however, that in order for the Hebrews to distinguish, as Bultmann suggests they did, between the usual and the unusual, requires already a concept of 'patterns of regularity' – a picture of what is 'normal' as a backdrop against which to see the unusual. Men knew well – for instance the conservative Sadducees – that 'dead men do not rise', long before science formulated biological 'laws'.

They knew that resurrection is not normal, or 'natural', and that only a mighty act of God, executing a specific purpose, could bring renewed life out of death. Undoubtedly, therefore, although the Bible does not 'objectify' nature nor dissociate it from God, the distinction was clearly made between the normal and the miraculous within the total unity of the acts and purposes of God the Creator, who works out His will within the universe He created.

It can be convincingly argued, indeed, that the birth of modern science owes more to a development of this Hebrew distinction between Creator and creation in which God is understood to have a separate, personal existence as Creator who is before and beyond or above the whole universe which is His creation, than it does to the Greek idea of the world as a 'cosmos', of which Bultmann speaks. In Greek thought, as he says, "The world is a unitary organism. Its strict observance of the laws of cause and effect make it so, and therefore rationally intelligible. For the Greek mind this meant that the world was itself divine."[10] God was merged with nature, and became essentially a part or aspect of the 'objective' cosmos.

The psychological importance of the Hebrew concept of creation for the origins of modern science has been stressed by many theologians. John Baillie, for example, noting that the point is

51

being emphasised by an increasing number of historians,[11] argues that the development of the modern view of nature, necessary for science, was made possible by the Reformers' rediscovery of the biblical doctrine of creation with its emphasis on the radical *distinction* between God and His creation. If what we now call 'nature' was conceived as a part or aspect of God Himself, (as in Greek thought, according to Bultmann) simple reverence or primitive fear would inhibit the believer from engaging in or supporting the sacrilege of seriously trying to investigate Him (and it) experimentally. The possibility of developing empirical science would then be largely contingent on the prior establishment of an atheistic attitude in the society concerned – and atheism is not normally characteristic of 'primitive' societies. To distinguish clearly between God and nature, Creator and creation, would seem to be a psychological prerequisite for the development of empirical science in a community. In historical fact it was only when mediaeval Christendom, so deeply influenced by Greek thought-patterns, was released into the freedom of the Hebrew/Christian distinction between Creator and creation, God and nature, that modern science was born. As T. F. Torrance says: "The Reformation of the sixteenth century certainly involved a profound change in the attitude to nature." Such a change was badly needed, away from the Greek-influenced mediaeval view of nature as a sort of cyclic emanation from a relatively static and changeless God, back to the biblical view of nature as the creation of a dynamic, active Creator-God. "This was what was brought about by the Reformation," Torrance writes. "With it the whole outlook upon nature changed. It is that change in the concept of nature that is so characteristic of the whole of modernity."[12]

Thus we can say that the absolute distinction between Creator and creation which emerged from biblical, Hebrew thought was present along with the objective/subjective distinction, derived from Greek thought, at the birth of modern science: and that many of the ailments in the body of human thought which modern theology (like modern philosophy, history and science) has been concerned to diagnose and heal, have stemmed from the wrong use – as absolute and normative instead of merely relative and functional – of that distinction between subjective and objective aspects of truth and reality which comes from Greek thought and which dominates modern science.

WORLD-VIEWS AND IMAGES OF GOD

If now, as an aid to popular understanding, we try to represent diagrammatically the outline 'form' of the Christian world-view, it is clear that the only possible base upon which it could properly rest is: The *Creator God* – who acts. Of course the universe of nature, as the *creation* of the pre-existent Creator-God, who remains transcendent beyond and above it while also being immanent and active within it, must be represented not only as standing upon God as its foundation but also as wholly contained within His reality. With what diagram can we represent God as containing within His own creative and sustaining reality the whole natural universe?

At this point some scholarly readers will wish to explode with protests against this idolatrous sin of trying to represent *God* – YHWH whom no man has ever seen; of whom the prophet Isaiah asks, "To whom then will you liken God, or what likeness compare with him?" (Isaiah 40:18) – and then pours ridicule on the very idea! "You shall not make yourself a graven image, or any likenesss of anything that is in heaven above . . ." – so states the Second Commandment: and the whole Bible makes it clear that to worship any God that you can represent with an image is idolatry. Of course, we do not now make *metal* images to worship. What we go in for, rather, are *mental* images; and these also, by clear implication, are obviously prohibited by the Second Commandment. Do not think that anything you can imagine is really like God; do not make imaginative representations of Him, for they will certainly be false. Just this, many theologians would want to say, has been one of the main faults of the Church throughout the centuries, and the time has come to put our house in order in this respect.

"Our Image of God Must Go!" – this was the 'motto' on which J. A. T. Robinson's best-seller *Honest to God* was launched in 1963. The words appeared first as the headline above a pre-publication article written by the Bishop for a London newspaper; and the editorial comment preceding the text of this article stated that the main theme of the book was "to question the traditional image of God". We must grant that the Bishop does make critical reference to one or two caricature 'images' which he calls traditional views of God (e.g.

"the mental image of an old man in the sky" on page 13 – and, with reference to belief in God as incarnate in Jesus, "God dressed up like Father Christmas" on page 66). He also considers and rejects the idea that God is a person. Yet it will be clear to the discerning reader that what is primarily and radically questioned and rejected in *Honest to God* is not so much an image of God Himself, as a *world-view* which represents God as being related to the natural world in a certain way, as 'supernatural', or as 'transcendent' in a way other than merely by a special quality of immanence.

There is, of course, a very great difference between making an image of *God* on the one hand and depicting on the other a *world-view* which indicates in a purely formal way the relationship of God to the world, without giving imaginative content to 'God'. For whereas no Christian can properly believe that anything he can imagine about God (apart from Jesus Christ, who is "the image of the invisible God", Colossians 1 : 15) is an accurate or true representation, yet surely every intelligent Christian has an obligation to think out, with the Bible, the nature of God's relationship to this world in which He acts. To aid clarity of understanding it is important, if possible, to represent this in a world-view comparable with other world-views which have been constructed from different view-points and with different presuppositions.

One important cause of the tragic confusion of contemporary theology is undoubtedly its failure to do this in an effective manner. This failure has left the way wide open for R. Bultmann, J. A. T. Robinson, L. G. Geering and others to set forth – as illustrating (they say) the traditional and not-yet-superseded biblical and Christian world-view – a primitive three-decker cosmogony, with heaven literally above and hell literally below the earth.

They would probably concede that most biblical or traditional Christians today have accepted the 'round-earth' view in place of the old 'flat-earth' view; but they argue (with more than a little truth) that this leaves some Christians confused and puzzled as to the proper modern interpretation of, for instance, the word 'above' when referring to 'God' and 'heaven'. This confusion, however, is by no means necessarily inherent in the presuppositions of biblical theology. These New Theologians surely realise full well that although they, like the rest of us,

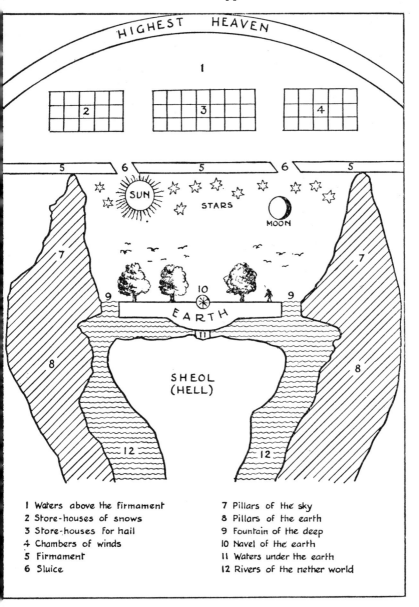

1 Waters above the firmament
2 Store-houses of snows
3 Store-houses for hail
4 Chambers of winds
5 Firmament
6 Sluice
7 Pillars of the sky
8 Pillars of the earth
9 Fountain of the deep
10 Navel of the earth
11 Waters under the earth
12 Rivers of the nether world

PRIMITIVE BIBLICAL WORLD-VIEW

Based on a diagram by T. H. Goster in his article on Cosmogony in *The Interpreter's Dictionary of the Bible*. Copyright © 1962 by the Abingdon Press. Used by permission.

continue to speak of the rising and setting of the sun, yet neither they nor we believe still (as did primitive and mediaeval men until the time of Copernicus) that the sun literally does circle the earth each day, rising 'up' into the sky and going 'down' in the sunset. They must therefore agree that it is both possible and common to use such 'pre-Copernican' terminology without thereby being committed to the pre-Copernican world-view. Yet because traditional Christianity speaks of God as being 'up above' or as 'supernatural' and so on, they claim that this proves it to be inseparably committed to a primitive biblical and pre-Copernican world-view! And, since modern theologians have failed to think through the Faith in terms of a diagrammatic world-view that can be accepted as both comparable and compatible with the world-views of science, but have offered only *words* about God – words usually as abstract and negative as possible ('non-objectifiable', 'wholly other', 'non-temporal' and the like) – confusion and dismay have spread among intelligent Christians in face of the ridicule heaped by the Secular Theologians on this so called 'traditional Christian world-view'.

"There are several modern writers who pour scorn upon any idea of God being *up* or *above*," J. B. Phillips has written. "They are confusing literal spatial position with a mental image which must be common to nearly all thinking human beings. Why should we talk of 'high' ideals or a 'high' purpose? Why should we talk of a 'rise' in salary? Why should sales be 'soaring'?...and so we could go on. It is a common and quite understandably symbolic way of speaking..."[13] This is well said. Much more doubtful however is the validity of Phillips' conviction that Paul "uses expressions of height and depth as useful symbols but not geographic locations", and that neither he nor the Ephesian Christians to whom he was writing understood the Resurrection and Exaltation of Jesus to God's right hand "in physical terms".[14] Is there not in most of us – when we are thinking about the created world of nature and also about its relationship with the supernatural Creator and the risen and ascended Christ at His 'right hand' – a sort of compulsion (perhaps a necessity for thought) to use 'concrete' mental images of a spatial sort? Are they not deeply embedded in the wording of the Second Commandment itself: "You shall not make for yourself a graven image, or any likeness of anything that is in *heaven above,* or that is on *the earth beneath,* or that is in the water *under the earth*"? (Deut. 5:8).

With the physical emptiness of the tomb and the *upwards* impression made on them by the ascension of our Lord, is it reasonable to suppose that the first century Christians, whose contemporaries undoubtedly accepted some sort of three-decker world-view, somehow avoided the conviction that Jesus had literally, spatially, gone up to God in heaven? Must we not agree that this *is* probably the way in which the first Christians interpreted the Resurrection and Ascension, and Heaven? But what follows from this?

If, in place of this first century conception of space and matter our contemporaries today have adopted a different view of these things, why cannot we Christians relate our understanding of the Resurrection, the Ascension, the belief that God is 'up' in heaven, and so on, to the world-view of *our* contemporaries? To flee from spatial terms into a language of pure subjectivist spirituality is to run into inescapable trouble. If the Resurrection and Ascension and the 'super' status of God are real, then we must accept the task of translating the three-dimensional flat-earth physico-spatial view of these things held by St. Peter and St. Paul into terms of our four-dimensional (or N-dimensional) view of space-time, our energy/matter view of physical reality and our problems about the relationship to these of *personal* reality, self-consciousness, action, and the like. We must repudiate as absurd if not malicious the contention that the fundamental convictions of biblical Christianity to which we have referred cannot be understood physically or 'realistically' except in terms of the primitive first century world-view.

How is the modern Christian to understand the relationship between God as Creator and Saviour, on the one hand, and the world on the other? "It is the nature of this relationship which is in urgent need of exploration today," writes R. S. Barbour.[15] "Copernicus, Galileo, Newton, Darwin – all were acutely aware of the problem of the relationship between their astronomical and other scientific discoveries and the belief in a transcendent God, Creator of the universe and Author of Salvation; but today it appears to be possible, as it was not until recently, to suspend the question of God and to have a cosmology without a creator and without a soteriology. It is also apparently possible for Christians to suspend the question of cosmology, and to have a soteriology unrelated to the picture of the universe which their contemporaries – and they themselves by implication – hold. Are these in fact genuine possibilities? In particular, is the latter really a possible attitude for Christians? Or must we attempt to hold our doctrine of salvation and our view of the universe in relationship to one another?' After some discussion Barbour concludes: "On the whole we must assume that salvation and cosmology remain very closely linked. Without a suitable cosmology it is not possible to have a convincing doctrine of salvation."[16]

HEARING AND SEEING

There is an important distinction which is relevant here between language understood as linking thought with reality through visual or 'mimetic' imagery on the one hand, and through an 'acoustic' or auditory bond on the other. The visual interpretation of language is more appropriate to relatively static, spatial subjects – such as 'world-views' – but is unable to deal adequately with action and dynamic reality such as persons. For these the acoustic interpretation is much better fitted. Here again the Greek and Hebrew approaches were basically different.

Of this R. Bultmann writes: "Just as seeing (whether physical or spiritual) means perceiving at a distance an apparently stationary object, thus ascertaining its shape and measurements – so hearing is a sense of being encountered, of the distance being bridged, the acknowledgement of a speaker's claim on us. The Greek tends to think of the world as an objective closed system, susceptible of mathematical measurement. Thus for him sight tends to be the most important of the senses. For the Old Testament, however, hearing is the most important . . . Hearing is the means by which God is apprehended."[17]

This being so, it is important to keep clearly in mind that speaking about a Christian world-view is a different thing from speaking about God; and that whereas visual imagery and diagrammatic representation may be quite out of place and even sacrilegious in one case, it may be the only way to avoid inept and woolly thinking in the other. The danger lies in 'getting our lines crossed' as it were, and this has been another source of confusion in modern theology. This is well shown by T. F.

Torrance, who quotes J. A. T. Robinson as saying that he "will always think and theologise in pictures". "Now if the relation between theological language and God is mimetic," Torrance writes, "if it involves a pictorial relation, then of course we are led to identify God by some pictures we have in our mind, and are forced to think of theological language as essentially descriptive. Thinking in pictures thus creates desperate problems, as we can see in Robinson's book *Honest to God* – his remedy is to keep changing the pictures and images, lest one image should harden into some idolatrous form and become substituted for God."[18] For talk of God, then, we must use language with attention primarily to its 'acoustic' significance, as relating to personal realities, to action, encounter, and the like; but we must not allow this fact to deter us from facing up to the need clearly to think through the problems of a Christian world-view which can be related to the world-views of modern science. "If we are really Christians," wrote James Denney, "we must know God; and our task, when we theologise, is to define our knowledge; to put it into scientific and systematic form, and to show, at least in outline, that general view of the world which it involves."[19] Again we ask, therefore: how can we represent diagrammatically the background realities of biblical theology in a world-view more adequate to modern thought than the pre-Copernican picture?

From a biblical perspective, the 'world' – the universe of nature – is essentially 'the creation', which is a dependent concept, derived from that basic faith-affirmation of Hebrew-Christian thought – the existence of the personal *Creator*, the living God who acts. It is impossible, therefore, to represent 'the world' alone, in a biblical world-view, as though it were self-subsistent and comprised the whole of reality. No *biblical* world-view for today will be possible unless we can indicate formally the fact, and something of the nature, of the relationship of the living God who acts – the Creator – to the world, which is His creation. Of course this formal representation of relationship must not be filled with imaginative content in visual terms – with an 'image' of God.

Since God was before the natural world as Creator, we represent His relationship to the natural world as the base or foundation on which all nature stands. Since He is today 'beyond' and 'above' the natural world, as its Lord, Redeemer and

Sustainer, we represent Him as greater in area than the circle of the natural world; though this certainly cannot be interpreted with quantitative literalness. In this sense we indicate the 'supernatural' or transcendent status of God. Since God cannot be adequately defined or described by man, or be confined within the limits of human understanding – (King Solomon declared almost three thousand years ago: "Heaven and the highest heaven cannot contain Thee" – I Kings 8:27) – we therefore represent Him by a broken or dotted line encircling and wholly enclosing the natural world.

The natural world, in such a modern biblical-world-view, would have to contain all that is real and true according to science, subject to acknowledgement of the relativity and impermanence of many 'scientific facts', and also (I think) to the provisional exclusion of some scientific theories such as that of the 'steady-state, eternal-matter' view of the world.[20] And of course everything would be viewed as the creation of God. Knowledge of God would have to be viewed as having come into the world from God by personal revelation, and the revelatory acts of God in nature and history could be represented by means of arrows reaching into our four-dimensional space-time universe from the eternal dimensions of God's being, as 'miracles'.

It is important to note that the Christian world-view expressed in this *form* may be given a very considerable variety of theological *content*, as well as of scientific content. Indeed, the whole range of the historical interpretations of the Christian Faith can be represented on this diagram, from the literalist beliefs of the biblical 'Fundamentalist' who accepts without question as historically true every miracle account in the Scriptures, to the radical doubts of the Liberal theologian who doubts every miracle, but still acknowledges that miracles as acts of God *could* possibly happen, because he has not yet denied the relevant reality of the living Creator-God. And not only all varieties of Christian orthodoxy through the centuries, but all the Christian heresies also, from the beginning of Church history up to that variety of modernist Liberalism which Karl Barth so tellingly criticised as 'heresy' – all can find a place in this Christian world-view. But not 'Secular Christianity'. This new view whose fundamental presupposition entails the 'a priori' denial of the living Creator-God who acts in the world, and so, without further examination, of all miracles – this view *starts* at the point where, on the Christian world-view, faith has finally died; and, as we have seen, it requires a different form altogether for visual representation. Can it still properly claim to be really Christian at all?

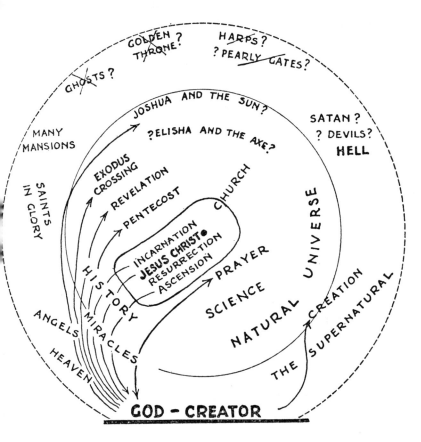

WORLD VIEW OF THE BIBLE AND THE CHURCH

The continuing use of some at least of the traditional Christian terminology by 'Secular Christianity' is regarded by many as an indication that it is just another 'interpretation' of Christianity rather than a denial of or substitute for it. But a consideration of the radically different, naturalistic and secular definitions given to some of these familiar words by the 'Secular Christians' has driven many to the contrary conclusion.

One specially interesting term which some secular theologians continue to employ (though others realise that it is really inappropriate for their position) is 'the acts of God'. They use it in a sense that seems intended to retain the 'acts', while dispensing with the Agent, as we shall now see.

CHAPTER 3

The Acts of God in 'Secular Christianity' and in Biblical Theology

In his book *Secularisation*, Arnold E. Loen describes the debate on secularisation as being focused precisely on the question of 'the acts of God'. "Formerly," he writes, "man was conscious of living in a world whose order pointed to God and in which God acted directly. Today that is no longer true: we are neither conscious of God in the cosmic order nor of his direct activity ... Is it true that God is withdrawing from the world? Or is he still present, today as yesterday, still showing traces of himself in the cosmic order and still acting directly? Or was he never present in the world at all, as little yesterday as today? Did the cosmic order never point to God and did he never act directly in it?"[1]

This analysis accords with the positions we have outlined: for we have seen that the root presupposition of biblical theology, on the one hand, is the reality of the living personal Creator-God who acts in nature and history; and that personal acts – the acts of God – are the basic units out of which this theology builds its 'world-view'. The primary presupposition of 'Secular Christianity', on the other hand, is that the empirical methods of modern science constitute the only ultimate source of truth and the only test of reality: and the units into which reality must be broken, to pass through the sieve of these methods, is 'events', understood as objective occurrences from which all possible subjective influence has been eliminated. It is therefore clear that except in so far as actions, and in particular the acts of God, can be reduced to terms of 'events', the secular man cannot possibly admit them as real, nor accept as true any accounts given of them.

If this is so, we may expect to find that 'Secular Christian'

63

writers either reject altogether the concept of 'acts of God', or else re-interpret it in a way which splits apart the complementary terms 'act' and 'agent', dispensing with God as Agent while retaining the term 'acts of God' for reference to natural *events* of some sort. Let us consider what a few of them have to say on this matter.

PAUL VAN BUREN. Perhaps the clearest and least ambiguous of the writers for 'Secular Christianity' is Paul van Buren. He, like the other secular theologians, uses some of the basic and familiar Christian words in strange, 're-interpreted' ways; but unlike some of the others, he makes real efforts to indicate his changed meaning clearly, when he is using an old word in a new way.

In the New Testament, van Buren tells us, "divine action is conceived as an intervention in this world by heavenly, transcendent powers. But men today can no longer give credence to such a way of thinking."[2] The early Christian Fathers insisted, he says, "that that which had taken place in the life, death and resurrection of Jesus was an act of God himself";[3] but, according to van Buren, we have been taught by Bultmann (and by Ogden who follows him in this) that "the mythological world-view has gone . . . in which God is said to have acted at a certain time in this world to change the state of human affairs."[4] Even these teachers, however, are not radical enough for van Buren. "Linguistic analysis challenges the qualified theism of Bultmann and of Ogden as much as that of more conservative theologians. Whether objectifying or non-objectifying, language about 'God who acts' must be interpreted in some other way."[5]

Thus van Buren, in secular loyalty to the empirical methods of science, deliberately parts company with the view of the New Testament and the Church Fathers, with the tradition of the Church through the centuries, and with what most modern theologians, at least until very recently, have agreed upon. He insists that 'acts of God' cannot be accepted as historically real by those who take science seriously – not, that is, if they are regarded as the purposeful actions of a transcendent living and personal Agent. The re-interpretation which van Buren then gives to the term 'acts of God' is determined by the fact that history, as he understands it, is simply "an answering of ques-

64

tions about *human actions* in the past . . . An account of 'how God works in history' is not history", and indeed has no real meaning, he maintains, since we cannot verify it empirically. Our definition of history, he says, "does not attempt to speak of 'God' as an 'actor in history' . . . It does not have room for transempirical entities . . ."[6] How then is the 'Secular Christian' to interpret the fundamental claim of the New Testament that Jesus "is not only the revelation of God but also the act of God: his history is God's decisive act of love for this world, . . . summed up typically in Paul's words: 'in Christ God was reconciling the world to himself' "?[7] Van Buren replies that to say something is an 'act of God' is really just to say that it is 'normative'. "He who asserts that the history of Jesus was a *normative* history of reconciliation means that he is committed to the *sort* of reconciliation revealed in that history . . . Wherever he sees at work in the world any reconciliation at all like that which characterised the history of Jesus of Nazareth, he will support it . . ."[8] It must be remembered that for van Buren the life and work of Jesus were purely and simply human, for he acknowledges no transempirical (or supernatural) personal God who could be working in and through Jesus. The secular man who says Jesus' loving and reconciling life was 'God's act', then, means no more than that he accepts it as normative for him, as setting a standard and direction for life which he will attempt to follow. (Just this, for van Buren, is what it means to be a Christian – a 'Secular Christian'.) The term 'act of God', therefore, refers to any individual effort or any social force working in the world towards that sort of reconciliation between people that Jesus fostered, as seen by one who thinks such reconciliation is 'good'.

The Christian doctrines of Creation, Providence, Redemption, and other doctrines which have always been regarded as requiring the personal action of God are re-interpreted in similar ways. Thus, for example, "The doctrine of Creation concerns God and his activity but . . . the doctrine is now used to assert that this world . . . is 'good' . . . The Christian doctrine of divine creation of all things 'through Jesus Christ' is . . . only another way of expressing the Christian's affirmative *attitude* towards the world (as opposed to a dualistic or world-denying attitude) . . ."[9] All 'acts of *God*' therefore, including the Creation, are really just the creation of the minds of *men* who have adopted certain particular attitudes or perspectives, according to Paul van Buren.

HARVEY COX in *The Secular City* is much less ready than van Buren to define in a precise way the main Christian terms he uses – and his meaning therefore emerges less clearly. Study makes it apparent, however, that his view of the 'acts of God' is not dissimilar from that of van Buren, especially in its essential connection with reconciliation among men. Any force working in the world to achieve reconciliation between people, such as Jesus worked for, is for Cox an act of God, or God in action.

Like van Buren, Cox indicates (though less directly) that his secular outlook has no room for the living God of biblical and traditional Christian theism – for the Bible's Living God who acts. "The God he (Camus) rejected, rightly, I believe," Cox says, "is the God of traditional Christian theism."[10] But confusion and misunderstanding are almost inevitable, since he continues to speak freely about 'the activity of God', without indicating how we are to understand the *activity* of a 'God' who is not the living, acting God of biblical Christian theism. Just what positive meaning he wishes to convey when he uses the word 'God', Cox seems not quite to know. It may be, he thinks, "that we shall have to stop talking about 'God' for a while, take a moratorium on speech until a new name emerges."[11] Meantime, "we speak of God to secular man by speaking about man, by talking about man as he is seen in the biblical perspective."[12] 'God' for Harvey Cox seems to be almost identical with 'social change' of a certain sort; and to change society is to change God. "Standing in a picket line is a way of speaking," he argues. "By doing it a Christian speaks of God. He helps alter the word 'God' by changing the society."[13] The primary obligation of the Christian and the Church is "to be broken and reshaped continuously by God's continuous action" Cox maintains: and "the action of God occurs" – note the impersonal form – "through what historians have sometimes called 'historical events' but what might better be termed 'social change'."[14] The Christian, Cox maintains with van Buren, will select the sort of social change which he is prepared to support according to the standard and pattern set by the one he considers to be "the lead actor" in human affairs.

"This actor has disclosed himself in the life of Jesus of Nazareth."[15] Thus, wherever he finds social change making for reconciliation such as Jesus of Nazareth favoured, the Christian will know that his 'politician-God' is acting, and that he must join in.

"Theology today must be that reflection-in-action by which the Church finds out what this politician-God is up to and moves in to work along with him. In the epoch of the secular city politics replaces metaphysics as the language of theology."[16] The 'metaphysical' or supernatural, living Creator-God of the Bible's 'mighty acts', having been dissolved in the acids of secular empiricism, is now replaced by 'Social Change'; and theology really becomes politics.

Whatever else remains obscure, this at least seems to emerge clearly, that, despite his constant references to 'the activity of God', there is no place in Cox's concept of the world – of the secular society and the secular city – for the 'mighty acts of God' in the biblical sense; nor will he acknowledge any God who is a living, personal Agent.

RONALD GREGOR SMITH in his book *Secular Christianity*,[17] expounds an Existentialist version of 'Secular Christianity'; and the words 'act of God' might be regarded as providing the key-term of his whole argument.

The Existentialist theologians are perhaps better known for placing their primary emphasis on 'the word of God' rather than on 'the acts of God'; although from their point of view, as Gerhard Ebeling has said, "With God, word and deed are one: his speaking is the way of his acting."[18] We shall further discuss the reasons for this tendency in Existentialist theology to identify 'word' and 'act' in a later chapter, when considering Rudolf Bultmann's theology. Gregor Smith, in making the identification, plays somewhat on the ambiguity of 'the Word' as meaning both speech and also Christ Himself. "Faith arises," he states, "as a consequence of certain events in history. These events are concentrated in the revelatory act of God in his Word."[19] But not only do the Word and Act of God coincide for him, it seems: both appear to be identical with God's *being*. "We believe that he *is* simply what he does," Gregor Smith declares under the chapter heading of 'An Act of God'. 'When we dare to speak of his acts we mean his acts as the expression of what he is ... His being is not separable from his action ... what he does is one with what he is ... We cannot speak of God being, but only of God acting."[20]

Thus God's being, action and word all coincide in a circle with 'Christ' as its centre – what could look more orthodox and 'biblical'? – and they have no reality apart from 'Christ'. But what does Gregor Smith mean by 'Christ', who is the Word, the Act, and the very Being of God? To such a question biblical and traditional Christianity would answer simply: "Jesus of Nazareth, true man, who was also and in history true God, the living supernatural Creator-God incarnate through His Son – Jesus Christ." But for Gregor Smith, as for Bultmann and other demythologisers, this is far too naïve and simple. For them, there remains "the burning question of the relation of the Jesus of history to the preached Christ" – sometimes called 'the Christ of faith': for that 'Jesus' and this 'Christ' are understood to be quite different.[21] "Are the history of Jesus and Christian faith simply like oil and water?" he asks.[22] And in order to say 'No' to this question, he finds himself obliged to give a very strange definition of 'history' (though he camouflages it somewhat behind the German distinction between *Historie* and *Geschichte*). "History," he says, "may ... be summarily described as what happens to *you*", as something that is "present to you".[23] "A past event which is not remembered is not history."[24] All that is actually remembered of Jesus – so that radical Form Critics maintain – is the bare fact that He lived and died and came to be adored as the Christ. A bare *point* cannot go in a different direction from a *line*, since a point has no direction: and the bare fact of Jesus' historical existence cannot conflict with any conviction about the 'direction' – the meaning and nature – of His life. There cannot therefore be any 'oil and water' conflict between this 'bare-fact Jesus', and 'Christ-of-faith' imaginatively painted in the Gospels (these radical critics believe) by the devotion of the early Christians. This faith-created (*geschichtlich*) Christ is present now as "something that happens to me", an aspect of my existential experience, an attitude in my general outlook, in Gregor Smith's view. But it is this subjective 'Christ' – constructed by the faith of the early Church, and an aspect of 'my' experience – and not the objectively real 'Jesus', who for Gregor Smith is at once the Word, Act and Being of God. Christ is to be found, he says, in my relations with others: and being in relation to others "is an action, not a state: it is the act or venture of mutual existence. In an analogous way, we suggest, we may speak of the relation with God."[25] Thus 'act of God' comes to mean simply 'being in relation with men' without acknowledging that there is any real living Creator-Being who is in relation with men! "It is in this being for others" (i.e. love) "that the act of God is to be apprehended."[26] Therefore, when we are speaking of our relations with others, as also when speaking of "what happens to us in the relation of faith, we are speaking of God's act. And when we speak of God's act we speak of what he is. But, it might be objected, . . . is the concept of God's being not unnecessary, indeed strictly not deducible from his act?"[27] Theology has traditionally "put on the brake" at this point, declining to draw this negative conclusion. Gregor Smith criticises theology's hesitation, and appears satisfied with a conclusion which retains some sort of subjective Word-Act-Being of God, while rejecting the Living, Acting and Speaking God of biblical theology. God's mighty acts, he writes, "can only be understood as breaking the sequence of events in the sense that the events are here both judged and forgiven."[28] But to ask *who* judges and forgives these events, and so acts mightily, would be to ask a foolish 'objectifying' question to which no answer is possible! For the word of judgement and forgiveness is identical with the mighty acts, and they are acts without an Agent: the 'acts' themselves are all that there is of the Agent!

Whatever remains obscure in the convolutions of this existentialist theology, one thing seems certain – that by accepting the presuppositions of secular man, Gregor Smith's *Secular Christianity* has parted company with the primary presupposition of the whole Bible – that God *is*; that this God who acts and speaks in nature and history is the living Doer of His acts and Speaker of His Word.

THOMAS J. J. ALTIZER in *The Gospel of Christian Atheism* injects into the stream of Secular Theology some interesting, although not easily intelligible, variety. Accepting with emphatic enthusiasm the empirically based secular attitude, Altizer presents his convictions in terms of an Idealist logic of thesis, antithesis and synthesis, as once stated by the philosopher Hegel.

In Altizer's somewhat exclusive opinion, the only true

Christians would seem to be the 'radical Christians',[29] of whom he is one. As such, he has repudiated altogether "the God who is sovereign Creator and transcendent Lord".[30] For "to cling to the Christian God in our time is to evade the human situation of our century..."[31] We must therefore accept "the necessity for a contemporary Christian atheism."

Of course, any thought of the man Jesus having been raised by an act of God to continuing personal life in the Resurrection is, for Altizer, sheer nonsense. What then (if anything) does he mean by an 'act of God'?

"God is Jesus, proclaims the radical Christian" – so Altizer informs us – "and by this he means that the Incarnation is a total and all-consuming act: as Spirit becomes the Word that empties the Speaker of himself, the whole reality of Spirit becomes incarnate in its opposite. Only the radical Christian witnesses to the full reality of Jesus or the Incarnate Word, because he alone responds totally to the kenotic movement of God. If Spirit truly empties itself in entering the world, then its own essential and original Being must be left behind in an empty and lifeless form."[32] "The God who acts in the world and history is a God who negates himself, gradually but decisively annihilating his own original Totality... The Christian who comes to understand God as a kenotic and forward-moving process will be delivered from the temptation to think of God as a wholly other and autonomous Being just as he will be freed from any form of theological dualism."[33]

It thus appears that for Altizer's 'radical Christian' who has accepted the freedom of secular man, the acts of God are 'acts' of a process and not of an Agent; and there is no Speaker of God's Word!

There may well remain a doubt in the reader's mind as to just what, if anything, Altizer's words really mean – but from this sampling of the views of the Secular Theologians about 'acts of God' it seems clear that God's acts emerge from secular thought as acts without an Agent. What is to be said about this concept?

David Jenkins has commented on a similar tendency in the writings of Paul Tillich, one of the forerunners of the Secular Theology. "Tillich's justly famous sermons," he writes, "are full of such things as exhortations to be aware that 'you are accepted' – passive verbs without any mention of an agent. To mention an agent would be to objectify God and this would in a sense go beyond the evidence ... But ... if there cannot be said to be an agent, it is extremely difficult to see what meaning can be given to the notion of 'being accepted'."[34] It is even more difficult, we may add, to see what meaning can be given in this sort of context to the basic term 'acts of God'; or what possible justification there can be for its retention by those who have dispensed with the Divine Agent. In such a situation, Jenkins goes on, "perhaps faith must either go further (and make claims about existence) or else cease to exist."[35] "For myself," he concludes, "I cannot see how Tillich's language will work unless the transcendent God exists both transcendentally and in an object-like manner (i.e. He is 'there' to be the agent)."[36] With this conclusion rational men must surely agree! But of course it puts a gigantic question mark against not only the arguments and conclusions, but especially the basic presuppositions of the Secular Christian position.

ANTHROPOMORPHISM AND ACTION

It is clear that the question of theological language, of how we can speak truly about God, is a very important one for modern theology. If the determination of the 'Secular Christians' to avoid 'objectifying' and anthropomorphic language about God leads them to conclusions which seem meaningless or absurd, is silence about God the only rational alternative? The question of theological 'objectivity' we shall consider in a later chapter. What of anthropomorphic talk about God, such as undoubtedly characterises the whole biblical story – is it altogether inappropriate and improper?

If it were not for the fact that God, who is essentially Other than the world and beyond the reach of man's searching, has come from beyond nature to reveal Himself to man through His actions, and especially in the person of Jesus Christ, anthropomorphic language could do no more than construct false images of God in the minds of men. However, as Helmut Gollwitzer has argued in an excellent discussion of 'Anthropomorphism and Analogy' : "The fact is, that with the approach of God the fruitless effort to evade anthropomorphism by means of abstraction, or by keeping as consistently as possible to 'nonobjective' talk of God, has become superfluous – and not only

71

so, but plain wrong: it is no longer a case of avoiding anthro-pomorphism as much as possible, but only (a) of examining what kind of anthropomorphic talk is appropriate and (b) of leaving no doubt about the 'improperness' of such talk."[37]

Gollwitzer insists that *all* our talk is anthropomorphic,[38] if this means that human language can refer only to what men have experienced and thought. If God had not submitted Him-self in action to be known as personal Agent by men, who are also personal agents, we could not have begun to come to know Him or to speak of Him truly at all. For "what the Bible says of God applies to One who is not attainable by any possible method of transcendence or abstraction, but who by *a special act* of approach enters transcendentally into the world as the One who does not belong to the world. It is special in this: that it is not identical with the relation in which the world ever and always stands to him from the start (from *its* start) – that is, with the relation of Creator and creature. Even this creaturely relationship is already *an act* of him whom the Bible calls God, transcending his self-contained being in free demonstration of his being Lord, for which reason the believer knows himself to exist along with the world in a being which he and the world constantly receive by God's free, transcendent giving. God does not belong to the world, but the world belongs to God, in so far as it is constantly dependent on this bestowal of non-divine being by God."[39]

The 'formal' representation of God's relation to the world as Creator to creation which we have offered already has, when it is analysed, dynamic *content*; for it represents an *active* relation-ship. Action, as the distinguishing mark of the personal, in-dicates God as personal Agent, to whom therefore we may apply the personal terms indicated as appropriate by His actions (of which speech is one special form). It must always be recog-nised, however, that these titles are 'improper', as applied to God, in the sense that they cannot be applied to God, the al-together unique One, in the same more or less adequate way in which they are applied to men. "Personal terms like father and son, mother and child, lord and servant, friendship and the like become applicable to our relation to him, but he is not sub-jected to them ... In what sense he is Father, Lord, Friend, etc., and how far these expressions are valid of him, can be ascertained only in view of his *actions*, not beforehand and without regard to them by means of a rigid definition of these terms."[40]

All other theological anthropomorphisms are dwarfed by this basic one which is contained in the fundamental presupposition of the whole Bible – that God *acts*, God is Agent. If this anthropomorphism must be disallowed, then the theology of the Bible and all subsequent 'biblical theologies' are constructed on a false foundation. As Heinrich Jacobi said: "God theomorphised in making man, therefore man must perforce anthropomorphise," when he speaks of God.[41] To speak anthropomorphically about God is *not* to create God in the image of man, unless it is quite false that God created man in His own image.

"Scripture, the so-called Old Testament," according to Martin Buber, "is among the writings of all peoples the only record of concrete action between God and the generations of men, touching in narrative form upon the origin of this action and in promissory form upon its goal . . . For this concrete action there is in the vast edifice of Plato's thought, in the vast edifice of Kant's thought, not only no place but absolutely no room."[42] This is even more obviously true of the modern empirical philosophies that claim to be 'scientific': and it is most interesting that not only the acts of God are excluded by these discursive philosophical systems and especially by the presuppositions of modern scientific method, but also the acts of men, to a consideration of which we now turn.

PART II

THE SECULAR OUTLOOK
AND ITS CONSEQUENCES

CHAPTER 4

Science and Human Action

One essential in the definition of *an act*, as relating to persons, is 'intention'; and intentions, or purposes, are not empirical entities or observable realities. From the point of view of empirical science, they are merely trans-empirical postulates, whose reality cannot be assumed.

There is one element in human behaviour which is not observable, John Macmurray has written in *The Boundaries of Science*. "What is observable in human behaviour is not characteristically human. It lacks the element of intention, which distinguishes the purposeful action of a human being from the mere happening of events in the external world ... Seen from the outside, objectively, a human action appears as an event happening. If science is to maintain the strict objectivity which its method demands, it must treat all observed changes as events. A psychology which is to carry science into the field of human behaviour must, therefore, treat human actions not as actions but as events which happen in the external world. It must seek for their explanation in their interrelation with other events which are equally objective and in laws to which such events conform. It must not refer them to subjective activities such as conscious purposes."[1]

Macmurray's contentions in this argument are most interestingly confirmed by Dr. Christopher Ounsted, a psychiatrist quoted by Ian T. Ramsey.[2] Because of the nature of human life, and also of science, Dr. Ounsted says, the psychiatrist "has two roles, and he must ordinarily play both simultaneously. *As a scientist he must disregard free will*; as a clinician he must constantly assert its claims." But if he loses balance, and affirms the scientific outlook not just as one aspect of thought, one source of truth, but as the sole and adequate authority for knowledge (as we maintain the 'secular man' has done): if, in Ramsey's words, he becomes "a scientific fanatic or bigot", then he will not be "torn two ways" at all. "And then it will happen," Ramsey concludes, "that law and morality are excluded from his considerations", and society, as he sees it, must become "amoral". But whatever the consequences, the scientist, as such, cannot recognise the reality of "metaphysical assumptions" such as personal freedom to choose, and so to *act*.[3]

This fact is of enormous importance. It means that *all acts*, simply as such, are forever beyond the reach of empirical science. It is impossible for empirical science, if it remains faithful to its presuppositions, to recognise any *agent* whatsoever. Therefore the ultimate and essential units with which biblical theology works are necessarily invisible to the eye that wears exclusively empirical or scientific 'spectacles'. That being so, it should not surprise or dismay the biblical Christian to learn that those (including the 'Secular Christians') who believe the empirical methods of science to be the only source of knowledge, *cannot* recognise the reality of God as Agent, nor the 'acts of God' as purposeful interventions in nature and history.

What is surprising, however, is that so many of those who claim to hold this secular outlook should casually continue to speak of *human* actions as though these had not been excluded from scientific recognition, by the same empirical presuppositions as led to the elimination of God's actions from the world of recognised reality. Such a blatant inconsistency at this crucial point cannot be allowed to pass. Let us examine the matter more closely.

An 'event', as viewed by science, is an occurrence in nature which is 'caused' by a preceding occurrence or state of affairs, and which in turn causes other events. Most modern scientists, in the contemporary mood of increasing scientific humility (which unfortunately has not yet percolated down to most of the would-be scientific, secular theologians!) prefer nowadays to speak of the 'invariable connection' of certain types of events rather than of their relation to each other as cause and effect, since the cause/effect terminology seems somehow to suggest that the nature of the connection and its supposed necessity is understood by the scientists – which it is not. But this change of terminology and of attitude makes no real difference to our distinction between events and acts.

We here regard as 'events' (and so exclude from the connotation of the word 'act') all such behaviour of living things as is not the result of a rational purpose. There is, no doubt, a certain attractiveness in the thesis advanced by Teilhard de Chardin who, speaking of "the *within, consciousness,* and then *spontaneity* – three expressions for the same thing", maintains concerning "the stuff of the universe . . . in every region of space and time" that "co-extensive with their Without, there is a Within to things".[4] But, without necessarily dismissing this as an instance of 'the pathetic fallacy', we must maintain that whatever truth there may be in the notion of a consciousness and spontaneity even in inanimate things, it does not affect the distinction with which we are concerned, between the intended *acts* of a self-conscious, rational human being and all else that happens in nature, as events.

Any attempt to approach a definition of 'action' in a form consistent with the basic presupposition of empirical science must proceed, inevitably, in terms of objective 'events'. Though we believe that this seriously prejudices the discussion from the start, foredooming it to insoluble problems (since actions *cannot* be adequately expressed in terms of empirical events), let us nevertheless follow this attempt along the paths where science and the secular attitude have led it.

By 'act', then, we must mean 'an event of a special kind, having among its immediate causes a rational, personal intention or purpose'.

At once a whole host of questions present themselves. What, in reality, is a 'purpose' or 'intention'? Is it some sort of 'event', an empirically observable reality? If so, why has it not been empirically observed and described? And if not, how can an unobservable purpose, which is not an event, enter into the causal chain of events in the objective world and cause observable changes in nature and history which, without that purpose, would never have happened?

It must be agreed that science can certainly, in principle at least, trace the chain of objective, physical or chemical events including the transmission of nerve impulses in and from the brain, which precedes and causes any event that is also an action. But can science ever describe how an invisible 'purpose' in an unobservable 'mind' can initiate empirical events in a brain, which will then cause obvious, objective changes in the physical world?

The answer is – No!

Empirical science, on its own presuppositions, cannot consistently acknowledge that beyond the empirical phenomena it examines, for instance, in the study of human behaviour (psychology), there are trans-empirical realities – a 'mind' which is distinct from the brain – a rational 'will' – a free 'agent'. Empirical science, to be consistent, must view man as an impersonal organism, reacting automatically to stimuli as all other organisms are assumed to do.

This view of the limitations of empirical science is confirmed, with an impressive display of evidence, by M. Polanyi in his massive book on scientific method. "Scientific theory," he writes, "must not go beyond experience by affirming anything that cannot be tested by experience ... In so far as a theory cannot be tested by experience – or appears not capable of being so tested – it ought to be revised so that its predictions are restricted to observable magnitudes."[5] Strange consequences follow from adopting "this view, which can be traced back to Locke and Hume, and which in its massive modern absurdity has almost entirely dominated twentieth-century thinking on science".[6] One of these which Polanyi strongly emphasises is the exclusion of rational man and his acts from the world which science acknowledges to be real. "A philosophical movement guided by aspirations of scientific severity," he remarks about the strict empiricism of 'secular man', "has come to threaten the position of science itself. This self-contradiction stems from a misguided intellectual passion – a passion for achieving absolutely impersonal knowledge which, being unable to recognise any persons, presents us with a picture of the universe in which we ourselves are absent."[7] Man, as a rational being, free to choose truth instead of error and right in preference to wrong (or *vice versa*), free to act – man in the distinctive difference of his reality – has no place in this world-view of *secular* science, of science as philosophically interpreted on the exclusive presuppositions of the secular outlook. Only the self-indulgent inconsistency of most would-be 'secular' theorists permits them to imagine that, having disposed of God as a supra-empirical or supernatural figment, they can still properly retain man, as free and personal, in their world-view. There is room only for man as an automaton, a sum of events.

"Many contemporary scientists," Polanyi elaborates, with the consistent secularists in mind, "insist that all intelligent behaviour is based on a machinery which, in organisms possessing a nervous system, operates on the principles of digital computers. This is the McCulloch-Pitts theory of neural network. It shows that a suitable linkage of neural circuits can account for the responses given by an intelligent person to the stimuli impinging upon his sensory organs. Adherents of this theory go so far as to assert that even the discoveries of Kepler and Darwin are but the output of a computing machine capable of solving a very great number of simultaneous equations. To represent Kepler and Darwin (and presumably also Shakespeare and Beethoven) as automata is, according to K. Z. Lorenz who puts forward this view, imperative for 'the inductive research worker who does not believe in miracles'."[8]

Any logically consistent person who adopts the 'secular man's' attitude of exclusive confidence (where knowledge is concerned) in the empirical methods of science must deny – as Lorenz says – the possibility not only of *God's* intervention in nature and history to achieve His personal purposes (by way of 'miracle') but also of *man's* intervention in nature and history (by means of 'action'), to execute rational intentions.

The prevalence of this attitude among modern psychologists was interestingly confirmed by J. Dorling at a discussion in Oxford, England, entitled "Men and Machines" and reported by I. T. Ramsey. "The mind is an entity we do not mention," Dorling said, speaking as a psychologist, "because we are not sure what anyone means by 'the mind' ... There are two related assumptions which the majority, or at least a very powerful minority of workers in this field make, and which certainly seem to run counter to traditional Christian views.

(a) That if we knew enough about the brain we would in principle be able to explain *completely* human behaviour and human experience.

(b) That in principle there is no aspect of human behaviour that could not be duplicated by an appropriately designed machine."

He went on to say that "the production of guided missiles was the first serious challenge to the conventional belief that *purposes and intentions* are the prerogative of human beings and cannot be displayed by machines. I admit that there is still a big gap between these simple mechanisms and *genuine* purpose or intention."[9]

Our contention is that this 'gap' is easily shown to be a 'boundary' which cannot be crossed, and the words 'purpose' and 'intention' are radically misused here, as applied to machines.

One especially interesting consequence follows logically from this 'behaviourist' view that sees man as an automaton – and we repeat that this is the only view of man that is logically consistent with the presuppositions of the secular attitude : If it is true, it cannot be true! The patent absurdity of this statement must not be allowed to divert serious consideration from the important point involved : because *this* absurdity is deeply and logically rooted in what Polanyi called "the massive modern absurdity" of the secular view, that the empirical methods of science are the sole and adequate source of all knowledge and criterion of reality. For if these empirical methods, consistently applied, require that *man as observed* by the scientist be regarded as an automaton, wholly 'conditioned' or 'determined' by the causal events of his past and in his environment, the same must be equally true of *man as observer* – of the observing scientist. Thus the scientist who puts forward a proposition or theory for others to accept as 'true' – such for instance as this 'behaviourist' view of man – must be regarded as putting it forward, not because he has freely and rationally chosen it as the *truth* from among rival views, but simply because his own past and present circumstances compel him to put it forward! His promotion of this theory must be viewed as merely an event in a biological chain of causal necessity, and not as a deliberate act in affirmation of the truth, rationally conceived. And the theory he champions moreover will have to be accepted or rejected by his hearers or readers in the same way : not because they are convinced by the evidence in a way that allows them to act deliberately in a rationally appropriate way, but because the stimuli which determine their responses compel them to believe as they do, for or against the theory in question.

The very possibility of 'truth' as a meaningful concept – as also of 'action' – presupposes a real freedom to choose. In order to act rationally a man must be free to affirm as 'true' one theory in preference to another, not because he cannot do otherwise, but because a consideration of the evidence has led him to a conclusion freely reached: and the same must be true of the choice between 'right' and 'wrong' action. To deny this freedom to man, as all consistent holders of the secular view must do, is to empty the concept of 'truth' of all meaning. If this view is true, therefore, it cannot be true!

The conclusion to be drawn from all this is that if the rationality and freedom of man are real, if the terms truth and error, right and wrong, really mean what they have always been taken to mean – involving the view of man as the morally responsible person assumed in biblical theology – then the secular presupposition with its *exclusive* devotion to the empirical method must simply be ruled out as false. The empirical criterion of truth and reality would then be given a limited place within the sphere of human 'knowledge', and other sorts of knowledge, including at least the possibility of revelation from God, could be recognised. If, on the contrary, the empirical secular presupposition is affirmed as correct (as by the 'Secular Christian') then it is totally inconsistent to speak of man as a rational agent, or as in any real sense 'free' and so blame- or praiseworthy when he 'chooses' right or wrong, truth or error.

This inconsistency may be very widespread in this secular age, with most of those who practise it quite unaware of the illogicality of their position. But it does not thereby become less objectionable in terms of truth and integrity of thought.

Among the 'Secular Christian' writers we have considered, it is interesting that van Buren alone, on whose superior logical consistency we have already commented, indicates any aware-ness of this problem. "Our empirical attitudes are such," he remarks with reference to the modern secular society with which he identifies himself, "that we are prepared to dismiss [the remark that God is not to be found in outer space] in a way in which we would not care to dismiss the statement that men are only machines."[10] He can see that the machine-view of man is entailed in the consistent secular attitude in such a way that it cannot be dismissed lightly, or indeed at all. The other secular theologians we reviewed, however, (together with most 'ordinary' people who like to think that they are logically consistent in their secular outlook) give no sign that they are aware of this enormous logical hole in the very foundation of their position;

and so they go on speaking freely – and inconsistently – about freedom and human action.

PHANTOM PROBLEMS?

Perhaps these 'Secular Christians' have been led astray by some modern scientists who have written on these matters. Professor C. A. Coulson says that he is following Max Planck when he dismisses as a 'phantom problem' this problem of free-will and determinism, or of action and event, which we have been considering. In the same way he dismisses parallel problems like those concerning the relationship between a purpose in a mind and the brain-event it causes, or between observer and observed in science.[11] He quotes Prince de Broglie and Gilbert Ryle in support of his contention, and Niels Bohr provides him with the concept of 'complementarity', (introduced by Bohr for use in physics primarily, though he also gave it wider application) which Coulson takes as the model on which to build his argument. Let us see how he dissolves these 'phantom problems' by the use of this concept.

The concept of complementarity is most often illustrated from the fact that two conflicting theories about the nature of *light* (as is true also of electrons, etc.) are currently held by scientists, both being supported by strong empirical evidence. Their 'complementarity' means that both theories are accepted as true despite their incompatibility, which is accounted for by saying that it results simply because observers looked at and described light *from different points of view*. Coulson extends the illustration, indicating how the path traced out by the ray of light from a penny in some water may be mathematically described with equal truth by two different equations, one general and relating to any observing eye that might see the penny, and the other particular, relating to an observer's eye in one specific place and reducing to a minimum a certain mathematical function in the equation. Though these two mathematical descriptions of the path of this ray of light differ significantly, both are accepted as true at once. They can easily be accepted like this when the different points of view involved are understood. It is in terms of this concept of complementarity, then, that Coulson claims to be able to dissolve the barriers that separate mind and matter, free-will and determinism, subject and object, observer and observed. And it is in terms of this concept that he explains how, as a scientist fully committed to the empiricist attitude ("what we may call 'the verification from experience' is central to my whole argument"[12]), he can also be a rationally believing Christian who accepts the reality of freedom and of God.

We note that one essential thing about these illustrations of the way in which this principle of complementarity is applied in physics is that both of the alternative descriptions refer similarly and equally to observable objective phenomena. It is *observed data* that are being interpreted in two different ways; and if it is maintained that there is an implied reference to the *observer* in the alternative descriptions (for there is no direct reference), then such a reference is equally present in both these complementary descriptions. But notice now how Coulson applies the complementarity principle to the problems with which we have been concerned.

To seek for "a clear description of the traffic which passes along the brain-mind highway is to court confusion", he writes. "How much better to have done with this dichotomy ... Mind and matter are different ways of looking at the same set of phenomena, or experiences (i.e. man) ... Man is matter, or mind, according to the situation you are describing ..."[13] And to end the 'famous debate' on free-will and determinism, Coulson's application of the complementarity principle issues in this conclusion: "Observed from without, the will is causally determined; observed from within it is free. The difference lies in the point of view ... *whether we are actor or spectator.* For man as *actor* the best concept is free-will: but for man as *spectator* it is determinacy."[14]

Now the real centre of the problem is that 'mind', 'action' and the 'will' cannot, even in principle, be *observed* by the scientist in the same empirical and 'objective' way as can brain and body events. We can easily accept, on analogy with its use in physics, the application of the complementarity principle to the various alternative descriptions that can be given of *man as observed*. Thus, for example, man's brain-events can be described in terms of physical changes (electrical, etc.) or of chemical or biological changes, or in some other way: and though from each point of view the account of man is different, all the accounts can be accepted together as true, as complementary;

for they are not mutually contradictory, allowing for the different points of view.

But Professor Coulson here quietly switches the application of this principle, and claims with the magic word 'complementarity' to have abolished 'the boundary of science' between observed, objective data and observing subject – between observable brain and hypothetical mind – between empirical determinism and the belief in freedom of the will which directly contradicts it – and between events and actions! This sleight of speech we cannot accept!

By "looking at the same set of phenomena" which gives the scientist his deterministic picture of the brain, Coulson maintains, he can see 'mind' also. But when has any scientist observed and described 'the mind' empirically, as many have 'the brain'? 'Mind' is not an empirical, observable reality at all: no one has ever seen a 'mind'. It is (for the empiricist) simply an hypothetical construct, a 'supra-empirical' postulate, which many strict empiricists would reject as sheer metaphysical speculation – and rightly so, if observable, empirical data are to be considered the only source of knowledge. "Man is matter, man is mind" – these are not (empirically speaking, as Coulson claims to be) complementary interpretations of "the same set of phenomena" at all. One is an empirical interpretation, the other a speculative assumption ... and the vital problem of their relationship is not a whit altered by the invocation of 'complementarity'. It remains radically inconsistent for the 'secular man', as a strict empiricist, to speak of mind, or of spirit, in realistic terms at all.

Coulson's 'solution' of the freedom-determinism problem, as it presents itself to the strict empiricist, is even stranger. 'The will', like the mind, is a postulate and not an empirical entity which can be 'observed', either from within or without. He, however, declares that "observed from without, the will is causally determined". To make any sense, this must be interpreted as meaning in effect: when you observe a *man* scientifically, you must regard him as a biological automaton, and therefore as not having a 'will' at all, as it has normally been understood. ('Will' according to the *Oxford Dictionary* is a "faculty or function which is directed to conscious and intentional action".) But what meaning can be given to the 'complementary' view of the will – "observed from within, it is free"? Coulson has earlier insisted (following Kant) that upon all that we 'observe', we ourselves impose patterns of 'law' in order to make things intelligible to us: we must fit them into such a pattern if we are to understand them.[15] Therefore, if 'will' could properly be said to be observed at all, then it could be seen only in terms of causal 'determinism', whether seen from within or without. But surely from 'within' the will is not observed but is *used*, and the observer or actor in using it knows himself to be free. This sort of 'knowledge' of the freedom of the will, however, is not derived from observation, in any empirically acceptable sense of the term. Such 'subjective' self-knowledge must be distinguished from and not (as by Coulson) confused with the 'objective' knowledge derived from scientific observation.[16]

Far from proving, by his use of 'complementarity', that these great problems of human thought at the boundaries of science are 'phantom problems', C. A. Coulson has in fact made more evident the fact that the solution of them claimed in terms of this principle is, despite the great names invoked in support of it, a 'phantom solution'.

All those therefore including the 'Secular Christians' who, under the sheltering academic umbrella of these scientific names, have assumed that they can consistently retain man as rational, free, and morally responsible on the basis of the secular-empirical presupposition, while rejecting the living acting God as a transempirical and unscientific concept, are shown to be in error.

If the empirical criterion of truth and reality is adopted in the exclusive way required by the secular outlook, then 'man' can be retained in the secular world-view only as a 'machine', a biological automaton responding in wholly predictable patterns to stimuli. If, on the contrary, the reality of freedom and personal action are taken to be basic and primary realities (as they are by both common sense and biblical theology), so that thought *must* make provision for them in any world-view that is to avoid absurdity and self-contradiction, then some other philosophical and epistemological foundation must be found than that of the secular man's *exclusive* empiricism.

This is not to suggest an atavistic rejection of science. But it is a call for honest and consistent thinkers to discard that philosophy of science which, as Polanyi has suggested, threatens to stultify modern science through sheer absurdity and internal inconsistency. Our undoubted knowledge of 'action' as a basic reality constitutes a logical rock of sufficient dimensions to wreck any philosophy – such as consistent secular empiricism – which tries to sail up the channel of truth with only 'events' marked on its chart. Some modern 'vessels' of theology have recognised this fact, and have tried to meet it appropriately. We consider two such efforts in the next two chapters, examining the relationship of Existentialism and of Linguistic Theology to the concept of 'action'.

CHAPTER 5

Existentialist Theology and Action

Existentialism, in its theological expression, is commonly named as one of the parents of 'Secular Christianity' which accepts, as the final source and sufficient criterion of all truth, man's empirical experience as refined and analysed by the methods of science. Some aspects of this connection have already been indicated when we considered the structure of Professor Gregor Smith's argument, as it relates to action, in his book *Secular Christianity*. Yet this insistence on the tie between 'Secular Christianity' and Existentialism may seem puzzling to those who are familiar with the origins – in philosophical and theological thought – of the Existentialist movement. For Existentialism arose primarily as a reaction against just those over-confident and exclusive claims, made for empirical science by secular men, which we ourselves have been opposing!

"Existentialism has appeared," according to John MacQuarrie, "as a philosophical reaction against the scientific humanism that prevailed in the early part of the [twentieth] century. It denies the claim of that school of thought that the only knowledge is that which can be scientifically verified, and affirms on the contrary that scientific knowledge is only one kind of knowledge, not privileged but specialised, and subordinate to the fundamental knowledge which is knowledge of existence."[1]

This would appear to be an admirably clear statement of the very conclusion towards which we were working in the last chapter. It might seem therefore as though Existentialism has already made the very same protest that we have been attempting to formulate, and that we are simply re-treading ground already adequately covered. But this is not so. And we must now show how the Existentialist movement in theology, though it has correctly identified the root problem for modern theology, has sadly failed with both the analysis and the solution of it. Existentialist theologians, indeed, have badly confused the basic issues, leading theology into futile side-tracks, as a consideration of their use of the concept 'action' can help to show.

The outlines of theological Existentialism in its classical form are to be seen most clearly in the work of the German theologian and New Testament critic, Rudolf Bultmann, who exerted an enormous influence over a great part of the field of Christian theology in the years immediately following the 1939-1945 war. Bultmann was intensely concerned about the fact that the biblical Christian Faith seemed to be in conflict with the principles of modern science, and that science was quickly gaining the un-critical allegiance of most modern men. He saw clearly that whereas empirical science describes everything it examines, in-cluding man, in deterministic terms of rigid causality, the primary essential for Christian life and truth is freedom to choose, to decide. But the secular champions of science were not prepared to share with religion the field of the 'objective' knowledge of reality, nor to recognise any real freedom in human actions in the observable world. Christianity seemed doomed by defection.

In the face of such exclusive and monopolistic claims made for deterministic empirical science, two courses are open to those who feel compelled to insist on the reality of human freedom, and the possibility of real choice and action. They must either *accept* the validity of the deterministic analysis given by science of all experienced reality as 'objective' (for as we saw in the last chapter, science presupposes a subject/object distinction), and then go on to show how freedom is possible in another area of reality – the subjective, which cannot be simply 'evaporated', as consistent secular thought supposes. This was the way chosen by Existentialist theology. Or else, from the start, they must challenge and *reject* the validity *as ultimate*, of the subject/object distinction required by science (and so also of the 'objective' analysis given by science), ac-knowledging that this distinction has a limited and important functional validity at the abstract level of discursive thought, while insisting also that at the concrete level of living and acting, reality is known to be *one*, uniting together 'subject' and 'object'. This is the course on which we have entered.

Existentialism accepts as 'given' the subject/object analysis presupposed by empirical science, granting to science the exclusive rights it demands in the objective area of observable phenomena, but at the same time claiming the left-over 'subjective' area for personal 'existence', for freedom, and (optionally) for religion.

We must pause here to note F. Gogarten's recent protest – with which we cannot agree – against those who accuse Bultmann's existentialism of 'subjectivism'. It is true that this accusation assumes Bultmann to have accepted the subject/object distinction, which as Gogarten says, was reinforced in philosophy with the work of Descartes. But for Existentialism today the relevance of this distinction derives directly – vertically as it were – from the manner of its current acceptance and interpretation in *science*, and not – horizontally – through the pipeline of philosophical theory. Its philosophical origins are of little relevance. It is the use made of it at any time that is important. Thus, for example, Søren Kierkegaard, the Danish theologian who is universally recognised as one of the ancestors of modern Existentialism, towards the middle of the nineteenth century expressed the same sort of reluctant acknowledgement and at the same time dislike of the subject/object distinction. Therefore, though we warmly agree with Gogarten that the transcending in some way of this subject/object distinction is very necessary, we cannot agree that R. Bultmann, whose thought clearly *presupposes* the distinction simply because of the way in which he has accepted science, can be said to have transcended it. And we find our interpretation of his position on this matter confirmed in the fact of Bultmann's warm commendation of MacQuarrie's book about him, in which his theology is expounded basically in terms of '*objective*-historical' and '*subjective*-existential' categories.[2]

With Schleiermacher (1768-1834), sometimes called the father of modern theology, Bultmann agrees that religion must resign all claims to having special non-scientific knowledge of the world with which science is concerned – the observable world. Thus on the objective side, Bultmann shares with secular man – as David Jenkins declares – "the modern scientific world-view, which ... takes it for granted that the Universe is a closed system with its own independent laws and patterns which are or can be open to discovery by observation and investigation ... The method [of science] can and does cope with everything observable without having recourse to any 'explanation' *outside* the type of observable things and happenings or *different from* the type of patterns of explanation which constitutes this method."[3]

How then, one wonders, can Bultmann possibly avoid acquiescing in the disappearance of all theism and the end of all talk about God? His way out, Jenkins maintains, is "by making a radical distinction between empirical experience and existential experience";[4] and by locating his 'qualified theism' (as Van Buren has called it) in the subjective existential area. We may say then of Bultmann's existentialism (like that of Heidegger and the philosophical existentialists who followed him), that it did not originate primarily because of a positive and spontaneous vision of new truth or reality, but rather as a reaction against, and an attempt to escape from, the monopolistic claims made for science by secular men in the area of our knowledge of reality. The validity of this judgement is confirmed when we consider also the background to Bultmann's demythologising activities. In the presuppositions which underlie this demythologising programme, John MacQuarrie maintains, we see "not the influence of existentialism but the hang-over of a somewhat old fashioned liberal modernism. He is still obsessed with the pseudoscientific view of a closed universe that was popular half a century ago, and anything which does not fit into that tacitly assumed world-picture is, in his view, not acceptable to the modern mind and assigned to the realm of myth."[5]

Both Bultmann's demythologising, then, and his retreat into the subjective world of Existentialism in search of space for 'freedom', are consequences of his initially *accepting*, on the level of unchallengeable presuppositions, the validity of the monopolistic claims made for empirical science in the objective world. Therefore, though we certainly share with the theological Existentialists a basic objection to the exclusive and monopolistic claims made for science in the area of knowledge of reality, we emphatically *reject* the claim (which they accept) that science is able to cope *adequately* with "everything observable", without calling upon 'trans-empirical' realities that are inconsistent with the empirical presuppositions of science. We maintain, on the contrary, that rational *purpose*, and *action* in the world, indicating a genuine *freedom* in the observable world, are essential to the logical possibility of science and of all knowledge; and that these are all trans-empirical realities which empirical science cannot consistently recognise, but which it cannot avoid employing. This does not, of course, constitute a denial of the value of science or of scientific knowledge, but only of the monopoly claimed for it as the sole source of knowledge of reality. The underlying conviction is that the proper place and true value of scientific 'knowledge' will be understood much more clearly when science is seen as but a specialised and in some ways distorted part of the whole range of the knowledge of reality which human freedom and action have opened for us, some of which comes to us in ways other than through the empirical methods of science.

As we turn now to consider some problems around the concept of 'action' which arise because of Bultmann's retreat, in search of freedom for religion and God, into the area of subjective existentialism, it will become apparent that it is largely because his efforts to be consistent with his empirical, science-accepting presuppositions have been better sustained than those of most other theologians, that his problems and 'solutions' have been seen as more interesting and more important than those of others in recent years.

Leaving to science the world of 'objective reality' which had been claimed for it by positivist zealots, Bultmann staked out a claim for freedom, for religion and for God in the 'subjective-existentialist world'. Let us see what sort of freedom and action are to be found in this rarefied atmosphere.

Bultmann understands existential experience, as subjective, to be quite distinct from objective, empirical experience. Existential experience is concerned with personal existence, with the fact that I am myself and not someone else, and with the question why this should be so. What aspects of my life are unalterably determined and cannot be changed? – and what sort of freedom, if any, is still open to me, for making decisions which will transform my situation, changing for instance my relationship with others, and altering the value of my existence? The basic question about 'existence', then, is "whether I am simply a determined object in the closed system of the world or whether I am a subject who can be set free from the threatening determinations of the world for freedom and fulfilment as a person with persons".[6]

For the Existentialist, a primary presupposition or affirmation of faith is that man *is* 'subject' as well as 'object' and that freedom *is* possible for him at the level of subjective existence, which includes at least his intellect, thoughts, words. Here, at least, he can choose between alternatives and exercise freedom in 'decision'.

But for Bultmann, as a *Christian* Existentialist, there is more at stake here than simply man's freedom. It is only in this subjective area, where freedom may be found, that it becomes possible for *God* to be known. Indeed human freedom as he sees it requires God for its actualisation, and is impossible apart from God. To become free, man must have an encounter with God, in the form of hearing the Word of God which alone, Bultmann believes, can call man effectively to make the decision of faith, to choose real freedom and authentic existence. It is at this level of words, of hearing and deciding for truth, that existentialist 'action' takes place. And the Word of God, which is heard in the preaching of the Gospel, focuses – of course – on 'the mighty acts of God'. How are these 'acts of God' (often called 'miracles') and also the responsive 'acts of human faith' to be understood from the Existentialist's point of view?

In connection with the 'acts of God', immediate and obvious problems arise for Bultmann. Since the observable world is for him a *closed* system of natural causes and effects, it is clear that he cannot acknowledge in it any objective action of God conceived as Creator and Ruler of the world, and therefore as above and beyond this world – as supernatural.

What then are we to understand by the 'acts of God', if they cannot be 'God-caused events' in the observable world? They must be understood as taking place simply on the subjective intellectual level of words – in the formulation, transmission and proclamation of a message (the 'Gospel', or the Word of God) which encounters a man in his subjective existence and demands from him a decision of acceptance.

But does this not in effect cut Christianity adrift from world-history, so that it can no longer claim to be an 'historical' religion? MacQuarrie draws attention to the way in which Bultmann tries to anchor the subjective-existential affirmations of the Christian Faith (as he understands it) to objective world-history, using the concept of the mighty acts of God as the anchor-chain, and the Cross of Jesus as the anchor. "We generally speak of the mighty acts [of God] in the plural," he writes. "Bultmann prefers to think of one unitary act centred in the cross, to which both the resurrection and the incarnation must be related for them to have significance ... The resurrection as the new life follows from the acceptance of the cross, and the incarnation means that God himself has spoken and acted in the cross ... The reason seems ... to be partly that ... the cross is the mighty act which is most easily intelligible as objective-historical happening."[7] 'Happening' – notice the word; it could have been 'event': but not 'act' in the sense of something 'intended and accomplished' in the observable world. For if it is to have a place at all in the objective world, as we have seen already, it cannot be thought of as due to the intrusion of a trans-empirical 'purpose', and especially not of a divine or supernatural purpose. It is, we notice, Bultmann's logical consistency which is shaping the argument. The Cross, more readily perhaps than any of the other recorded 'mighty acts of God', can be construed 'deterministically', or explained as a result of natural cause and effect, as an objective *event*, and not a purposed 'act' in which the subjective must be said to invade the objective world. If we can but call this one pregnant 'event' of the Cross an 'act' of God – or conversely call this one 'act' of God an 'event' and so drop an anchor from the subjective level to the objective world – then all the other 'acts of God' (incarnation, resurrection, and the rest) can swing around this anchor on the subjective-existential level as interpretations of it – parts of the message, aspects of the Word of God, without being entirely divorced from objective world history.

Men have spoken, explains David Jenkins, referring to Bultmann's viewpoint, "as if the acts of God were concrete interventions in history, and productive of scientific-like causes in changing or producing situations. But the existential and demythologised understanding of this is that God has always and only acted in his *Word*, whereby men who have heard this Word have been set free for authentic existence for God and for their fellows. There has been no act of God *as* an historical event but only ... the hearing of God's Word *in* historical events – which have, on the historical and scientific level, been historically and scientifically determined by their own autono-

95

mous historical and scientific causes. What finally and decisively makes plain that God acts in this way in his Word is Jesus"[8] – Jesus, and (as we have seen) His Cross. But 'Jesus', for Bultmann, we must add, means only the 'that' of His life and death, only the bare fact that He lived and died, without the 'what' of His character and achievements – *what* He was like and what He did – which means so much to the ordinary Christian believer. All the detailed contents of the life of the Jesus of the Gospels Bultmann attributes as 'myth' to 'the Christ of faith', whom he holds to have no objective historical reality, but to exist simply in the Word of the Gospel on the subjective-existential level. (Under the influence of what has been called the 'New Quest for the Historical Jesus' undertaken by his followers, Bultmann has apparently conceded a few more points to the 'what' of Jesus' life. But neither to him nor to his fellow-existentialist 'Questers', so long as they remain consistent with their presuppositions, can such details in the objective world be held to be of vital importance for faith, which for them exists solely on the subjective level, and requires no more to trigger it as an 'historical' faith than the bare 'that' of Jesus' life and Cross.)

Thus for Bultmann the 'acts of God' (which in biblical theology constitute the basic units for the whole Christian world-view) touch the world of objective reality only at a single point, like the tangent of a circle – at the point of the Cross of Jesus Christ. Apart from this, the 'acts of God' are confined by Existentialist theology to the separate, 'subjective-existential world' to which, in face of the monopolistic claims made for objective science, Bultmann retreated seeking a refuge for freedom, faith and God. Conceived now simply as 'Word', as parts of a message, and borne along in this rarefied atmosphere on the wings of Gospel preaching, the 'acts of God' are supposed – though having no reality in objective world-history or in nature – to exercise a wonderful function of liberation, setting men *free* for decision, for faith and authentic existence. What sort of 'action', we must now consider, is involved in the exercise by men of this freedom?

The 'act' of God in His Word, challenging men and calling them into freedom through the preaching of the Gospel, demands from them a responsive 'act' of faith. What are the possibilities of human action which are consistent with the presupposition that the whole of the observable world is a closed system, fully determined by natural causality and so in principle entirely predictable? If we agree with Bultmann that within the world in which men's bodies move and can be observed moving, the empirical methods of science "can cope with *everything* observable without having recourse to any 'explanation' outside the type of observable things and happenings", then we cannot speak of 'human action', in its common sense, dictionary and biblical meaning, as the causing of changes in the 'objective' observable world by means of 'subjective' and essentially unobservable 'purposes' expressed through our bodies. The intrusion through action of the dynamic purposes of *men* into the stream of observable events is in principle no less impossible or unreasonable on Bultmann's presuppositions than are the personal interventions of God through His mighty acts as proclaimed by biblical Christianity.

Men, of course, are visible, whereas God is invisible. But the distinctively human aspects of men – their 'purposes' and their personal reality as 'agents' – are no less invisible, no more to be claimed as 'empirical magnitudes', than the purposes of God and His personal, active reality. Though men's invisible purposes are inevitably regarded as somehow connected, and indeed integral, with their visible bodies, whereas we do not refer the purposes of God to any visible body, this surely cannot rationally be taken either as adequate proof that there is no God, or as somehow justifying the empirically inconsistent recognition of human action as real, while excluding the possibility of God's action. Unless the 'objective' nature of purposes, of mind, of freedom and action can be empirically discovered and shown to be inseparable from observable, physical bodies, this discrimination against the possibility of acts of God while admitting men's acts cannot be justified.

If these 'subjective' entities were located merely in shrinking 'gaps' in scientific knowledge, the foundations of Christian faith would indeed be in danger. But science *presupposes* the subject/object distinction, the distinction between the (subjective) observer and the (objective) observable world. And in terms of this scientifically necessary distinction the 'subjectively' known purposes, freedom and actions of 'persons', as also of the Living God, must not be thought of as waiting in a shrinking 'gap' in scientific knowledge: for they are in fact beyond the boundaries of science. No amount of advance in cybernetics or any other field can alter this fact. The present flurry of concern about the subject/object division in thought cannot end by somehow including all the *subjective* areas of knowledge within *objective* science: it can only result, logically, in the recognition that there *are* sources and criteria of knowledge other than empirical science, and open the way for the acknowledgement of a real unity of 'subject' and 'object' as combined in our experience of *action*.

But here, with Bultmann, we are still working with the separate subject/object strata required by scientific thought; and freedom, purpose and action must be understood as confined to the subjective-existential realm. What sort of freedom and action are possible for man at this level?

Addressed here by the Word of the Gospel (the Christian Existentialists claim) a person is free to respond with acceptance or rejection of the message and 'the myth' (Christ): his 'will' may engage in commitment to the preached Christ, or refuse the challenge and invitation presented. Thus the 'action' which is required of man is an 'act of decision'.[9] Such decision is an 'act' of the will or mind, an act of the 'self' as it may be conceived in subjective abstraction, and is said to lead to "a new understanding of the self", and a new relation of the self to other selves and to God. This concept of 'action', as the intellectual acceptance or rejection of a Word, a message, though astonishingly emaciated, remains basically consistent with the presuppositions entailed in the Existentialist's acceptance of deterministic science, so long as no attempt is made to leap the barrier between 'mind', 'will', or 'self' in the subjective-existential world, and to secure concrete implementation of the decision through real *observable action* which makes changes in the objective-historical world.

Bultmann has sometimes been criticised for a tendency "to over-emphasise the importance of decision" as a commitment of mind – of the self. But we should rather pay tribute to the logical consistency with which, having once accepted "the massive modern absurdity" of the determinist view "which has almost entirely dominated twentieth century thinking on science" (Polanyi), Bultmann tries to remain within the limits logically prescribed by his own assumptions, restricting 'action' to the level of 'decision'. Thus he largely resists the temptation to make easy reference to observable, objective bodily movements as being 'acts' of human freedom (since scientifically they must be regarded as 'events' in the wholly determined causal patterns of nature) and generally confines his view of human freedom and action within the subjective-existential area of thought.

But consistency with such rarefied positions is difficult to sustain. This existentialist view of freedom strips from the royal concept of 'action' all the regal robes of vibrant vitality which have always so much attracted those who delight to be *alive*, and not just to exist – to *act* in the world and change it, and not just to think about it. The Existentialists have, as it were, left 'Action' a naked monarch, clothed only with invisible, subjective 'decisions' and 'a new understanding of the self'. Like the loyal subjects in the old story of the king with the invisible suit of clothes, the consistent Existentialists try bravely to assure each other that their master, free Action, looks very fine in his robes of subjective decision. But what sensible man can rest long content with this absurd consequence of the absurd presupposition which requires the belief that personal intentions and purposes (because they cannot be empirically observed and therefore cannot be real) cannot issue in real, common-sense action and produce changes in the observable world? Thus we find that when they come to talk of history, Bultmann and other Existentialists break the chains of logical consistency and acknowledge the need to clothe Action in objective, visible garb. They remain however quite unable to show why they should now allow that the purposes of men can break into the observable world and cause changes through action, whereas the purposes of God can not.

"The historical method," Bultmann wrote in 1957, "includes the presupposition that history is a unity in the sense of a closed continuum of effects in which individual events are connected by the succession of cause and effect. This does not mean that the process of history is determined by causal law and that there are no free decisions of men whose actions determine the course of historical happenings. But even a free decision does not happen without a cause, without a motive: the task of the historian is to come to know the motives for actions. All decisions and all deeds have their causes and consequences: and the historical method presupposes that it is possible in principle to exhibit these and their connections and thus to understand the whole historical process as a closed unity.

"This closed-ness means that the continuum of historical happenings cannot be rent by the interference of supernatural, transcendent powers and that therefore there is no 'miracle' in this sense of the word. Such a miracle would be an event whose cause did not lie within history . . . It is in accordance with such a method as this that the *science* of history goes to work on all historical documents. And there cannot be any exceptions in the case of biblical texts if the latter are at all to be understood historically."[9]

Alan Richardson comments that "it is at this point that the basic fallacy of Bultmann's whole position is located. His fundamental presuppositions concerning history are not the presuppositions of historical method as such but of the positivist conception of history . . . The nineteenth-century positivist view is no longer the dominant conception amongst those philosophers and historians who have given attention to the problem. History is indeed a 'closed continuum' of causes and effects; but the *action of God* as a factor in historical causation is not to be ruled out on philosophical grounds in advance of the historical enquiry into the biblical evidence for it."[10]

Richardson's concern is that we should not allow the action of God to be ruled out of history because false presuppositions have been adopted; and this concern we share. But we are concerned also that since these same presuppositions logically require the exclusion from world history of the acts of *men*, this consequence too should be consistently drawn, thus underlining the absurdity of the presuppositions. We do not ask any exceptions or concessions in favour of biblical theology or the acts of God. But why should Bultmann, while denying such concessions with regard to the acts of God in the interests of consistency, make special and inconsistent concessions in favour of the possibility of *men's actions* in world history? He speaks of 'the science of history' in a closed system of empirical cause and effect: and yet he says, "Even a free decision does not happen without a cause . . . All decisions and all deeds have their causes." Of course they have! – human 'intentions' or 'purposes' being the unobservable but essential causes that make events into *historical* acts instead of just *natural* events. But how, with his empirical presuppositions, does Bultmann propose to 'exhibit', within the 'closed unity' of the empirical world, these 'trans-empirical' causes, showing their connection with the observable patterns of natural cause and effect? How can he, in other words, retain *human* action and history (without being inconsistent upon his presuppositions) inside the closed unity of 'the objective, scientific world'? He cannot, of course! – for as we have seen, these things are essentially beyond the boundaries of science. But if this is so, we ask again : by what logic can he acknowledge, as causal factors in objective world-history, the necessarily unobservable purposes of men, and at the same time exclude the equally unobservable purposes of God?

Either Bultmann must admit that the objective-historical world observed by science is open to 'invasion' from beyond it, in the form of personal purposes which cause action and change the observable world : in which case the possibility of the personal purposes and acts of *God* has as much right to be considered as those of men. Or else he must exclude from the objective world not only God's miracles but also human action : in which case he cannot adequately distinguish 'history' from 'nature'. For what Bultmann has really done, in withdrawing human freedom and action to the subjective-existential sphere and so removing them from the causal determinism of the observable world, is to regard man (in his freedom) as virtually 'supernatural', relative to the law-bound realm of 'nature'. Existential men, like their existential God, may be considered free to act – to communicate the word, to challenge one another and make decisions – in the subjective world alone. Their intrusion, through purposeful acts, into the objective pattern of cause and effect in 'nature' would be no less a 'supernatural' intervention than that of God. Existential 'faith', in the subjective world, is necessarily debarred from observable 'works' in the objective world : it is therefore a dead thing, and not the faith of biblical Christianity. Practical religion, together with human history, disappears!

Existentialist Theology must finally founder and disintegrate in absurdity on the rock of real 'action', concrete and observable, as practised by every man in the life of common-sense, and as presupposed also throughout biblical theology in the mighty acts of God and the responsible acts of men. Or (to change the metaphor), the subjective-existential world to which Bultmann and his followers have retreated from the deterministic problems of the objective-scientific world, proves to be merely an imaginary refuge. When we rise from our cogitative theological armchairs and throw open the windows of our life-knowledge, this 'subjective-existential world' disappears from the screen of our belief, like a theological Wonderland dispersed by the light of our irrefragable knowledge of world-changing, bodily action, through which we execute free and rational purposes.

The commonly alleged 'parental relationship' of Theological Existentialism to 'Secular Christianity', then, is rather an odd one. For the Secular Attitude is both father and child of Existentialism! With the wounds of increasing criticism presaging the probable demise of Theological Existentialism, it seems to some that its offspring, 'Secular Christianity', is the heir apparent in the theological world. But of course the deepest root problems of theological Existentialism, which we have considered in connection with 'action', arose from the initial uncritical acceptance by Existentialist theologians of the monopoly-claims made for deterministic science in the 'objective' world: and these remain unsolved and indeed accentuated in 'Secular Christianity'.

Only a fresh analysis of truth and reality, reaching deeper than the subject-object analysis presupposed by empirical science, is likely to open the way to a more comprehensive and acceptable world-view, which can rationally accommodate freedom and action together with determinism and science, and which can recognise God (if He *is* real and personal) as well as man.

The modern preference, in philosophical and theological circles, appears to be to forget about 'reality', as far as possible, and to concentrate on 'truth', in so far as we can know it through concepts and language. 'Linguistic Theology' therefore, working with the tools of linguistic analysis, seems to have become, in the interest of theologians, the main rival to Existentialist Theology in recent years. Linguistic Theology also, notably through Paul van Buren, is named as a parent of 'Secular Christianity'. We turn now therefore to examine briefly this emphasis in modern Christian thought.

CHAPTER 6

Linguistic Theology and Action

"It is remarkable," observes Dr. Hugo Meynell, "that the criterion of *true faith* stated by Bultmann – that its content should not be subject to verification – is the same as the criterion of *meaninglessness* advanced by the Logical Positivists", who were early representatives of the Linguistic Analysis school.[1]

Logical Positivism and the Linguistic Analysis movement which grew out of it share extensive common ground with Theological Existentialism, since both start by accepting the exclusive claim to knowledge made for empirical science by secular men. For the Logical Positivists, however, talk about non-empirical matters – such as God, the Gospel, faith and freedom, allocated by Bultmann to the 'subjective existential' area of life – is just nonsense, because it cannot be empirically verified.

Though the development of Linguistic Analysis has modified the provocative dogmatism of Logical Positivism as expounded, for instance, by A. J. Ayer in *Language, Truth and Logic* (1936), the basic insistence is still that only propositions which can (at least in principle) be verified or falsified by the empirical methods of science are properly *meaningful*. It therefore remains largely true that "the criticism of religious belief by contemporary empiricist philosophers is not so much that it is false, as that the question of its truth or falsehood does not even arise. The trouble with religious statements, it is claimed, is that they do not make sense."[2]

This means that statements about trans-empirical things, such as freedom, purpose, and God, though they may *appear* to be statements of fact (or of error) – e.g. 'God acts in history';

'men are morally free'; etc. – must be denied any real factual meaning. If they have any sort of meaning, it must be non-factual. Thus they may be regarded as hypostatised expressions of feeling or of attitude. As such they may be considered to be important and interesting nonsense. But they cannot be acknowledged as having any status on the level of fact, of truth and error, under the empirical-verification criterion.

There are, however, exceptions to this prevailing contemporary attitude amongst linguistic philosophers and theologians. Thus Anthony Flew (whose version of the Absentee Gardener Parable is used by Paul van Buren as the launch-pad for his linguistic argument in *The Secular Meaning of the Gospel*) considers that in large part Christian beliefs do comprise "a collection of cosmological assertions",[3] and that the indications from observation are that they are false, rather than meaningless. Ronald Hepburn also, in his interesting book *Christianity and Paradox* acknowledges that many basic Christian statements are certainly intended as statements of fact, and that since they *contradict* other generally accepted statements of fact, they must be assumed to be either false or else 'paradoxically' true, rather than meaningless.

"When," he asks, "is a contradiction not a mere contradiction but a sublime Paradox, a Mystery? How can we distinguish a viciously muddled confusion of concepts from an excusably stammering attempt to describe ... an object too great for our comprehension, but none the less real for that?"[4] The 'paradoxical' claims of Christianity can be accepted as true and genuinely paradoxical, rather than false, he maintains, only if they as well as the statements they contradict can be supported by good empirical evidence (like the two rival theories of light). Not surprisingly – since he continues to stand firmly on the exclusive empirical presuppositions of secular thought – Hepburn fails to find adequate empirical evidence to verify even the basic Christian claim that the Living God exists; and so, with agnostic reservations, he presumes it to be false.

Hugo Meynell (from whom we have been quoting) is another linguistic theologian who insists that many Christian affirmations are indeed what they are set forth as: statements of historical and cosmological *fact*, not of feelings and attitudes: but he maintains that an unprejudiced inspection of the available evidence tends to confirm the *truth* of these statements.

Not only among its unsympathetic critics, however, but also among those who claim to be trying to defend and preserve Christianity, the dominant linguistic fashion today is to regard even what appear to be statements of trans-empirical facts as really just disguised expressions of some sort of feeling or attitude. R. B. Braithwaite, for example, in *An Empiricist's View of the Nature of Religious Belief*, thinks that religious statements about God and His acts, about eternal blessedness and the like, though empirically meaningless, should be understood as expressing personal commitment to certain policies of loving conduct towards others, embodied in some of the 'stories' of the Christian Gospel. Although as a Christian he must 'entertain' these stories, Braithwaite maintains, the person who makes such a life-commitment is not thereby required to *believe* them to be true in fact.

R. M. Hare sees more of an 'objective' reference in theological statements than is allowed by Braithwaite; but it is in terms rather of an *attitude towards* objective reality than of *beliefs about* it. Thus statements which purport to be affirmations of belief are really expressions of what he calls a 'blik', involving the adoption of a particular attitude towards the world, whether a Christian attitude or some other. Seen through this 'blik', as though through a pair of tinted mental spectacles, events in nature and history will inevitably be given a distinctive subjective colouring. This is the understanding – or misunderstanding – of the meaning of affirmations of Christian belief that is taken up and developed by van Buren as 'the secular view of the Gospel'. On this interpretation of the Christian Faith, affirmations about God, about the world as His creation, miracles, and so on, no matter how factual their form, cannot be either true or false, but are simply indications of the standpoint from which a person speaks, or of his general orientation and attitude towards life and the world.

ACTION

We have already noticed, in considering van Buren's linguistic analysis of 'the acts of God', that by the word 'act' when it is in a theological context, he means something very different from what the word would ordinarily be taken to mean. What sort of analysis, we now ask, would a linguistic theologian or philosopher give of the word 'act' in ordinary use?

The verification principle which is so basic in empirical linguistic analysis assumes the unlimited validity of the methods of science, and these in turn presuppose a subject/object distinction within reality. 'Action', however, transcends (or perhaps 'underpasses') the distinction between subject and object, binding together purposes or intentions (in the 'subjective' world) and the observable events which they cause (in the 'objective' world). The problem this sets for science is bound to be a problem also for any linguistic analysis which depends wholly on the empirical verification principle. But the linguistic analyst faces additional problems of his own with respect to 'action' statements. By the very nature of his discipline, which confines him to language, he can never observe or deal with the real *action* of a personal subject, but only with the *predicate* of a grammatical subject. In living speech, no doubt, the dynamic activity of real life *can* be largely communicated through the verbal forms of language. But when linguistic analysis inserts its logical scalpel into an action statement, frozen into immobility for inspection, nothing can be found there but inert concepts and the static relationships between them.

John Macmurray has drawn attention to some of these problems in an admirable discussion on "What is Action?", which is worth quoting at some length.[5]

"In language, action is that which is expressed by verbs. The distinction between substantives and verbs is the most fundamental distinction in the field of language. The substantive is primarily the linguistic form which denotes an object. This at least suggests that the distinction between *object* and *action* is a fundamental distinction in reality. How otherwise could the necessity for a grammatical distinction between substantives and verbs be accounted for? ... Substantives are qualified by adjectives. Verbs are modified by adverbs ... Modern ethics is accustomed to examine statements of the form 'This action is good', or 'This action is right'. Such statements refer to action by means of substantives and to the ethical modalities of action by means of adjectives. Action then appears to be an object, and its characteristics appear to be qualities or properties of an object, 'adjectival' to it ... Yet the natural form in which to express moral judgements is rather 'X acted rightly' or 'X did well' ...

"But here we find a seemingly insuperable obstacle. The

available means of logical analysis do not provide us with the means to [analyse such verbal forms] ... Unfortunately the ... process of logical reformulation gets rid of a good deal more than the emotive element in expression. It loses the verbal and adverbial forms also. Traditional logic retains only the verb 'to be', limiting it to the present tense" (a mere copula, which *may* perhaps express existence, but certainly not action). "... Contemporary logic has got rid of the last vestige of the verbal form and substituted the idea of a relation between terms which are substantival or adjectival in character ... Any attempt to think the world through logical forms which do not recognise verbs runs the risk of failing to express action altogether ... There is a danger that the conceptual representation of the world which such a logic necessitates will imply that all action is unreal : or, in other words, that there is no such thing as action."

The term 'action' is ambiguous, Macmurray points out, in the same way as terms like 'perception'. "It may mean either 'doing' or 'deed' ... The question 'What is action?' must therefore be resolved into two questions, viz. 'What is acting?' and 'What is an act'?" What is to be said of the relation between 'acting' and 'act'? Of the parallel relation in the case of 'perception', it has been conceded, he states, "that there is no inherent necessity to believe that what is perceived depends for its existence upon the perceiving of it. But this is not so in the case of action. To act is to effect a change in the external world. The deed is the change so effected ... What is done, in action, would not be at all but for the doing of it."[6]

We may expect, in the light of these facts about language, that unless it proves possible to develop a new logic that can somehow accommodate the dynamic 'doing' aspect of verbs, the concept of 'action' will continue to present insoluble problems to the Linguistic Theologians. The situation is not adequately met by sweeping action statements under the carpet of a static logic – though this seems to be, in effect, what the empirical philosophers have usually done. What would seem to be necessary is a recognition, from the analysis of language, that there are, in connection with action, these linguistic problems which seem insoluble in terms of formal and relational logics; and an admission that within the totality of our knowledge of reality there are 'boundaries of logic' or of discursive linguistic thinking,

boundaries beyond or beneath which we must acknowledge another type of direct or intuitional *knowledge* which includes the
knowledge, through action, of reality as one (without subject/
object division), of freedom, of other persons, and of God.

One contemporary linguistic theologian who has started an
important enquiry into this area of language, touching on action,
is Dr. I. T. Ramsey; and he has set it in the particularly interesting context of a discussion on miracles as 'acts of God'.[7] In
his Inaugural Lecture at Oxford in 1951, Ramsey analysed
'scientific language', of the sort to which van Buren has conceded a monopoly in 'truth'. He notes its "permanent in-
completeness" and its "peculiar selectivity". "Having in mind
the general character of scientific language as we have described it," he says, "we can readily see why there is no room
for the word 'miracle' within it ... The scientist is bound, as a
condition of using scientific words, to exclude 'miracle' from the
start."[8] But this does not mean that there cannot be any
miracles. It means only that science cannot recognise them or
acknowledge them, and that if they are to be rationally recognised and spoken about, it must be on a different 'level' of
language, using a different 'logic', and seeing a broader – or at
least different – picture. Different levels of language, each with
its own 'logic', are postulated for science, history, religion, and
so on, and some are more inclusive than others.

Ramsey goes on to distinguish certain words which may be
said to belong to the 'index' class of words, the most widely
usable and most necessary class in the language hierarchy;
words which therefore belong "to no one level though they can
be used at all levels of languages".[9] The one specific example
he mentions here is 'activity'! "I believe that all languages" –
i.e. scientific, historical, metaphysical, religious, etc. – "will
throw up the word 'activity' ... Without going into detail I
would claim that the traditional puzzles philosophers have found
about activity, e.g. the problems of Movement, Change, Cause,
Will, and so on, have really arisen from an attempt to work
the word activity by an inadequate model instead of recognising
that it is a word presupposed (so I would suggest) at all
language levels."[10]

The main reason why these puzzles, together with similar
problems, are presented so acutely to modern thought in terms
of the subject/object division, is that the highly-rated logical

language of science cannot consistently acknowledge this ultimate concept of 'action', which is necessarily presupposed by all thought, because of its objectivist presuppositions. Yet 'action' or 'activity' certainly seems to be, as Ramsey claims, the word most capable of drawing different language levels together towards unity, or of focusing and illuminating the rational grounds on which disunity and division may be understood and accepted when the very conditions of our thinking prevent their reconciliation.

Among the concepts most obviously in need of being united are the subject/object concepts of 'I' and 'me', divorced by the objective requirements of scientific thinking: and the 'selective' and 'incomplete' language of science clearly cannot be expected to effect a re-union. "In every situation, when 'I' and 'me' have been distinguished, 'I' cannot be given an exhaustive 'objective' analysis without denying ourselves in fact, or without supposing that the subject/object relation in language is merely a subject/predicate relation, which seems a quite unnecessary and indeed a quite disastrous assumption."[11] How then are we logically to reconcile 'I' and 'me' in thought and speech? The suggestion offered by Ramsey "is that as a first approximation, which also recalls the importance we have given to the word 'activity', we might try 'I actively related to me'."[12] That is to say 'I' (as myself viewed subjectively) may be seen as united with 'me' (as myself viewed objectively) in 'activity' or 'action'. The same sort of thing is true with regard to the concepts 'persons' (others known also to be 'I's, or 'subjects') and 'people' (others viewed objectively). "We have urged," Ramsey continues, "that 'I' has its public counterpart in 'me' which characterises the Other. Then may it not be plausible to suppose that, as the logic of 'me' implies another logic for 'I', so also observation logic about 'individuals' or 'other people' implies another logic for 'person'?"[13] The analysis of language, Ramsey is saying, seems to compel us to acknowledge that, in addition to man seen objectively through the empirical methods of science as 'me' and 'people', we must recognise also man as 'I' or as 'person', subjectively known (through activity) as free agent, even though science and scientific language cannot deal with this aspect of reality: and that in 'activity' we may know these divided aspects of man's being to be *one*. Neither objective 'scientific' logic, nor subjective 'existentialist' logic, we may conclude, is able to recognise consistently the real unity of man's life in thought and action. It must be through a 'logic of action', if such a thing be possible, that 'I' and 'me' will be thought together (as they are already by pre- or sub-logical common sense) since it is in 'activity' that they are known to be one. But perhaps, without such a logic, 'I actively related to me' is about as close as linguistic analysis can get to giving an adequate account of this level of 'personal' reality, in terms of static logic.

Ramsey approaches this problem again in *Religion and Science*, and here it appears that the nearest we can get to analysing 'action' linguistically, because of the logical separation between subject and object, is to try to analyse, as Subject, the 'I' *who* acts; since the presuppositions of the search prevent us from getting to the 'I' as Agent *in* action. Thus when Ramsey analyses the difference between the statements: 'He's dancing' and 'I'm dancing', his attention becomes fixed on the personal pronouns, which point to the 'Subject' – on the 'he' and the 'I' – and he never reaches the action, the dancing.[14] Action, and the Self as Agent, as we see again here, lie not only beyond the boundaries of science, excluded by its narrowly objectivist emphasis, but also beyond the boundaries of logical analysis, as presently practised. This is true of human acts and agents, no less than of God and His acts.

MIRACLES

This, then, is the area of language to which 'miracle' properly belongs, in Ramsey's opinion. "From the historical point of view," he writes, "a miracle is an event of great *relevance* and *significance*; a focal event which somehow demands description in terms of *God's activity* ... So the question: can we place 'miracle' anywhere on our language map? becomes: can we place 'God's activity' anywhere on our language may?"[15] He indicates an important distinction between (on the one hand) "God 'generally' active = providence", this being on the same 'objective' language level as 'me' and 'people'; and (on the other hand) "God 'personally' active = miracle", which being on the 'I' and 'person' level of language, is not susceptible of 'scientific' formulation, but requires what he calls 'metaphysical' language.[16] Now these two levels of language pass each other, as it were, without meeting. Thus, Ramsey concludes, "the so-called conflict between science and miracles is a pseudo-conflict which only arises when complete adequacy is claimed for the language of science."[17]

This might indeed become a 'pseudo-conflict' if the pseudo-claim of complete adequacy for science and its language were not pressed by its secular supporters. But it is just this mono-polistic claim that is in fact being pressed by 'secular man' in his basic presupposition (i.e. in his attitude and the conclusions it leads him to, even if he does not directly state the claim.) Even within the Church today, this claim is being urged by the 'Secular Christians'. And so long as it is seriously advanced, we cannot avoid a *real* conflict between religion and the secular view of science, illogical though the secular claims may be.

Biblical theology, with pre-scientific (or sub-scientific) com-mon-sense, *presupposes* that at a level of personal reality where 'subject' and 'object' are still united, purposeful action by whole ('I-me' or 'people-persons') agents is possible in the real world, and so it avoids the logical tangles into which thought is inevitably led when the objective emphasis of science is affirmed as normative. For when one side of this subject/object distinc-tion is affirmed in such a way as either to exclude or 'absorb' the other – as the objective is exclusively affirmed by the secular attitude – confusion and absurdity are bound to follow. It is also unsatisfactory, however, as we have seen in connection with Existentialism, when both sides are affirmed separately in a dualistic way, so that they may in a sense pass each other on their different levels without coming into conflict. For then no rational account can be given of that real unity which we know as binding us to the world, and know also within ourselves as living, acting persons to whom any suggestion of an ultimate 'I-me' dualism sounds absurd. It is similarly unsatisfactory to have multiple languages and logics avoiding conflict with each other simply because they fail to meet: for we know that truth must be one and undivided; but we have no way of indicating or understanding the nature of its unity, unless we can show how the different language levels are related to one another, and that within these relations there is still no conflict. Thus, until we can see at least the 'ground' of the real unity of all thought and language, and assess therefrom the relative 'weight' and au-thority of the different levels of language, we cannot rest content with the conclusion that since science cannot join issue with religion on its different logical level, therefore the conflict between science and miracles is a pseudo-conflict.

Dr. Ramsey's linguistic analysis, in pointing us to 'activity' as the key to the necessary unity of logical thought, has been of great value. It is therefore unfortunate that in later books he does not go on to develop significantly this early insight concerning the vital function of 'activity' for understanding the unity of all 'logical languages' within the totality of knowledge. Thus in his major discussion of religious language,[18] it seems that objective scientific language is no longer regarded as merely one among many of different levels, but has been given the status of the *basic* language for truth, becoming the 'norm' by which other logical languages must be measured. The 'precision language' of science is taken to be normal and proper, and religious language is constantly referred to as 'odd' and 'improper' in a logical sense, since the things to which it refers involve a 'something more' beyond the range of meaning possible for the precision language of science. The presumption, therefore, is that instead of science being regarded as a specialised limitation, and in some measure a distortion, of truth which is more broadly and deeply described in personal language or religious language, scientific 'object' language sets the standard, and religious language must try to justify against this standard the 'more' of which it wants to speak. The language of religion, Ramsey writes, "will be object language and more, i.e. object language which has been given very special qualifications, object language which exhibits logical peculiarities, logical impropriety. Now have we had any guide to this oddness, this impropriety? Well, does not the way in which distinctively *personal* situations parallel those which are *characteristically religious*, suggest close logical kinship between 'I' and 'God'? Both, by the standards of observational language, are odd in their logical behaviour . . . At any rate, 'I' will never cease to be a useful guide to us when we are confronted with puzzles about 'God'."[19]

This is very true, and very important – *if 'object language' must be the norm*. But why should it be? Does it not make much better sense of life, action and thought, to say that in normal communication, (as used and studied quite apart from the efforts of Aristotle, Hegel, Russell and others to make men systematically 'logical') ordinary *living* language can be and is used to speak simply and meaningfully of persons, actions, God, miracles, and the like? 'Object language', and especially scientific object language, is 'living language but *less*', language which has been specialised by the deliberate exclusion of its subjective over-tones and implicit references to purpose, action, freedom, persons, God, etc., as well as to feelings. Similarly, 'subjective language' will be normal, living language but less, diminished in specialised and logical ways. Ramsey, however, in common with secular thought generally in this modern period, accords *primacy* to scientific 'object language', and is left with the problem of justifying religious language against this norm.

Instead of looking to the reality of *action* to re-unite the subjective/objective, I/me division in understanding, and to deal with the problems which arise when God and the world come together in 'miracle', Ramsey now looks to reflective 'disclosures', which are *subjective* occasions of illumination, of 'light dawning': and they are inadequate to the task.

Thus, when he turns to consider again the 'oddness' of miracle, as 'a non-conforming event',[20] Ramsey concludes that: "Miracle stories are stories of a characteristically personal activity, with 'God' substituted for a person-word."[21] Therefore, "we may see 'miracle' and 'free will' as logical parallels ... A 'miracle' situation ... claims about the *objective* features of a certain situation what free-will claims about the *subjective* features of other situations: it makes (we may say) a 'free-will' claim about the Universe ... In a miracle the Universe declares itself personal at a point where persons are not."[22] "What a miracle claims about the universe is," Ramsey declares, "that on some occasion the universe 'comes alive' in a personal sort of way."[23]

There is a serious logical confusion and distortion here. Instead of seeing a parallel, as before, between human 'free-will' action and God's miraculous activity (both understood as somehow transcending 'subjective' and 'objective' by uniting them through purposeful activity in the real world), a parallel is now alleged between human 'free-will' as simply *subjective*, and divine 'miracle' as *objective* changes in the world. Only an outlook which has submitted to the strange, split-level distortions of existentialist thinking, however, can accept as adequate a view of God's 'activity' which declines to affirm God's existence as personal 'Agent', or a concept of 'free-will' which confines it wholly to 'subjective features', as Ramsey suggests. Common sense and common language mean by 'free-will' the ability of man to effect intentional changes in the *observable* world; and conversely, belief in 'free-will' acknowledges the propriety of deducing from certain observed changes in man's objective environment that there are other living, personal human beings besides the 'observer' who also have, and exercise, purpose or 'free-will' in 'action'. In parallel with this, faith claims from certain 'objective features' of an observed situation that there must be a living, personal God who has freely acted in the world. Miracles make a 'free-will' claim for *God* who created and works in the universe, and not for the Universe 'come alive'! This failure to draw the acknowledged 'parallel', and speak of the Personal God acting, instead of 'the Universe coming alive', can claim no *logical* justification at all. It suggests, rather, that Ramsey has now adopted presuppositions which preclude the possibility of recognising any real 'acts' in the observable world, or any supernatural Agent to whom such acts could be attributed. But it also demonstrates – does it not? – the inadequacy of Ramsey's subjective-intellectual 'disclosures' as the key to truth, and of 'I', analysed in static terms of existence or being rather than in dynamic terms of action, as the logical 'model' from which Christian statements of faith may be elucidated.

The root problem which logic must consider as it analyses religious language is really the nature of 'action', and not one of the derivative problems on which attention has usually been focused. The acts of man and the acts of God belong logically together in many respects; and any logic whose presuppositions lead to the conclusion that action-talk is 'odd' or 'improper' must surely for that very reason be judged inadequate as an ultimate criterion of truth. Must we not agree, then, that the action-recognising presuppositions of common-sense thinking and every-day speech – as also of biblical theology – are 'normal' and 'proper', and that it is the deterministic declarations of strict empiricism which must be declared 'odd' and 'improper', no matter how important and useful they may also be in their own limited way? One is reminded of John Locke's famous dictum that God was not so mean that He made men merely two-legged animals, and left it to Aristotle and his system of formal logic to make them rational. "He has given them a mind that can reason, without being instructed in methods of syllogising: the understanding is not taught to reason by these rules: it has a native faculty to perceive the coherence or incoherence of its ideas, and can range them right, without any such perplexing repetitions."[24] Nothing is more certain to sane men, whose mental vision has not been distorted by sophisticated 'objectifying' techniques, than that men can and do *act*, and that it is in and through their free, purposeful actions in the world that truth can be discovered and knowledge may grow.

Perhaps it is a belief that the dialectical logic of Idealism can deal more effectively than other available types of logic with the dynamic realities of action that has led W. Pannenberg, whose vigorous theology of the acts of God has recently attracted so much attention, to adopt Idealism as the philosophical framework for his theological exposition (which we shall consider briefly in a later chapter). And certainly the new action-based and dialectical logical forms outlined by John Macmurray in *The Self as Agent* are intended to overcome some of these problems.

DIALECTICAL LOGIC AND MODERN MAN : SCHAEFFER'S THESIS

Some reference must here be made to the extreme criticism of dialectical logic recently expressed in the name of evangelical Christianity by Francis Schaeffer, in two books which have been widely acclaimed among evangelical Christians.

In many respects the analysis of modern man's predicament put forward by Schaeffer is very similar to that which is emerging from our study of 'action'. He speaks of a chronic dualism in Western thought, claiming that modern man has now given up in despair all hope of solving it rationally, and has fully embraced sceptical irrationality. "The essence of modern man lies in his acceptance of a two-level situation, regardless of what words or symbols are used to express this . . . Between these two levels there is no point of contact."[25] Previously, he declares, "educated men would not give up rationality and the hope of the unified field of knowledge. Modern man has given up his hope of unity and lives in despair – the despair of no longer thinking that what has always been the aspiration of men is at all possible."[26]

Søren Kierkegaard is identified as the first man to go below this 'line of despair', and so is "the father of modern secular thinking and of the new theological thinking".[27] Working with the dialectical form of logic proposed by Hegel, 'Kierkegaard came to the conclusion that you could not arrive at synthesis by reason. Instead, you achieved everything of real importance by a leap of faith. So he separated absolutely the rational and logical from faith."[28]

Some of the theological consequences of this conclusion by Kierkegaard have already come under consideration, during our examination of Existentialism particularly, but also of Linguistic Analysis. Schaeffer illustrates the impact on modern life of this despairing dualism with· an interesting range of illustrations drawn from a wide spectrum of activities in Western Culture today – philosophy, art, music, literature, theology, etc. – and cogently argues the urgency of the need for a solution, if there can be one.

When he seeks to isolate the basic causes of this sad situation of modern man, however, we must part company with his reasoning. For he does not trace these problems back (as we have done) to the essential *content* mistakenly placed by Descartes (in his *cogito, ergo sum*) into the 'bowl of knowledge' he had just emptied, which Kant was later to melt and mould into its classical form as the 'Critical Philosophy', and into which the contributions of virtually all succeeding Western thinkers, including Hegel and Kierkegaard, have been poured. He goes back only as far as Hegel, and focuses the responsibility for man's present predicament almost entirely upon the dialectical form of logic introduced by him.

"Hegel has removed the straight line of previous thought and in its place he has substituted a triangle. Instead of antithesis we have, as modern man's approach to truth, synthesis."[29] When Hegel propounded this idea, Schaeffer declares, "he changed the world."[30] By changing the way in which people think, he changed the known world. Here, in the very foundation of Schaeffer's argument, we find a strange affirmation and a strange self-contradiction.

The world is not changed, and sound thinking is not changed nor even 'made valid' by logic. As John Locke said so memorably in the words which we quoted above, men did not have to wait for Aristotle and his logical principles – probably the first ever formulated – before they could think validly and formulate truth effectively. Not even by this great occasion in the history of human thought was the world changed: for Plato and his predecessors had already been thinking, long before then, in the ways advocated by Aristotle's logic. Logic simply analyses and formally describes the valid thinking processes of which men are already capable and which (usually) they are already practising: it does not change the manner of man's thinking nor the nature of his world.

Now Schaeffer recognises this. Up until Hegel's time, he says, all thinking men believed in 'the rational' and thought in terms of antithesis. "If a certain thing was true, the opposite was not true ... This is something that goes as far back as you can go in man's thinking ... *As a matter of fact it is the only way man can think*. The sobering fact is that the only way one can reject thinking in terms of an antithesis and the rational is in terms of the rational and the antithesis ... That is the way God has made us and *there is no other way to think*."[31]

The odd thing here is that, while he states this fact, the linchpin of Schaeffer's whole argument is – not just that Hegel's logic wrongly describes the processes of human thinking, but – that the dialectical logic has actually changed the manner of modern man's thinking so that he now *does* think in another way! "The mass of people have received the new way of thinking through mass media without analysing it ... The reason why Christians are not understanding their own children is because the children are being educated into the other way of thinking. It is not merely that they think different things. They think differently."[32] And the water-shed in thought is the new 'dialectical' way of talking about and arriving at the truth, Schaeffer maintains.[33]

If a new way of thinking had indeed been found by modern man, who has performed such wonders in recent years in the areas of science, technology, and so on, these modern children might well be expected to believe – and with good reason – that it is a better way of thinking than that formerly employed among men. Schaeffer argues, however, that the new way of thinking which is characteristic of modern man is a false way which cannot lead to truth: and only the conservative Christian who refuses to become a 'modern man', and clings to the good old-fashioned logic of antithesis, can safeguard truth for the future.[34]

117

For modern men, "the only way out of their dilemma is to move back to the methodology of antithesis",[35] and to keep well away from the dialectical logic, with its talk of synthesis.

The obvious self-contradiction at this crucial point in Schaeffer's argument should function as a 'red stop-light' for all who have been inclined to follow Schaeffer's lead in blaming the intellectual predicament of modern man mainly upon Hegel and the dialectical form of logic. If we are correct in believing that the key which will open the door to a solution of today's great problems is the dynamic concept of 'action', is it not inherently unlikely that the need now is to go back from Hegel's dialectical logic, with its relative dynamism, to a much more static form of logic? Might we not expect, rather, to have to go forward to a more adequate and more concrete, more empirical and less idealistic and theoretical form of dialectical logic?

It is towards such a logical form that Macmurray leads us in the development of his analysis of man as agent.

STATIC AND DYNAMIC IN LOGIC: MACMURRAY'S THESIS

The logic in terms of which Macmurray presents his personaalist philosophy of action is dialectical: but it is neither a Hegelian or Idealistic form of dialectic, nor yet a Marxist or Materialist forms. It is, he claims, the logical form of the personal.

The creation of the positive sciences, which has been the outstanding feature in the modern development of knowledge, as Macmurray says, has always involved a reciprocal relationship between philosophy and science. "The result of this interrelation between science and philosophy is that modern philosophy has completed two distinct phases, which correspond respectively to the creation of the physical and the biological sciences ... The key-concept of the first phase is 'substance'; its form and method are mathematical ... Pure mathematics provides the ideal form of all valid knowledge, and whatever cannot be determined in this form is unknowable." Working with the mathematical 'straight-line' logic, this process of thought "distinguishes between what is objective and what is subjective in experience. The objective is valid: the subjective is unreal, illusory or imaginary."[36]

The 'first phase' attempt to understand all reality in terms of the material world, mathematically, collapses into scepticism, especially in its attempt "to conceive the self as substance and to determine it through the mathematical form".[37] The mathematical form – which in logic finds somewhat primitive expression in the traditional (Aristotelian) logic and more sophisticated expression in the modern relational or mathematical logics such as that associated with Bertrand Russell – is utterly unable to deal with "the element of spontaneous construction, of self-determining and self-directed development which is present in the activity of the Self, but which is excluded from the conception of the material.

"The second phase, seeking a more adequate form, turned its attention from the material to the living . . . Its key concept is not substance, but organism, and its problem is the form of the organic. In contrast with the mathematical form, which is a combination of identical units, the organism is conceived as a harmonious balancing of differences, and in its pure form, a tension of opposites; and since the time factor – as growth, development, or becoming – is of the essence of life, the full form of the organic is represented as a dynamic equilibrium of functions maintained through a progressive differentiation of elements within the whole. This proved to provide an adequate conceptual form for the development of the biological sciences."[38]

When this form is universalised, as a basic philosophical concept must be, and applied to the self and to thought, we find that "the logical form of thought is no longer mathematical but dialectical; not analytic but synthetic; a progressive synthesis of opposites."[39]

This phase in turn has ended with a relapse into scepticism, as Macmurray shows, through the emergence of a new problem, formulated in strikingly different ways by Kierkegaard (as the problem of the existing individual) and by Auguste Comte (as the problem of persons in society) – a complex problem which the dialectical logic of Hegelian Idealism is incapable of solving. But there is no reason to suppose that this phase of scepticism is any more final than the others which philosophy has overcome in the past. If these thinkers discovered "that philosophy is incapable of formulating, in either its individual or its social aspect, the nature of personal experience, this need not mean that philosophy is invalid, but only that an organic conception of the personal is inadequate to the facts. Since philosophy must include the personal in its field of enquiry, this can only mean that we must abandon the organic form as inadequate for the philosophical purpose, and initiate a search for the form of the personal."[40] This leads to an analysis of 'action', as the real *differentia* of persons, and to a philosophy based on the concept of the self as Agent, replacing the Cartesian concept of the self as thinking Subject on which both the earlier phases of modern thought were based.

Macmurray's attempt to outline the form of logic which is required for the philosophical treatment of these problems of the personal life – individual (psychology) and social (sociology, history, etc.) – produces a clearly dialectical form. "The Self that reflects and the Self that acts is the same Self: action and thought are contrasted modes of its activity," he writes. "Action is a full concrete activity of the self in which all our capacities are employed: while thought is constituted by the exclusion of some of our powers and a withdrawal into an activity which is less concrete and less complete. Indeed . . . action and thought are the positive and negative poles of a personal experience which moves, in its actuality, between them . . . The concept of 'action' is *inclusive* . . . 'Action' without thought is a self-contradictory conception . . . 'Thought', on the other hand, is an *exclusive* concept, and therefore negative . . . Action is primary and concrete, thought is secondary, abstract and derivative. This must mean that the distinction between 'right' and 'wrong', which is constitutive for action, is the primary standard for validity: while the distinction between 'true' and 'false' is secondary. The 'I think' is not ultimate: it is the negative mode of the activity of the Self, and presupposes the 'I do' . . ."[41]

Now I must confess that I feel far from happy with the terminology of this dialectical form of logic which Macmurray employs in expounding his philosophy: but I cannot now suggest more satisfactory terms. I am particularly reluctant to agree that 'thinking' is well described as a 'negative' activity, though I can see the sense in which Macmurray comes to use the term. But I am confident that the problems which are here being dealt with are the real problems with which modern man must grapple, in order to escape from the dualistic difficulties which fence him into his present painful predicament of confusion with regard to the most important realities of his life as a person. And although the logical forms of each earlier phase of thought are retained in the succeeding phases, and not rejected (for man is both a material thing or object and also a living animal as well as being a personal agent); yet it seems to me extremely unlikely that the simple, 'straight-line' thought-forms so dear to Schaeffer, though most effective in solving less complex problems, will ever prove capable of giving an adequate account of action and of the forms of personal life, such as are of the essence of history, and of theology.

With reference to theology, which is our special interest, and the question as to whether the Christian God has acted in history, it is clear that only a type of logic which can rationally recognise the acts of *men* in history can be expected to yield a rational judgement on such a matter. We turn now to consider some of the problems to be faced by historians in this connection.

CHAPTER 7

History and Action – On a Secular Base

Science, with its empirical methodology and its concentration on nature, developed to relative maturity (by objective standards) some two centuries before history underwent its transforming revolution in the nineteenth century. By this time the historical dualism inherited from the mediaeval period (history 'sacred' and 'profane', running largely parallel to the mediaeval 'supernatural/natural' dualism) was under scholarly attack, and 'sacred history' was being dissolved in the acids of scientific criticism. With regard to the predominant stream of 'profane' history, it is scarcely surprising that the immense prestige already enjoyed by the empirical, natural sciences resulted in an attempt to formulate methods for regulating history that would make it truly 'objective' and scientific. "Modern classical-rationalists," Alan Richardson states, "accepted the nineteenth century positivist view of history as a search for regularities amongst particular historical instances and they thought of historical enquiry as a quest for scientific explanation in terms of general laws."[1] The pursuit of 'scientific history', which developed particularly in Germany, was led with distinction by Leopold von Ranke, who regarded history as involving the disinterested pursuit of 'facts' from the past, using empirical methods of verification as similar as possible to those of the natural sciences.

This revolution in historical method has had great importance for theology. For instance, the problems of Rudolf Bultmann's theology, at which we have already glanced, resulted largely from his acceptance of this 'scientific' understanding of history with its exclusively empirical methods, and its presumption of universal causal-determinism. "The historical method," Bultmann wrote, "includes the presupposition that history is a unity in the sense of a closed continuum of effects in which individual events are connected by the succession of cause and effect."[2] But Bultmann was by no means alone in both accepting this view of history and at the same time reacting from it theologically, and seeking a way to escape from its exclusive claims, so that Christian Faith might survive. In company with him there were many others, including Tillich, Brunner, and Barth; all of whom, according to Richardson's well-documented contention, "carried over the old assumptions of the positivistic attitude towards history, without subjecting it to radical criticism . . . Instead of asking what the fact of divine revelation through historical events implies for our conception of history, they have exhibited a tendency to assume the 'scientific' validity of positivist notions of history, and then, finding that there is no standing-ground for revelation within such a conception of history, to look around for a sphere of super-history or of existential encounter in which the salvation events may have taken place."[3]

We shall consider in the next chapter the obvious implication that there are 'new' assumptions proper in the study of history today which make the assumptions of nineteenth century positivist history 'old'. Here we ask how it happened that this concept of 'scientific' history, which aimed to end the mediaeval dualism by retaining nature without 'the supernatural' and profane history without 'sacred history', gave rise among theologians to a new division of history into two levels, with God, His acts, faith, and the like, all finding refuge on the level of existential history or supra-history of some sort.

The acceptance of this new historical 'dualism' – though they would not have agreed that it was such! – was made easier for the German theologians by the fact that where English has but the one word 'history', German has two words: *Historie* referring to bare facts, and *Geschichte* meaning the interpretation of the facts from a particular point of view. These two words figured in the title of a lecture given before a pastors' conference in Germany in 1892 by Martin Kähler, which can be translated "The So-called Historical Jesus and the Really Historical Christ". "The two German words for the adjective 'historical' in this title," Daniel Fuller comments, "are taken from the two German words for 'history', *Historie* and

Geschichte. Kähler employed these words in order to distinguish between two ways of knowing history: *Historie* is known through an application of the historical method, with its underlying supposition that nothing can be known in history except what is capable of bearing an analogy to ordinary human experience, while *Geschichte* is history known in some other way, depending on the particular theologian in question."[4]

Fuller shows well how the pressure to split history again into two levels was at least in part a consequence of the elimination of the distinction between 'natural' and 'supernatural' reality, which had formerly been accepted as axiomatic within the Christian Faith. Biblical criticism by Liberal scholars showed one after another of the biblical documents to be undeniably based on the assumption that, in addition to the natural world acknowledged by the scholars there is a supernatural world, and in particular a supernatural God who acts in the natural world and in history. Since their positivist view of history could not admit the supernatural within history, they had therefore to class as historically unreliable one part of the Bible after another.

As the flood-waters of scientific criticism, dammed up behind the wall of naturalism, rose and covered more and more biblical territory, the Liberals continued to retreat and take their stand on the diminishing areas of the New Testament which they still held to contain genuinely historical (*historische*) material. St. Mark's Gospel, long supposed to give a basically historical and non-supernatural picture of Jesus, was their last island of refuge. But such critical conclusions as those of Johannes Weiss and Wilhelm Wrede soon flooded even that ground. "Liberalism had failed in its attempt to find any one part of the Gospels that was not tainted by the supernatural and would thus set forth a 'human Jesus' who would serve as its support. The idea of the supernatural permeated every Gospel so thoroughly that no human Jesus" – i.e. *merely* human Jesus – "could be found there ... Either Jesus was indeed supernatural, or the idea of this supernaturalness was the product of human thought in which either Jesus thought he was the apocalyptic Son of God or the early Christians thought him to be such."[5] The 'Form Criticism' is one of the main methods that has been developed to prove (what the Liberals presuppose) that the latter alternative is the case – the early Christians, through their loving imaginations, 'created' the 'Christ of faith' of whom the

Gospels speak, out of their memories of a Jesus who was really 'merely human'. But that is to anticipate – we must return to Kähler's lecture.

Kähler and his sucessors saw in effect, that if the supernatural/natural distinction is to be excluded from the Christian Faith because 'scientific' history cannot acknowledge the reality of the supernatural, then either the Bible must be abandoned as basically false, or else a new, two-level distinction must be permitted in history, with respect to the point of view from which events are regarded: whether objectively, as *historische*, or subjectively, as *geschichtliche*. Thus Kähler declared: "The resurrected Lord is not the historical (*historische*) Jesus behind the Gospels, but the Christ of apostolic preaching, which is the content of the whole New Testament."[6]

It is important to be clear about what has happened in the development of this change. Instead of speaking of the 'two natures' in Jesus Christ, representing *two levels of reality* – human and divine, natural and supernatural, created and creating – we are asked now to speak of *two points of view* from which the one-and-undivided reality of Jesus, and of all things, may be seen; for there is, we are told, no supernatural reality present and active in our world. F. Gogarten, in his book *Demythologising and History*,[7] has discussed the root-causes of this change, arguing that it is part of the process of the rejection of mediaeval metaphysics by modern man in favour of an historical outlook. Metaphysics and history seem to be regarded by Gogarten as mutually exclusive alternatives rather than as complementary ways of looking at the world. It appears to be accepted (on Heidegger's authority)[8] that to take as it were a cross-section through time and analyse, in the present, the ultimate constituents of reality as Creator and created, supernatural and natural, etc., is intellectually improper or at least old-fashioned and outmoded, representing a 'static' view of the world instead of the 'dynamic' view of the historical outlook. Therefore, apparently, we must *presuppose* that all reality is one and undivided, and is accessible in all parts – in principle at least – to investigation by the methods of empirical science. Only limited distinctions of historical process within this total unity, as seen from different points of view, may be permitted. Metaphysics, then, is to be *replaced* by history; and natural and supernatural by *Historie* and

Geschichte. And although the latter two points of view give quite different pictures of reality, they are both to be called 'historical'. Thus it happens that the Critic who is convinced that in historical fact (*historische*) Jesus was merely human, can also now affirm that properly understood, or as seen from the 'truly' historical perspective (*geschichtliche*), He was indeed divine – and so can claim still to be faithful to the biblical emphasis!

It will be obvious, however, that this new distinction concerning points of view will very easily be 'objectified' so that it comes to be understood and spoken of as though it were a 'real' distinction in the objective world, or in history. Thus we may come to speak of 'general history' and 'salvation history', for example, as though they were on different levels of *reality*, instead of saying and meaning, 'from the scientific point of view' and 'from the point of view of faith'. We shall not try in this study to analyse exactly the mixture of an ontological meaning with the epistemological one in the thought of the theologians to whom we refer: but this distinction is clearly a pregnant source of confusion.

Theological ambiguity and double-talk inevitably accompany the use of this split-level concept of history: for it gives to the one English word 'history' two different and sometimes incompatible meanings; and theologians differ widely in the definitions they give to the two German words. This double-talk has in fact recently caused a debilitating confusion among Christian people. Here, surely, is one of the roots of the present sickness of the Church. For by use of this double-concept, both in affirmations and in denials of the historicity of the acts of God – for example the Resurrection – two theologians who use the very same form of words may really believe and intend to express altogether incompatible views! Today a 'secular Christian' and a biblical Christian may both solemnly say: 'I believe in the truly historical resurrection of Jesus Christ', one of them mentally splitting the word 'historical' and meaning that he believes it only as he subjectively interprets it – i.e. *geschichtliche* but *not historische* – while the other uses it in its usual, common-sense and undivided meaning to refer to an 'objectively' real *and* intelligently interpreted, 'fully historical' happening. Only intensive probing, often, discovers that they are using identical words to express contrary views. E. L.

126

Mascall, Professor of Historical Theology in London, has rightly said that in this sort of situation, "discussion of religious and theological issues becomes extremely difficult: if you want to know what somebody believes, it is no longer sufficient to listen to what he says about God and Christ ...: you have first to find out whether he is using these words in the sense which they have always had in the past or in one of the senses of the new theology ..." Thus, he says, "Dr. van Buren sets forth a version of Christianity in which ... we are to go on saying 'Jesus Christ rose from the dead' but we are not to mean by this that he did rise from the dead: what we are to mean is that after he had died on the cross his followers had a new kind of experience and that this experience has been passed on from one Christian to another down the ages like an infectious disease."[9]

It does not require much imagination to see the desperate confusion which must follow in the Church when it becomes widely realised that this deliberate ambiguity has become embedded deep into words like 'historical' and 'Resurrection' as used by theologians today. Just such confusion, indeed, can now be seen around the Church far and wide – and it is not confined to the unschooled and simple-minded. For, as Carl Henry has written, "Many graduate students find the current climate of conflicting exegetical claims so confusing that they are tempted to identify the 'assured results' of historical research simply with 'what most scholars (now) think'. The definition of history remains so much in debate that more radical students think of history only in terms of historical documents plus the imagination of historians."[10]

The importance for the Church today of this basic ambiguity with respect to the concept of 'history' in theology, as focused especially on the Resurrection of Jesus Christ, is indicated in G. W. H. Lampe's recent Statement on Easter where he refers to what he considers to be at this time "the fundamental question about Easter".[11]

"This is the question whether what happened at the first Easter was an objective event in the external world or whether it was simply a change of mind, radical and dramatic but not necessarily sudden, on the part of the disciples. Was the resurrection an event in the life of Jesus, so that we can say God actually raised him from the dead? Or was it only an event in

127

the lives of the disciples – a change in their outlook as they came to realise through further reflection upon their dead and buried teacher, that his influence still lived on, that his teaching had been true, that his life must be their example and his character a pattern for themselves to follow ... When we say that Jesus was raised from the dead ... do we mean that he was raised in the minds of his disciples, ... or are we making a factual assertion, not only about the mental processes of the disciples, but about Jesus himself?"[12]

All who are genuine 'Secular Christians', together with Bultmann and those sceptical Existentialists who follow him, can believe in the historicity of the Resurrection only in this subjectively 'supra-historical' or 'existential' sort of way, as being constituted only by the subjective experience and changed attitudes of men, and not as an 'objective' act of God: for their presuppositions leave no other possibility open to them, unless it is to acknowledge that they simply cannot accept the historicity of the Resurrection. While continuing to use the old familiar words of the Christian Faith, they not only may, but must – if they are going to remain consistent with their presuppositions – mean something very different from what has been commonly understood through the centuries and in the Bible by 'the Resurrection of Jesus Christ'.

That 'Liberal' theologians should adopt such a position is now accepted by many. But it comes as a surprise and shock to the conservative Christian to find – so great is the academic prestige of the German giants of theology who have led this way! – that some theologians who are in other respects unambiguously conservative and orthodox in their beliefs are now following them in this matter of split-level historical thinking; and following them also, therefore, in accepting the validity for objective world-history of the positivists' deterministic analysis, as well as in the addition of à 'supra-historical' level to accommodate the 'acts of God' and the like. Thus G. E. Ladd, who "confessedly writes from a conservative or evangelical point of view, and believes the Bible itself is the inspired Word of God",[13] refers with deference to Bultmann as a 'scientific historian'; and after quoting his view of historical method as presupposing a closed continuum of causes and effects (which we have already criticised, see p. 99f. above) Ladd writes: "We must acknowledge that *everyone* uses this approach in his study of most of ancient history."[14]

What, he asks, is the conservative Christian to do in this situation? "Is the Christian theologian to construct his own definition of history and ask the secular world to accept it? Or is the theologian to accept the basic validity of the modern secular understanding of history, and attempt to interpret his faith in terms which will at least communicate with those who do not share his faith?... It would appear to be ... better ... to admit the basic validity of the prevailing scientific historical method, but to insist on its limitations at the point of *redemptive* history where God has entered into history in self-revelation and redemption."[15] Thus Ladd concludes that "while the historical method possesses general validity, there is one stream of history which transcends the competence of this method. If there is a personal, living God who has acted in history, the nature of his acts might be expected to be beyond 'historical', natural human explanation."[16] It is clear therefore, from what he has stated in defining his terms, that Ladd would *say* with Bultmann and the 'Secular Christians' that the Resurrection of Jesus Christ and the other acts of God 'are not really historical events' like the death of Jesus or the destruction of the Temple: yet the context of his discussion of history in this otherwise excellent book makes it very clear that (unlike Bultmann and the 'Secular Christians') he deeply *believes* that the Resurrection and the other acts of God really *did happen* in some strange sort of objective way. Thus a theologian today may *deny* the historicity of the Resurrection and yet still believe that Jesus Himself *was* raised and is really alive today: and again, a theologian may declare today that he *believes* in the Resurrection as "truly historical" and yet hold that Jesus is dead and buried and that nothing actually happened to *Him* in the Resurrection, but only to His disciples! For the ordinary straight-forward Christian who expects 'yea' to mean 'yea' and 'nay' to mean 'nay', confusion becomes worse confounded.

THE THEOLOGY OF HOPE

That Jürgen Moltmann's 'Theology of Hope' should be considered in the context of split-level theologies will surprise some, for it has been reviewed with such unstinted praise by some conservative scholars.[17] Thus in the evangelical fortnightly *Christianity Today*, February 16th, 1968, a brief review by David P. Scaer of Concordia Theological Seminary stated (*inter alia*):

"With clear and decisive strokes, Moltmann shows that for both Jews and Christians history is rooted in actual events and sets its sights on a *real* future in accordance with God's promises. Christianity does not concentrate on the Hellenistic concept of God as an eternal presence but sees God going before his people, leading them to a goal. History is the framework for the promise that is the basis of hope. Hope is the other side of faith and more than anything else is the unique characteristic of Christianity ... This work, a masterpiece both in theology and in language, has already become a milestone in European theology, providing a positive, corrective influence by showing that the Church's real life lies not in the present but in the future ..."

This estimate of what Moltmann is saying seems to me to involve a serious misunderstanding of his basic position. He appears to write from a standpoint of post-Hegelian Idealism,[18] which, though it was the predominant academic philosophy at the beginning of the twentieth century throughout most of the Western world, is now not easily comprehensible to those whose basic training in thinking has been in the empirical tradition – which probably includes most of the theologians whose native language is English.

Moltmann's logical starting point is the same as for the other twentieth century split-level German theologians – an acceptance of the basic validity of the positivist approach to 'world' history, with a subsequent looking around for some refuge in which the salvageable remnants of the Christian Faith may be defended. But instead of fleeing like the others we have considered to a supra-historical plane or a subjective-existentialist level of history, which may be imagined as *parallel* to their basically positivist world-history, Moltmann takes refuge in the unborn and still unreal future, *after* the deterministic history of the scientific historians has run its course. This pattern can be seen in Moltmann's fine discussion of "The Historical Question of the Resurrection of Christ and the Questionableness of the Historical Approach to History"[19] from which with some brief quotations we shall try to convey his main argument.

"In face of the positivistic and mechanistic definition of the nature of history as a self-contained system of cause and effect, the assertion of a raising of Jesus by God appears as a myth concerning a supernatural incursion which is contradicted by all our experience of the world ... A theology of the resurrection can try several ways of solving the problem of history then presented to it. If, as is plain from the above few references, the risen Lord does not fit in with our concept of the historical, it is possible to grant that the report of the raising of Jesus by God is 'unhistorical' and to look around for other ways for modern, historically determined man to approach to and appropriate the reality of the resurrection ... The resurrection of Christ does not mean a possibility within the world and its history, but a new possibility altogether for the world, for existence and for history ... In view of what is meant and what is promised when we speak of the raising of Christ, it is therefore necessary to expose the profound irrationality of the rational cosmos of the modern, technico-scientific world. By the raising of Christ we do not mean a possible process in world history, but the eschatological process to which world history is subjected ... The raising of Christ is then to be called 'historic', not because it took place *in* the history to which other categories of some sort provide a key, but it is to be called historic because, by pointing the way for future events, it *makes* history in which we can and must live. It is historic because it discloses an eschatological future ... A theology of the resurrection can no longer speak of facts of the resurrection, in terms of a metaphysic of history, but in terms of a metaphysic of subjectivity it can certainly still speak of an Easter faith for which 'resurrection of Jesus' is merely an expression of faith, and one that can be left behind in the course of history. In this form the resurrection faith that makes no assertion of the resurrection fits in exactly with the modern world's view of reality and is in a sense the ultimate religion of our society. If theology on the other hand strives to attain a theological view of history and a revolution in the historical way of thinking, then there is justification for the objection that theology is thereby driven into the ghetto of an esoteric church ideology and can no longer make itself intelligible to anyone else."[20]

Moltmann's purpose appears to be – without denying the adequacy of 'scientific determinism' with reference to the history to which it lays claim (past and present, made and in the making) – to achieve a 'revolution' in the theological way of historical thinking, by claiming the *future* for God and Christian faith with the concept of 'promise' – "a key-word of Israel's 'religion of expectation'."[21] "It is not evolution, progress and advance that separate time into yesterday and tomorrow, but the word of promise cuts into events and divides reality into one reality which is passing and can be left behind, and another which must be expected and sought. The meaning of past and the meaning of future comes to light in the word of promise."[22] If the future – "a reality that does not yet exist"[23] – is accepted as being 'in' time, then we can say that Moltmann's 'split' is not (as it were) horizontally in 'levels' but by a vertical division across the time-line. Within the future thus separated from history, so long as it remains a non-existent 'reality', faith may construct on the foundation of hope "its own peculiar history";[24] but of course as soon as this 'history' becomes an existent reality, it is claimed by – and must, Moltmann concedes, be yielded to – the historical determinists. For what it is worth, then, "the promise binds man to the future and gives him a sense for history. It does not give him a sense for world history in general, nor yet for the historic character of human existence as such, but it binds him to its own peculiar history".[25]

It is fascinating to see the brilliant use which Moltmann makes of this new sort of split-history, in face of the problems of contemporary theology. The fact that secular history cannot admit the reality of acts of God in the past (including the resurrection) nor in the present need not trouble the Christian: for God is not in the past or present but in the future. Also, if we will accept Moltmann's solution of the problem of history, then together with the 'Secular Christians' we can accept with equanimity the widespread modern conviction that, in the present, God is dead – there *is* no living God: for Moltmann's God is essentially not in the present, but in the unborn future: God 'is' a 'reality' that does not yet exist, but for Which (Whom?) we may hope. The same must be said of the Risen Christ: He does not (yet?) exist in the present, He is not *now* the Living Lord: but we may hope for Him in the future, which of course can never become present reality without wrapping up Our Lord again in the deterministic grave-cloths of natural death, and burying Him again in the past. If we will but leave the great things of the Christian Faith in the safe sanctuary of the future, we can keep them for 'hope': but to claim them as realities in past history, and challenge the scientific historian on his own ground is 'uncritical' and will inevitably lose them even to hope.

On this ground Moltmann criticises Pannenberg's vigorously historical theology. "The uncritical use of such terms as 'historical', 'history', 'facts', 'tradition', 'reason', etc. in a theological sense, appears to show that the methodical, practical and speculative atheism of the modern age is here circumvented rather than taken seriously. If this very atheism – as it has most profoundly been understood by Hegel and Nietzsche – derives from the nihilistic discovery made on the 'speculative Good Friday', that 'God is dead', then the only real way of vindicating theology in the face of *this reality*, in the face of this reason, and in the face of a society thus constituted, will be in terms of a theology of resurrection – in fact in terms of an eschatology of the resurrection in the sense of the future of the 'crucified Lord'."[26] Thus the Christian who lives by hope rather than faith ("faith ... depends on hope for its life"[27]) agrees that in the present, God is dead and the Risen Christ is not alive: they are only a hope in the future.

Because of its novelty, and the importance that has been accorded to it even in conservative circles, we have spent some time considering the basic theological position which Moltmann adopts: but our immediate interest is the question: how well can this theology deal with 'the mighty acts of God', and with the concepts of God as Agent, which are so basic to all biblical theology?

It is surely beyond dispute that the present, NOW, is the only possible time for real action. We cannot act in the past, for it is gone and has in it only remembered 'acts' but not living 'action'. And we cannot possibly act in the future until it becomes present and is no longer future. We can remember actions in time past and plan actions for the future: but the reality of action is inseparably tied to the living present.

For Moltmann, however, as we have seen, we are not to seek God in the present or in the past, but only in the future. In the opening pages of his Introduction he indicates that the God of the theology of Hope "is no intra-worldly or extra-worldly God, but ... a god with 'future as his essential nature',

...the God whom we therefore cannot really have in us or over us *but always only before us*...'[28] It is therefore not surprising that for Moltmann the revelation of God comes to men not through the mighty acts of God experienced in the living present by his people, and remembered with thankful faith from the past: for "his revelations are essentially promises..."[29] Not the mighty *acts* of God but "the promises of God initiate history for Israel and retain the control of all historic experiences".[30] "There is therefore only one real problem in Christian theology...the problem of the future."[31] The problem of action, with which we have been concerned, does not even come within sight; and certainly it could never be adequately dealt with on the basis of the presuppositions of this 'theology of hope'. Moltmann's theology no doubt offers answers to some of the criticisms currently levelled against the Christian Faith by secular men. But we must say of his 'futurising' of history, as Berkhof has said of Bultmann's 'existentialising' of history: "The proverb 'the medicine is worse than the ailment' is applicable here."[32]

We must therefore apply to Moltmann's theology of history as to those of Bultmann, Tillich, Barth,[33] Ladd, and all others who radically split the concept of history, the following criticism, which Richardson levels against Brunner's theology.

Brunner escapes, he says, "from his entanglement in positivist notions about general laws of history by flight into the realm of *Heilsgeschichte*, or supra-history, where the critics cease from troubling and the faithful are at rest. But he also evades the biblical affirmations about the living God who acts in the history of this world. Against all such attempted solutions of the problem of criticism and faith, we must insist that there is only one history, and that if it is incredible that the acts of God were worked in it, then the revelation in Christ cannot be salvaged by recourse to a *Heilsgeschichte* that runs parallel to secular history, never really intersecting it, and inaccessible save through some extra-historical perception known as faith."[34]

It may seem that we have not made much progress in our search for an adequate view of history which can include, without logical inconsistency, recognition of the reality of (at least) *human action*, and with this at least the possibility that God also may have acted in the world in the past. We have, however, mapped and cleared the ground somewhat, and eliminated some of the theories applying for recognition as adequate. Let us pause to review the argument.

The 'secular' view of history, which came to sharp expression through the Positivists in the nineteenth century, demands that the verification methods of empirical science be applied with all possible strictness in assessing every asserted occurrence in the stories of man's past. This view of history, which is held by its supporter to be – and all the prestige of natural science appears to add weight to the claim – the only possible *rational* view of history, yields a deterministic account of man's past in which all real freedom to choose and to *act* must be denied to man. But as we have already seen, in discussing the scientific view of man, this position logically results in the conclusion that if it is true it cannot be true. Now to deny logic rather than question the adequacy of the determinist 'secular presuppositions' from which this conclusion follows would indeed be irrational. Moreover, as A. D. Ritchie has well put it, "The view of history as the working out of impersonal causes like physical causes, if held consistently, as it seldom has been, ... makes men into mechanically operated puppets. If men are puppets, it makes no difference whether you say the strings are pulled by God, necessity or chance."[35] Whichever you choose, history thus seen cannot be about the *acts* of man – for the possibility of human action has been excluded by the presuppositions. If man is to be regarded as simply a machine (which van Buren considered not impossible)[36] then one cannot without radical logical inconsistency define 'history' (as he does) as "an answering of questions about human *action* in the past" : for a machine cannot *act*.[37] 'Secular History', in this deterministic sense, is a self-contradictory, self-denying concept.

Such considerations have made it seem reasonable for historians to proceed on the assumption that by *limiting*, as merely part of the story of man, this scientific-determinist point of view, and supplementing it with another interpretation given from a non-determinist point of view – existential, suprahistorical, eschatological, etc. – a better result may be achieved. The obvious requirement, both in biblical theology and in the traditional Faith of the Church, that free and responsible action (both the acts of God and the acts of men) be acknowledged as real, has spurred several modern theologians to offer 'split-level' views of history in an attempt to meet this need. These

135

we have now judged to be inadequate and in error in their central concept of 'split-history'.

The scientific-objective approach to history (*Historie*), whether on its own, or as supplemented with a subjective or religious stream of supra-history (*Historie* plus *Geschichte*), is quite unable to meet the requirements for a rationally adequate view of history. A unified, non-dualistic and action-recognising approach to history is necessary. And when Richardson said, in the remark which we quoted, that the positivist presuppositions about history, assumed as basic by the Germanic leaders of theology in this century, are 'old' presuppositions, he had in mind attempts which have recently been made to approach history in this more rational way. In the next chapter we shall consider the views of theological history developed by some recent writers who claim to be working with new and better presuppositions.

PART III

TOWARDS A MODERN BIBLICAL THEOLOGY

CHAPTER 8

History and Action – Towards a Better Foundation

History is not one of the sciences; for the objective methods of the 'exact sciences' are not adequate for it. History is a unique discipline, and needs its own special methods of working. It is this conviction that was midwife at the birth of post-positivist modern history. Thus in an article on modern theories in the Philosophy of History,[1] P. L. G. Gardiner starts with the information that since the end of the nineteenth century the attention of philosophers concerned with history has been directed particularly to the task of "trying to delineate the specific character of historical knowledge and understanding", and to indicate ways in which history is unique. During the nineteenth century the positivists had assumed that history was really just another branch of science, seeking complete 'objectivity' through the exclusion of all 'subjective' influences such as personal purposes, motives, and so on: and academic historians, especially on the Continent, struggled to be truly 'scientific historians'. But now it came to be increasingly realised that history is different, dealing with man in a broader and more inclusive way than 'objective' science can; it needs its own different methodology.

Three men in particular are commonly named as among the leaders in this new movement of historical thinking : W. Dilthey, B. Croce, and R. G. Collingwood. "Like Croce before him," Gardiner tells us, "[Collingwood] wished to see history released from what he termed 'its state of pupilage to natural science', arguing that historical explanation radically diverges from the model of understanding proposed by the nineteenth century positivists and that the historian explains events, not by showing them to be instances of universal laws or regularities, but by

139

exhibiting them as the expressions of past thinking on the part of purposive agents, thinking which he must imaginatively re-construct or 're-enact' in his own mind."[2]

History, therefore, is essentially about actions, motives and *purposes*, about *persons* and their lives in the past, individually and in communities; and the strictly objective interests of science, as we have seen, are quite incapable of dealing in any adequate way with such matters. "The true aim of the historian, and his reward," as Alan Richardson says, "is the understanding of humanity in its concrete wholeness ... Nor is he disturbed by the criticism that historical judgements are rarely verifiable by methods comparable to those of the natural sciences, or that they are frequently incapable of being falsified. History is *sui generis*, and historical judgements cannot be reduced to any form of scientific generalisation, because historical characters are not laboratory specimens, but men and women who in their historical individuality are the objects of human regard and compassion."[3]

The subject/object distinction which is essential to the method of the natural sciences, with their search for objectivity and empirical verification, makes it impossible (as we have already shown) that from the scientific point of view man could be seen in his 'concrete wholeness'. Science, positivist philosophy, and secular man who uncritically accepts these as his sufficient standards, can see man only as 'object' (if they are logically consistent), and not also as 'subject'; nor indeed as 'agent' in whom this distinction is 'under-passed', as we shall see later. The logically consistent 'secular man', if he could be found, would see man's actions only as a series of events in a causal pattern : for he would be logically debarred, by his presuppositions, from acknowledging that a rational (and therefore free) purpose in a man's mind can somehow actually cause observable changes in the 'objective' world. He therefore could not consistently study man's actions as such at all, whether past or present, but only 'human events'; and the modern concept of history would be beyond his reach.

Hardly more adequate (we have argued) for the purpose of rationally undergirding modern historiography with its interest in the 'concrete wholeness' of man in his actions, is the existentialist division of history into two levels : for although it holds in view a subjective aspect of history as well as an objective aspect, it cannot 'think them together'. (We shall later consider and refute Gogarten's claim that Bultmann does in fact do this.) None of the 'split-level' theologies of history – those of Barth, Brunner, Tillich, Moltmann and others – can in this matter serve us much better. Linguistic Analysis also, while it works with the forms of logic currently available, is unable to deal adequately with action, or with the modern view of history in which action is paramount (as it is also, of course, in biblical history and theology). The philosophical streams of our age seem to run dry before reaching the pasture-land of human history with its crops of action. In a later chapter we shall further consider the need, indicated so clearly by Macmurray, to dig a new intellectual well for a philosophy of action which takes the self primarily as Agent rather than Subject, and the world as Other rather than Object; and from which the pastures of modern historiography may receive rational refreshment and philosophical confirmation.

But if, in the meantime, no effective *philosophical* support can be found for the aims and methods of the modern historian, he must still continue, on the basis of common-sense convictions, the work of uncovering and explaining to man his own racial history. For just as thinking, and sound thinking, went on amongst men before Aristotle formulated simple 'laws' or presuppositions for rational thought in his 'formal logic'; and just as Monsieur Jourdain in Molière's *Le Bourgeois Gentilhomme* had spoken prose already for forty years before he learned with delight that that was indeed what he had been doing; so also, we may assume, history – and good reliable history – has often been written apart from, and even in spite of, the efforts of philosophers to formulate an adequate philosophy and consistent methodology of history.

The modern style of history is really a return to common-sense. Whether or not we can prove or explain it, we *know* that in the past men were able to and in fact often did *act* for rational reasons, and that human purposes have changed the observable world in the most astonishing ways. If deterministic positivist presuppositions assume this to be impossible, if existentialist presuppositions hold man's freedom of action to be real only in the subjective realm of 'decision', and every act is turned by Idealism into a 'conceptual event' fully determined by the structure of the Whole – then so much the worse for these philosophies! Common-sense sounds out the ground-bass on the organ of truth, and the rising and falling philosophies of the years must be pitched in harmony with the notes it sounds, if they are not to be quickly discarded. History in this modern 'action-mode' that accords with common-sense must – and will – continue (as also will the steady, strong belief of ordinary Christians in the biblical God who acts) while changing patterns of philosophy and theology form ever new and interesting chords – and discords! – in humanity's ear. Thus while the brilliance of Continental speculation and scholarship in the nineteenth century led into the strange dissonances of positivist philosophy and of history as a science patterned as far as possible on the physical sciences, with 'Christian history' emerging among theologians as a separate stream of history, English historians were producing a less spectacular symphony of history in full harmony with a common-sense view of action, developing the 'theme' announced in the work of Edmund Burke (1729-97). Richardson outlines the development of this quiet stream of English historians, through S. T. Coleridge, Macaulay, and others, leading up, in the Church, to a 'school' of Liberal Anglican historians of which Richardson himself is obviously now a member:

"It would seem to have been the 'Liberal Anglicans' who, by providing a non-positivist attitude towards history, rendered it unnecessary for English theologians to embark upon that unfortunate strategy of disengagement from history" – we have called it a 'split-level view of history' – "which has characterised Germanic theology from Ritschl to the disciples of Barth and Bultmann. Because of their influence, the methods of historical science, properly so called, were not in England believed by theologians necessarily to presuppose the assumptions of positivism. The great English scholars of the nineteenth century, Lightfoot and Hort – critical scholars, said Lord Acton, surpassed by neither Frenchman nor German – together with Westcott, the third of the great Cambridge trio, were able to accomplish their biblical and historical work without feeling constrained to make any concessions to positivist conceptions of what might not be allowed to be historically possible. In an age of rebellious bewilderment, they demonstrated that the wholehearted acceptance of modern critical methods was entirely compatible with a serene and confident allegiance to the unreduced faith of the Catholic Creeds."[4]

The task of the historian is not, like that of the scientist, to observe patterns of regularity in human behaviour, and to formulate more and more general 'laws of history' which may be taken to indicate with increasing accuracy what may and what cannot happen in history : for instance that 'men cannot fly to the moon', or 'God cannot act in our world – there are no miracles'. His task, rather, is to examine *all* the evidence available in situations that arouse historical interest – without having prejudged possible reasons and causes – and in the light of all his own experience and learning about life and the world, to say what he believes *really* happened, and how and why. The honest historian knows full well from his own experience that men's actions have *reasons* (of purpose) and not just *causes* (in events); but also that the reasons expressed and the motives declared are sometimes found not to be the ones really operative. In fact, not only is what we say and do influenced by our prior interests and preconceptions, but even what we see and hear – what we unconsciously select for conscious attention, and so 'notice' among the many things that happen around us and which, in an unregistering sense, we 'see'. Thus a countryman in the city, for example, will hear amid the roar of the traffic a chirruping cicada which is quite unnoticed by the equally acute hearing of his city friends; his attention, shaped by his different interests and background, has made a different selection from among the multiple noises.

Similarly it happens at the level of things historically important that one man will notice and report things in a certain situation which another man also present will not even 'see'. A convinced Secularist and a committed Christian, though working side by side, are likely to report very differently the proceedings of the same Church Council meeting, or the same Rationalist Society meeting, no matter how objective they try to be; for each selects the things that *he*, being himself, believes to be real (and therefore 'credible') and important. A man in the seventeenth century and a man in the twentieth century, if they could exchange places, would notice things very differently from those around them – and on the basis of their own experience each would select and comment differently from those around them on the available reports of events in earlier times. This is why history must ever and anew be re-written for each generation, though the things that actually happened do

143

not change. Each different point of view will see as probable, or as incredible, a different range of 'possibilities'; and will include different areas of 'blindness'. The interpretation of history which best makes sense of *all* that is most reliably reported to have happened should be accepted as the truth about history.

It does not require much research to demonstrate that, for example, the often claimed 'impartiality' and 'objectivity' of the genuinely 'secular' historian, as contrasted with the alleged 'bias' of the Christian historian, cannot be taken for granted. "Western man," Lesslie Newbigin has written, "is at the moment going through a period of acute embarrassment about his Christian past which makes him unwilling to recognise the place that missions have had, and still have, in the making of modern history. As an interesting example of this, I might refer to the massive volume reporting the UNESCO conference of 1962 on Education in Africa. At a time when something like 85 per cent of all the school children in that continent were in mission schools, this volume contrives to provide a survey of the total situation without conveying the impression that such a thing as a mission school exists."[5]

In similar vein John Foster, of the University of Glasgow, writing of the astonishing expansion of Christian influence in the world through the modern missionary movement from about 1790 on, remarks: "Most writers of history books seem to have left out this missionary movement. *The Cambridge Modern History,* for example, gives one of its fourteen volumes to the French Revolution, and another to Napoleon. The index volume mentions the word missionary as occurring only once. This is the entry: 'Missionary Hill, fighting at, 1864'. It is a battle in the American Civil War. Yet this contemporary movement was to do at least as much to change the world as the French Revolution and to have far more permanent effects than Napoleon."[6]

Such omissions are not due to any lack of documentary evidence, but to a selection made, without intention of bias, by historians or reporters whose presuppositions and attitudes predispose them to see certain things as important and true, and to dismiss as insignificant or even fail to notice other things. Obviously the historian, seeking an accurate understanding of what actually happened, must try, as Collingwood said, to "imaginatively reconstruct or 're-enact' in his own mind" the thinking and doing, the selective prejudices and presuppositional biases which have helped to shape the various reports we have of past actions and events. The impartial historian who is seriously in search of truth, when wondering what to believe about the historicity of (for example) the Resurrection of Jesus Christ, and how to assess the views of our contemporaries and also of the relevant first century documents, will have to bear in mind not only the bias likely to result from a deep commit- ment to the Christian Faith, but also the secular sort of biased twentieth century blindness, instanced above with regard to missions. No less than other (including Christian) historians, the 'secular' historian pre-judges (on so-called scientific grounds) what can and what cannot happen, what is and is not im- portant, in history. That he does it all in the name of 'objective impartiality' does not mean that he is right and they wrong !

The really 'modern' historian, then, realises that contrary to the claims of the positivistic historians, "there are no un- interpreted facts which form the raw material for the scientific historian : the assumption that there are such facts prevents historians from asking the right questions. It is not the historian who sticks to the facts – the facts stick to him : 'the really de- tached mind is a dead mind, lying among the facts of history like unmagnetised steel among iron filings, no synthesis ever resulting in one case or the other to the end of time'."[7] Certainly there can be, at the technical level of chronicling events, a broad consensus about 'what really happened', having many ragged edges cut by the prejudices of the interested parties : but this consensus is not 'history'. History requires a *synthesising* of reported happenings – after the most rigorous critical appraisal of their status that the historian can make – into a coherent pattern which makes the best possible sense of all that he has experienced and learned about life and the world, past and present.

The version of history which must be accepted as true – Communist, Positivist-Secularist, Existentialist, Idealist, or Christian, etc. – is that which is judged to give the most credible and coherent account of all the evidence available, without resorting to some sort of two-level scheme as a means of retaining as 'historical realities', reports which will not fit into the dis- ciplined pattern of world history.

"Once we abandon positivist notions," as Richardson says,

"there is no need to dissociate the historian and the man of faith, or to imagine that there will ever exist a 'scientific' or 'ultimate' history which will leave no room for Christian faith in the interpretation of history. For history is a matter of interpretation in the light of personal commitments, accepted values and existential understanding in a way in which natural science is not thus a *personal* interpretation of nature. There is a public and verifiable scientific interpretation of nature, but it does not answer our deep existential questions; there is no such public and verifiable interpretation of history... That is why there can be a Christian interpretation of history but not a Christian chemistry."[8]

The important question which in the end must be decided by every historian, and indeed by every person to whom it comes, is whether or not the Christian view of history is the *truest* one, the one that makes better sense of everything than any other view does. Is the view of history which presupposes the reality of the biblical Creator-God who acts, and who has revealed Himself in Jesus Christ, better able than any other view to account rationally for all the available evidence about man and his world?

This much, at least, can initially be claimed for the biblical (Christian) view of history: it *does* recognise the reality of free and responsible human action (whether it can now provide acceptable philosophical justification for it or not): and this, though common-sense demands it, most of the rival theories cannot consistently do on the basis of their presuppositions; including, of course, 'Secular Christianity' and its view of history.

The various members of the common-sense 'school' of English historical theology through the years have no doubt espoused various systems of philosophy; but never – like their Continental brethren – in a way that would lead them to deny (by implication) such common-sense convictions as that men can act in the world with responsible freedom, or that history is one and undivided. If God acts, it must be in this one world and one history of ours and in ways analogous with human action: and if He does not act in this world and in man's history, then indeed we must say that 'God is dead'. Has God really acted in history? The fate of Christianity depends on the answer. We turn now to consider briefly the views of two other influential modern theologians who deal with this great question – Oscar Cullmann and Wolfhart Pannenberg.

Oscar Cullmann's brilliant book *Christ and Time*[9] broke important new ground in modern theology, in an area – the understanding of 'time' – which is of fundamental importance for a discussion of history and of action. God's 'eternity' as understood in the Hebrew tradition that runs through the Bible, is not a *timeless* state, as in Greek thought, without 'before' and 'now' and 'after'; in which therefore action, as a deliberate changing now of what has been before, is inconceivable, and 'history' is without real meaning. God's eternity, Cullmann maintains, is time with the quality of God's presence and God's action in it; and God is a God who acts in *our* time and history, which is contained within and permeated by His own eternal time.

In *Christ and Time* Cullmann claims to be simply expounding what is already in the Scriptures, without re-interpreting it to fit alien presuppositions of modern thought.[10] The same claim is repeated in his later book, *Salvation in History*,[11] in which he is concerned also to defend his development and interpretation of this basic theme of the Bible – that God has acted in man's history – in face of the criticism which had been levelled against it, especially by Bultmann and his followers. "I would like to convince my serious partners in dialogue (above all Bultmann himself . . . that their objections and way of raising questions, departing very much from my own, have caused me to deepen and make more precise my own position."[12] In his eagerness to be relevant to the position of Bultmann and the Existentialists, and to meet them on the ground of a common terminology and shared concepts, however, Cullmann seems in fact to have slipped into an unwilling and unconscious acceptance of far more in their presuppositions than is compatible with his claim of philosophical neutrality. This 'existentialising' of his position has reflected adversely on his exposition of the centrality of the acts of God in history, in various ways, of which we instance three.

BASIC TERMINOLOGY – ACT AND EVENT. "The whole content of the New Testament (and of the Old as well) is God's acting, not his being," Cullmann declares: and this – God's acting – is to be his major theme.[13] Certainly a Being

– an Agent – is revealed in this acting, he agrees. "This being may and must be an object of dogmatic reflection, but not of *exegetical* exposition",[14] and as it is simply with exposition that he is concerned, he will focus attention on God's acting.

It is surprising, therefore, that throughout this book the word 'act' ('act of God' and its cognates) occurs but rarely – and not at all in the Index. The heavily predominant term is 'event' ('divine events', or some parallel). In view of the nature of the distinction (which we have shown to be fundamental) between 'actions' and 'events' – a distinction especially important for the modern concept of history, as we have seen – this use of words by Cullmann in a discussion of history and of the acts of God certainly calls for examination.

Ordinary common-sense conversation, today as always, can properly and uncritically speak in the one breath of both 'act' and 'event', without trying to relate them in any exact way to one another. For we all know perfectly well both that people do act and that events do happen; and we seek reasons for actions and causes for events. As long as theology and history are content to stay uncritically with common-sense, problems here remain few. But when we try to think with philosophical comprehensiveness and precision, 'acts' and 'events' appear to constitute aspects of a dualism, which demands unified rational formulation of some sort. The obvious and perhaps the only available forms of unification here are either that acts should be regarded as a special sort of event, or *vice versa*. Now to Cullmann, despite his intention not to become involved in philosophical matters, these considerations become important because of his wish to avoid the appearance of 'splitting' history in the manner of the nineteenth century *Heilsgeschichte* school, as Bultmann and others had accused him of doing.

How can the unity. of history be maintained? In the pre-scientific outlook of the Bible (as we have already seen – p. 49 above) it was *action* – 'the acts of God' – that was adopted as the primary and basic category for explaining the world; and what we now call 'natural events' were distinguished within the activity of God as a sort of 'fixed order' activity (cf. Jeremiah 31 : 35, 36 etc.). A simple exegesis of the biblical texts, uncoloured by alien presuppositions and philosophy, would undoubtedly have to speak in terms of 'actions' as primary, with 'events' as derivative and secondary. But in his dialogue with Bultmann, for whom such thinking is simply 'mythological' and primitive, Cullmann's exegesis apparently balks at the possibility of being accused of such primitivism. With Bultmann, therefore, he appears to opt for a supplemented version of the Positivist presuppositions, by which everything is reduced to a common denominator of 'events', among which some may be distinguished (with reservations) as a special sort of event called 'actions'. Those who pursue this course are not avoiding philosophical bias. On the contrary, they are really just formulating consistently the implications of Descartes' thought-centred formula *Cogito ergo sum,* as developed by Locke, Hume, Kant and others (which we shall further discuss in a later chapter).

Cullmann, in accepting these 'positivist presuppositions', accepts the possibility, which we have already disputed in the name of modern historiography, of 'naked events' and 'simple facts' which are known but not 'interpreted'.[15] In the Old and New Testaments, he writes, "the mythical elements are intended to make a kerygmatic meaning clear, but this is a kerygmatic meaning of *events* . . . In the Bible we have, of course, *only* kerygmatic interpretations before us, and not a simple report of facts that could influence us as the events of the present influenced them [i.e. the eyewitnesses]. It would seem that we approach their understanding in faith if we at least *dare to make the attempt,* however uncertain its success may be, to place the events alongside the interpretation in such a way that in the naked events disclosed to us the interpretation of those events is forced upon us as it was upon the biblical witnesses . . . So we should not look at form criticism so onesidedly, as if its only aim were to impress us with the possibility of bridging the distance between kerygma and history."[16]

It seems clear therefore that despite modern historiography, Cullmann, along with Bultmann, accepts as in some sense 'knowable' a bare and uninterpreted substratum of *historische* events which are separated by a 'distance', a gap, from the interpretations that may be given of these events – including as an interpretation the 'mythical' concept of 'acts of God' in the observable world. The specific nature of 'action' as distinct from 'event' is apparently not recognised by Cullmann. Thus the word 'act' either becomes a synonym for 'event' in a rather careless usage; or else it indicates the mythical *meaning* of events which are claimed as 'acts of God' – and so presages a two-level view of history in the Existentialist style.

Already in the Foreword Cullmann has these words apparently working as synonyms. Thus he refers to a criticism levelled at him by Barth and others for overstressing "the horizontal line of salvation". "These critics say that the crucial thing in the New Testament is the vertical *saving act* of God in Christ. In what follows," Cullmann replies, "I shall try to show that I do not dispute the verticality of the *saving event . . .*"[17] 'Saving act' has become 'saving event'! Again, within the space of ten lines, when discussing the anti-Gnostic debate, he says: "For Marcion the Gospel is punctiliar, unbound *event*, vertical and not horizontal . . . Bultmann wishes to see the saving *event* only punctually, and not connected with salvation history . . . the Old Testament reveals God's *action* in salvation history."[18] Even where the context makes it clear that 'act' is the proper word, Cullmann usually has a phrase with the word 'event': "a sequence of events brought about by God"; "a divine, if not also an historical, event", "the plan of God accomplished in *events*"; "an *event* that has been accomplished by someone else (Christ) without our help" – and so on.[19] (Cullmann's italics). The fact that he so often puts the word 'event' into italics in such phrases suggests that he is aware that there is something rather odd about this usage; but he does not discuss it.

He does not discuss, either, the status of *human* actions, as distinguished from acts of God. Are they also to be regarded as 'vertical events', seen as expressing a personal freedom of 'intention' that somehow breaks into the causal sequence of events? Or are human acts merely 'horizontal events' – natural events like the rising of the tides, with the term 'vertical' reserved for 'divine events'? In either case Cullmann faces difficult problems.

To discuss this sort of question, concerning the status of action as such, is *not* to wander off into the paths of "alien philosophies": for this is the basic 'native' term of biblical theology, and it is no doubt partly through his failure to discuss it that Cullmann has in fact adopted a terminology and outlook alien to that of the Scriptures. The Bible does *not* speak of bare, impersonal, naturally caused 'events' to some of which, by 'revelation' superimposed, God gives a special divine meaning or quality, as Cullmann seems to suggest. "According to the

150

New Testament faith, God selects only specific events, bound together by a developing connection. This saving connection God reveals to the prophets and apostles in an act which itself belongs to salvation history."[20]

The fact of the matter seems to be that by failing to grapple with the linguistic and logical problems (and their metaphysical implications) which arise in connection with the concepts 'event' and 'action', Cullmann has indeed drifted, in spite of all his efforts at resistance, into accepting linguistic usage based on presuppositions which are not only alien to the Bible but even in conflict with the basic presupposition of all biblical theology – the assumption that *God acts*. His wish, obviously, is to speak in defence of this primary biblical assumption and theme : but what he actually says, in dialogical embrace with Bultmann, seems rather to be in confused contradiction of it.

SUBJECT AND OBJECT. Fundamental in all philosophy, especially since the time of René Descartes (1596-1650), and to-day a crucial issue in theology, is the subject/object distinction to which we have already referred several times in the passing, and which we shall later consider more systematically. Cullmann returns to it time and again as one of the issues on which he believes himself to be most at variance with Bultmann and his school.[21] He takes seriously the claim of F. Gogarten and Bultmann that theological Existentialism has transcended or otherwise dispensed with the subject/object distinction, following the suggestions of Dilthey, Heidegger, Buber and others. "The hermeneutics of today," he writes, ". . . include the person of the exegete right at the start. A resigned acknowledgement that our exposition can never be completely free from presuppositions is not felt to be enough. Today, under the influence of the works of W. Dilthey, B. Croce and R. G. Collingwood, who have dealt with the problems raised in interpreting history, the inclusion of the interpreter's own person in the question brought to the text is raised to an exegetical principle requiring the deliberate abrogation of the distance between subject and object . . . The effort at objectivity is intentionally dropped in the case of the questions with which one is faced . . . The object is deliberately no longer seen alone, but only in relation with the subject in the 'address', in the 'encounter' . . ."[22]

Now we shall later show that this extravagant claim of the

Existentialists is false (as indeed Gogarten seems indirectly to admit). For though the subject/object way of thinking *must* be somehow transcended (or 'under-passed') if thought is ever adequately to encompass action and history – which is about *agents acting* in the world – yet it is logically absurd to suggest that it can be eliminated with reference to the exegete and his texts, the *thinking subject* and the objects of his study. What Cullmann is so concerned to defend here, therefore, is in fact what is really basic to the subjectivist position of the Existentialists, (as we have already argued at length) into which they found themselves obliged to retreat in search of room for freedom and religion, when they initially conceded the claims of the Positivists with respect to universal determinism in the objective world of nature. He is, in a sense, shadow-boxing here: for what he disagrees with is really just the unjustified claim of Existentialism to have dispensed with the subject/object distinction: and what he so strongly defends is really their essential position, with its fundamental error in accepting the positivist assumption that we may know 'objective', uninterpreted historical facts in *historie*, within a basic pattern of natural causality; and its added 'subjective' area of so-called 'real' (*geschichtliche*) history, which includes the meaning or interpretation of these facts. If this is indeed so, we may expect to find in Cullmann's view of history a significant 'split' into two levels, despite his claims of unity.

THE DISTINCTION BETWEEN GENERAL HISTORY AND SALVATION HISTORY

In the Introduction to *Christ and Time*, Cullmann declares that for the Christian, his concept of 'salvation history', "is also the measuring standard of general, so-called 'secular' history, which when seen in this light ceases to be secular to him ... For the problem here treated must not be rendered inoffensive in the way in which this so readily happens among non-Christians and Christians alike: both groups often surround the Biblical history with high walls so that all access to general history is made impossible."[23] In *Salvation in History*, however, he refers to the necessity today laid on scholars by the work of the demythologisers to distinguish "between the historical and non-historical levels" in biblical history. "For our modern thinking,

152

the distinction between the two levels is unavoidable."[24] A radical distinction exists between history and salvation history. "For secular history, historical events are not interpreted by their relationship to a wholly different event, occurring on a non-historical level, which is nevertheless thought to be just as real as the events it interprets. A fundamental distinction exists here *a priori*."[25] Nevertheless, Cullmann insists, "a positive relationship to history is established by the fact that salvation history involves a sequence of events taking place within history. Salvation history is therefore not a history *alongside* history (a notion that has wrongly been attributed to me); it unfolds in history, and in this sense belongs to it."[26] Obviously Cullmann is finding it very difficult to keep salvation history within general history, and to prevent it from separating or climbing to a different 'level', after the style of the split-level histories we have mentioned.

All history, Cullmann agrees, consists of events in connected series.[27] 'General history' connects events in an uninterrupted causal series: but what is the principle of connection between the scattered events of 'salvation history' which links them into a real history? It is "the divine selection of a few events out of the whole of history".[28] This principle of selection and connection in salvation history is "traced back to the progressing divine revelation in events and the interpretation of them. All biblical salvation rests upon the tacit presupposition that the selection of events is reached by the decision of God."[29] Thus, instead of saying that these events were 'done' or 'caused' by God, or – which is the only satisfactory way of saying it – that they were 'acts' of God and not mere events at all, (so that he can find the principle of connection in God as Agent), Cullmann speaks of God choosing or selecting 'a few events' and then revealing to men that they are connected 'divine events'. One receives a strong impression that, drawn willy-nilly into the existentialist whirlpool, Cullmann has now ceded all 'objective' general history to impersonal causality, retaining only 'the act of revelation' as the sphere of God's action, a single, vertical, punctual and verbal or 'subjective' event; which is what he rightly believes to be Bultmann's position, and disclaims for himself! "According to New Testament faith," he writes, "God selects only specific events bound together by a developing connection. This saving connection God reveals to the prophets and apostles in an act which itself belongs to salvation history."[30] It looks as though the 'events' become 'divine events' because of the revelation, and not because in any real way they were in history the acts of the living God. Again we see how, given the subject/object distinction of all scientific thought, and the priority of 'objective events' as the units out of which to construct the world as we know it, we seem to find ourselves in an unsatisfactory and frustrating intellectual 'dead end'. Surely the proper conclusion to draw is not that we must altogether give up the concept of 'action' – God's action included – as a real exercise of freedom in the world, and make do with 'events' only; but rather that we must go back and review the foundational presuppositions of all critical modern thinking, and consider again (as we shall do in a later chapter) the possibility of acknowledging *action* as that which is primarily 'given', with *events* as derived and subordinate.

We have noted that in spite of the name of his recent book, Cullmann's thinking seems to have moved away somewhat since he wrote *Christ and Time* from the Bible's activist emphasis on 'salvation in history' towards a view of salvation history as ultimately a matter of conceptual revelation – of the interpretative 'Word' of God coming to man. In some senses this brings him closer not only to Bultmann and his followers, not only to Barth, Brunner and the theologians of the Word, but also to W. Pannenberg and his recently influential circle in Germany. This last point is noted by J. M. Robinson in his essay on Pannenberg's work, titled: "Revelation as Word and as History".[31] Here he refers to "Cullmann's new book, whose title *Salvation in History* stands in striking parallel to that of the symposium of the Pannenberg group, *Revelation in History*". Cullmann himself, discussing the relationship of the two points of view, comments that by Pannenberg "the problem is actually seen from the vantage point of revelation rather than that of salvation. But as Pannenberg himself recognises in passing, the two concepts can hardly be separated ... Pannenberg's work seeks to rehabilitate history as the source and place of revelation, and its clear statements are a contrast to much of the modern theological literature of Germany, obscure in its sophistication. In distinction to the theology influenced by existentialism, history, and not a single act of God, is designated as the revelation of the one God, indirect, but uniquely complete ...

154

Although Pannenberg rests his position in a commendable way upon the exegetical studies of the Old and New Testament scholars who belong to this group," Cullmann remarks, "it is still clear that the premises of his thought are taken mainly from a philosophy of history."[32] We have seen that, in fact, the sort of history which yields revelation for Cullmann himself seems to be a special sort of history designated as such by (if not a single act, then) a relatively few special 'acts of revelation': and that his own exegesis, especially in its neglect of 'action', is not nearly so free from alien philosophical presuppositions as he thinks it is.

We turn now to consider Pannenberg's view of history and revelation in the light of our common-sense knowledge of 'action', and of history as composed of actions.

WOLFHART PANNENBERG'S vigorous Idealism is quite different from the reluctant Existentialism which seems to colour the recent thought of Oscar Cullmann. John B. Cobb, in his contribution to the recent American symposium on Pannenberg's thought says this of it:

"Pannenberg sees in German idealism a powerful apprehension of the truth he wants to bring home to our day ... It is through the immense undertaking of re-establishing for us the persuasive power of major aspects of this philosophical tradition that Pannenberg proposes to set the context for the appropriation of the truth of Christianity." Many will share the reservations Cobb expresses about this prospect: "To one committed like Pannenberg to the importance of speculative thought and to the quest for comprehensiveness of vision, but schooled far more in the empiricism and naturalism of the English-speaking world, this vast undertaking appears awe-inspiring, but also somewhat foreign."[33] The knowledge of Pannenberg's philosophical commitment, however, gives us a very welcome indication of the perspective in which his theological arguments must be seen.

In Pannenberg's writing, as in Cullmann's, the words 'event' and 'act' appear to be largely interchangeable. Pannenberg, however, makes much more frequent use of the word 'act', so that it becomes a key-word in his vocabulary; and the *concept* of God's action is obviously fundamental for him. Yet in the title of his (1959) programmatic essay, "Redemptive Event and History", it is the word 'event' that is prominent; and

155

'event' (both the word and the concept) is by him given a status more basic than that of 'act', so that acts are seen as special events, distinguished as 'accidental' or 'contingent' events from among the 'necessary' and 'connected' events of the causal pattern in nature. It must surely be admitted that for a concept as unique and positive as that of 'action', properly understood by common-sense to be an exercise of personal freedom in the world, such a derivative and negative status seems hardly satisfactory; such 'action' does not seem adequate to carry the weight of a full 'system of theology'.

Speaking of the way in which Christianity once traded its dynamic view of the living God for "the Greek concept of a God who remained unchanged and could not act as a person", Pannenberg believes (as reported by Daniel Fuller) that instead, "Christianity should have shown how its God, who acts as a person and thus brings about contingent events in history, could have delivered Greek philosophy from the absurdities and contradictions to which its idea of an impersonal, static God had led it."[34] Here, it would seem, is an outlook, a view of God and the world, urgently in need of a dynamic action-based vocabulary and logic, but confined still in the static 'stocks' of an event-based vocabulary and logic.

Essential to Pannenberg's theology, with its idealistic structure, is his insistence on the indivisible Wholeness of history and all reality. The acts of God and the acts of men, as accidental or contingent events, must take place in the very same world in which the necessary and connected events of nature occur: no split-level concepts of history or of nature can be tolerated. But this seems to result in a blurring of the important distinction between nature and history and between event and action – a distinction which in terms of critical thought must be considered to be fundamental and irreducible. "If all reality, and not only the level of human life, is marked by historicality," Pannenberg writes, "then the divinity of God can only be thought of in relation to the whole of reality understood as history, and in this sense in relation to history."[35] In a way rather reminiscent of the pan-psychism of Teilhard de Chardin, Pannenberg seems to suggest that all process should be included in *history*. In a *theology* which took as primary, not events but actions – the acts of God and of men – and from them derived (as subordinate) the event-processes of nature, such comprehensive inclusiveness could be rationally acceptable – and precisely this *is* the new form of theology which seems to be so urgently required today. But it is into idealistic Thought and not into Action, (or into God as Subject and not God as Agent, as we shall see in more detail later) that Pannenberg is here absorbing events: and this no empiricist can admit as proper.

This insistence on the wholeness of history, however, means that, for Pannenberg, "a splitting up of historical consciousness into a detection of facts and an evaluation of them (or into history as known and history as experienced) is intolerable to Christian faith, not only because the message of the resurrection of Jesus and of God's revelation in Him necessarily becomes merely subjective interpretation, but also because it is the reflection of an outmoded and questionable historical method. It is based on the futile aim of the positivist historians to ascertain bare facts without meaning in history. Both neo-Kantianism and the philosophy-of-life school have accepted historical positivism as one of their presuppositions and have merely supplemented it by an 'evaluating' contemplation or by the interpretation of the facts according to their expressive value. Against this we must reinstate today the original unity of facts and their meaning. Every event, if not taken artificially out of context, . . . brings its own meaning for each particular enquirer . . ."[36]

Pannenberg refers to Cullmann's treatment of "the events which are reported by the Biblical writings as decisive acts of God", and comments: "the exclusion in principle of this series of events from the rest of history, which Cullmann has effected, is questionable, for it creates the appearance that these events were different from the others not only in their historical peculiarity, but also *qualitatively* different in another, metaphysical sense . . . In my view of things every interpretation of an event must be justified from the context in which it is experienced . . . Only in this way is a speaking of definite events as divine acts possible, and indeed not in a supernatural sense, but in a phenomenological one . . ."[37]

"Supernatural", for Pannenberg, is a pejorative term. When used of revelation it apparently denotes for him a quality of super-rational (and therefore almost anti-rational) authority, superimposing a special divine meaning upon certain events, facts or words;[38] and when applied to history or nature it is taken to indicate an inadmissible split (spatial or temporal as well as qualitative) in the unified wholeness of reality. Thus, in what is obviously a further reference to Cullmann's view which he has dismissed as 'supernatural', Pannenberg insists that God must be in all of history, or in none. "The very concept of history, precisely as human and profane history, is constituted by the presence of the infinite in the midst of the finite, and in this sense by 'God's action'. History is not initially conceivable as complete in itself, as if God's action in history were then added somehow 'vertically from above'. So conceived, any talk of God's action in history would be superfluous; there would be no further occasion for it, if everything that happened were comprehensible without it."[39]

D. P. Fuller reports that Pannenberg "deplores what he has termed a two-storey view of God's working in which one part is supernatural and the other part is natural, for if such were the case God would be fully revealed only in the supernatural, not in the natural, part of history, and thus not all of history would be the medium of revelation . . . Pannenberg feels that he can keep his contrasts" – i.e. necessary events and contingent events, etc. – "happily on one floor of history, while the admission of the supernatural would split history into two floors."[40] Pannenberg rejects also, as "supernaturalism", the "dualistic-sounding antithesis" in time which J. Moltmann makes between past and present, on the one hand, and the future on the other; and which, as we have seen, he then uses with reference to the resurrection of Jesus and the existence of God in ways which we found to be objectionable. For, as Pannenberg says, "a future that is *only* opposed to the presently existing world cannot be a 'promise' for it, but can only mean threat and destruction."[41]

The maintenance of this unity and wholeness of time, past, present and future, is essential to Pannenberg's idealistic position; for nothing can fully be what it is, or be known to be what it is, until the Whole is complete, and there is no more future still bringing in ever new things. "If one is at all justified in speaking of God as the power over everything, it is only in view of the *whole* of reality, and not of certain special experiences." Thus "the words of the prophets and . . . their special experiences . . . have the character of revelation not in and of themselves but at most as the anticipation of the whole of reality . . ."[42] Even what is sometimes called 'the finished work of Christ' is, in Pannenberg's Idealism, a special sort of 'mere anticipation': "The history of Jesus, precisely in the form of mere anticipation, is the final revelation."[43] Nothing that has happened in the past, nothing present, is fully real nor can be definitely known for what it is, until the future is also complete.

Those whose background is in an empirical tradition of thought inevitably begin to wonder how '*real*' nature and its events, history and its actions – and especially the acts of God – are understood to be within this sort of 'system'. How far has everything been reduced essentially to the "mental acts" of thinking subjects?[44]

Kendrick Grobel raises a related point with Pannenberg in the American symposium and draws a reply on this matter. "The acts of God in history! Good! But when is an event in history *eo ipso* an act of God?" he asks. All present in the same situation witness the same event, yet whereas some see an act of God, others do not. "The piercing of the barrier should have been for *all* or *none* – unless the recognition of an act of God was neither solely, nor even basically, a matter of sense, but was instead a product of a higher function of the mind than perception, viz. that combining power we call thought. The brute fact, the external event, was *there* – no one in the crowd denies it – and to some that brute fact was the vehicle of revelation : but *how* the individual took it, experienced it, understood it, assimilated it into his own being, did not come *from* the fact but was brought *to* it."[45]

Now without departing from our conviction, already stated, that there are no 'uninterpreted facts' known as such to men, we may – and most people do – maintain that there really are 'external events', brute facts which must inevitably be interpreted *somehow* by everyone who experiences them, but which are 'there' and 'real', whether they are experienced and known to be there or not. Those who believe this will draw little satisfaction from Pannenberg's reply to Grobel's contention that the experience of the facts "did not come *from* the fact but was brought to it". "This formulation," Pannenberg says, "leaves untouched the crucial point that the true cognition of an object is not added externally to the object, but expresses its very essence, and does so in a way that becomes demonstrable in the object itself . . ."[46] One suspects that in an Idealist system of this sort, both 'events' and 'acts' are in the end brought to a

common denominator as 'ideas' of thinking Subjects. The undivided unity of history and nature are saved at the cost of
evaporating *reality*, and especially full-blooded, living action
in the real world, into a mist of ideas. Again we are reminded
of the saying that the remedy is worse than the ailment. Better
an unresolved 'dualism' in a context of reality – better 'events'
and 'actions' unreconciled, subject and object, history and
supra-history, nature and the supernatural – than a 'solution' that
dissolves them all into acts of cognition, or whatever the ulti-
mates of Idealism are to be called!

From this impasse, at the end of the modern split-history
trail, our thoughts run back to the situation which led Kähler,
in his 1892 lecture to German pastors, to suggest that Christians
must look at history in two different ways: *historische* or objectively, and *geschichtliche* or subjectively. The Liberal New
Testament critics, having in effect accepted the positivist assumption that there is no supernatural, had continued to claim that
their non-supernatural view of Jesus could be supported from
the 'inner core' of the New Testament, until it became clear
that even Mark's Gospel, the last remnant of their 'core' was
also, in fact, permeated with a supernaturalist view of Jesus
– and of God. With the New Testament now acknowledged
to be everywhere and inseparably committed to supernaturalism,
the Critics, as Kähler saw, had come to the place where they
must either abandon all claims of being loyal to the biblical
foundations of the Faith, or else accept, in place of the discarded two-level (ontological) concept of reality, a two-level
(epistemological) view of history, such that the same event (or
person) could be looked at from two different points of view –
whether with scientific objectivity, yielding 'knowledge', or with
theological faith-filled subjectivity, yielding Christian beliefs
which may be claimed by Christians to be the 'real meaning'
or the 'proper interpretation' of the event or person, and which
in the Bible are expressed in a supernaturalist, 'mythical' form.

We have now glanced at some of the salient points along
the course of this 'split-level history' concept, which from time
to time has tended to objectify from an epistemological distinction of points of view into a distinction among events in reality
itself. We noted the move in modern historiography to abolish
this two-level 'facts-and-meaning' distinction, and to unify history around the concept of rational human action: and the

historical tradition of English theological Liberalism, with Alan Richardson as its modern champion, was indicated as having accepted this unification, along with many non-theological historians. But it is noteworthy that while accepting the unity of *history*, these 'common-sense English historians', as we have called them, also accepted the distinction, in *reality*, of natural and supernatural. Thus they *retain* that fundamental biblical distinction, the rejection of which by German theologians in Kähler's time forced them either to split history or to abandon the Bible entirely.

O. Cullmann we have judged to fall into a somewhat ambivalent intermediate position, claiming that history is one and also apparently that reality is one and undivided; and yet appearing sometimes to accept a two-level view of history, and sometimes to admit a distinction of natural and supernatural in reality.

Here, however, with Pannenberg, we have come to a theology which claims to dispense with both the double-view of history and also the natural/supernatural distinction, and yet still to be faithful to the New Testament, in a religion without 'miracle'! We must now consider further this question of miracles and the supernatural.

CHAPTER 9

The Supernatural and Action – 'Miracles'

W. Pannenberg, whose vigorous reaffirmation of the reality of the acts of God in history has recently evoked a keen and sympathetic interest especially among the more conservative theologians of the church, rejects both the supernatural and the supra-historical in his theology, and also (says J. M. Robinson) the concept of 'miracle', because it is in tension with the concept of creation.[1] Such a rejection of the supernatural and miracle would normally be taken to mean a denial of the Christian conviction that God, who as Creator is 'above' all nature and history, has personally and directly acted in the world. How can one *affirm* the acts of God in history, and at the same time *deny* miracles and the supernatural?

The definition of terms is obviously crucial here. What is meant by 'miracle', 'supernatural', 'supra-historical' and 'acts of God'? J. M. Robinson, elaborating on Pannenberg's views about miracles, relative to creation, writes: "In Pannenberg's opinion it would ... be difficult to argue that an occurrence is to be regarded as *miraculous in the common connotation of the term as referring to a breaking of the laws of nature*."[2]

This 'common' understanding of miracle dates back at least to David Hume (1711-1766) who in his famous essay, *Of Miracles*, defined miracle as "a transgression of a law of nature by a particular volition of the Deity, or by the interposition of some invisible agent." Now if it is agreed that the essential thing about a miracle is that it involves breaking a law of nature, then we are compelled by definition to begin any discussion of miracles with the tacit acknowledgement that, whatever else is doubted or denied, the reality which must be accepted as 'given' and pre-supposed is *nature*, understood as

162

a system of events in patterns described by 'laws of nature'. We are debarred, by the presuppositions embodied in this definition, from starting with the assumption that acts rather than events are the ultimate constituents of nature, or that God rather than nature should be assumed as initially 'given' reality, God as Creator through whose act of creation nature receives its being and form. The definition of miracles in terms of the breach of natural law *presupposes* the naturalistic, secular world-view, therefore logically compelling Christians to speak of God either dualistically, by adding Him as an extra above nature – as 'super-natural'; or pantheistically, by identifying Him with all nature, understood as everything there is; or else to identify Him with some part or aspect of nature – e.g. as the 'ground of being' or 'the depth of existence' (love?) – and so to contain Him fully within nature as wholly immanent. This process very obviously begs the question against the biblical position, which starts by assuming the personal reality of God who acts, and sees all nature and all events as contained within and dependent on that primary reality.

It is, of course, no more proper for theology to beg the question against naturalism than vice versa. For instance, to define miracles as 'the known acts of the supernatural God in history' *presupposes* the existence of God as living personal agent; and a discussion that remains within the terms of this definition, though perhaps denying the historicity of some claimed 'acts of God', could not logically deny the existence of such a God if some participant wished to do so. What is needed here, therefore, is the mutually acknowledgeable neutral concept of 'action', which recognises in a rationally rigorous way that personal purposes can and do make changes in the observable world, through a dynamic meeting between the Self as *Agent* (not merely as 'observer' or Subject) and the world as *Other* (not merely as Object). This is urgently required to provide common ground between modern history and the sciences, as well as between both of these disciplines and theology. It is properly the task of philosophy, which so often today behaves like a minor department of linguistic studies or as a mere handmaid of technology, to formulate such a 'common-ground concept', and in the next chapter we shall consider a most interesting attempt which has been made to do this. With reference to our present concern, such a concept would provide opportunity to discuss whether, among the 'acts' observable in history and nature, some appear to be the acts of an Agent who is not confined within nature, but is supernatural Lord and Creator of nature. Without it, however, we can only return within the circle of Christian conviction to discuss the view of miracles as 'acts of God' over against the contrary views of miracles as 'events which break natural laws', or as 'events which cause surprise because their cause is unknown'.

CHANGING CONCEPTS OF NATURE

The concept 'supernatural' is obviously derived from and dependent for its meaning upon the concept of 'nature': and this presents problems in theology because of the considerable changes undergone by the concept of nature during the centuries. To assume that the word 'supernatural' has only one continuing meaning, while the word 'nature' is used to refer to various quite different views of the world, is obviously fallacious. It is always necessary to be clear what view of 'nature' this 'super' is supposed to transcend. The 'nature' of primitive animism is different from that of Old Testament thought, and both must be distinguished from the mediaeval view of nature. This again is different from the view of nature that was developed in connection with the mechanistic outlook of classical science which reached its zenith in the Newtonian period; and truly modern science, with its nuclear physics and allied disciplines, has yielded yet another concept of nature. Each of these, and others that could be mentioned, would have related to it a different view of the 'supernatural', and some care should be taken by scholars to ensure that their use of the word with reference to different periods of religious history does not overlook important distinctions.

The mediaeval view of nature was derived largely from theology, which in that day was 'queen of the sciences'; whereas the classical-scientific concept of nature, as a system of reality showing patterns of regularity that can be described in terms of scientific or natural laws, "came less from theology than it did from Sir Isaac Newton and his colleagues in the scientific revolution, who showed that the operation of the universe could be explained rationally in terms of the laws of nature, without bringing in any external intervention."[3] Nature in this period was thought of as a closed system which was 'governed' by permanent laws that could not be broken, except perhaps by God's intervention : it was a closed continuum of natural events related to one another in a deterministic pattern of causes and effects. 'Supernatural events', relative to such a system, would be events which cannot be fitted into the patterns of natural law, but which appear to have 'broken' the laws of nature, therefore requiring a reference to God as the cause of them : though as Lerner says, scientists (as such) concluded that in nature there are no such events, and science does not need to make any reference to external intervention at all.

It is, of course, to *this* scientific concept of nature, as a closed and law-bound continuum of causes and effects, that the meaning of the term 'supernatural' has normally been tied during the last century or more in Protestant theology; though the issue is complicated by the fact that in Roman Catholic theology the pre-scientific Thomist view of nature may still sometimes predominate. Reformed theologians, who though familiar with the views of science still believe in the theological necessity of the term 'supernatural' for describing the manner of God's transcendence over nature, find an anachronistic irrelevance in many of the arguments formulated against the supernatural by Bultmann, Gogarten and others who apparently assume that the term is still normally used in Reformed thought with a mediaeval connotation.[4]

The word 'miracle' has often been taken to be synonymous with 'supernatural event' as defined above; an event requiring reference to God's causality. But this word, too, is open to various definitions in which it is related to different understandings of 'nature' and of 'God'. Some of these meanings have recently been ambiguously exploited, to the confusion of 'the faithful' who comprise the simply-believing majority in most churches.

THE "NEW VIEW OF MIRACLES"

Typical of the course followed in much modern theological thought about miracles is that outlined by A. R. Billings in a short article on religious education in schools. "It is becoming fashionable," he wrote, "for many teachers of divinity to deal with the problem of miracles by emptying the word miracle of its conventional theological meaning. The conventional definition is that a miracle is an event usually fairly spectacular and astonishing, whose cause is supernatural. That is, whereas with a natural event there is a direct causal relationship between that event and a previous one within the natural order, with miracles no such natural cause could be found, and we must postulate a cause beyond, above, outside the ·natural order, a supernatural cause." But, he argues, "belief in supernaturally caused events seems to contradict the fundamental presuppositions of science, that all events can take their place in a pattern of regularities described in terms of general laws." Billings apparently assumes, in common with many others in the secular age, that anything which is inconsistent with these scientific presuppositions must be false – that there is no area of reality or truth to which these presuppositions do not apply. Miracles, therefore, as 'supernaturally caused events' must somehow be 'explained away' in terms of natural causality, if they are not to be simply denied. And so he goes on to discuss "the new approach, the re-defining of miracles with the emphasis not on the cause but on the effects which these events produce on those who witness them."[5]

Thus an event is to be called a miracle, not because it is caused in a surprising (supernatural) way, but because it causes surprise in those who experience or observe it! The *psychological* attraction today of this new approach lies in the fact that it accords well with the already dominant secularism of the modern outlook, which does not recognise the reality of the supernatural. This new definition allows a person – for example a 'Secular Christian' – to say "I believe in miracles" (and so to retain the *words* of orthodox belief), without necessarily implying any belief at all in the supernatural or in the living God of the Biblical Faith – God who acts. The main *logical* strength of the new view of miracles, as seen by many wavering believers in traditional biblical Christianity, is probably in the fact that to attribute to the pre-scientific believers of biblical times a view of miracles which involves 'laws of nature' and their being broken supernaturally, is obviously anachronistic: compared with this, the new view is much more credible. Several of these points are well stated or well exemplified in L. G. Geering's book *God in the New World*, as in the following quotation:

"The image of God as a supernatural being, who from time to time interferes in the affairs of the natural world in clearly recognizable ways, and who can suspend or reverse the usual behaviour of natural phenomena, if He so wishes, in order to perform His will, is one which has become less and less tenable as the new world has emerged. As the sciences have moved from one apparent success to another, and paved the way for the rapid advance of technology, the ordinary man has felt more and more confident that he understands the natural forces and processes with some degree of certainty . . .

"This leads . . . to the fact that secular man neither expects nor believes in the miraculous intervention by God in the times of his desperate need. At this point the word 'miracle' needs to be more carefully analysed. The word originally meant a marvel, something which was so extraordinary as to attract attention, wonder and even awe. In this sense the word still has a valid meaning for us, since there are many things in our experience which make us marvel. The advent of television, penicillin, nuclear fission were all marvels. When modern surgery restores sight to a blind man, when a drunkard is re-formed, when what appears to be certain catastrophe is averted, then the word 'miracle' arises naturally to our lips in order to describe them.

"But if the word 'miracle' is used to describe a supernatural intervention by God, which is possible only through the temporary suspension of natural laws and forces, then we are talking about something else. It is this kind of definition which lies behind much popular talk of miracles. But it is a view of miracle which does not properly belong to the ancient world, where there was no clear understanding of permanent natural laws, and where they could distinguish only between the usual and the unusual. Certainly the Bible bears witness to the wonderful works of God, the signs and miracles of His grace, but it is anachronistic to read into these affirmations a much later understanding of miracle, one which belongs particularly to the medieval view of the interpenetration of the two worlds – the natural and the supernatural. The receding of the sense of the supernatural world, characteristic of the secularizing process, is bringing an end to that idea of miracle which implies a temporary suspension of natural law."[6]

Here we see illustrated the way in which the concepts 'miracle' and 'supernatural' can be shuttled between the centuries – from today (nineteenth-century-science version) to the first century, to the mediaeval period, and so on, with a rather careless play made on the differences of outlook in the different periods. Also of importance is the indirect indication of awareness that a modern understanding of miracle naturally works with the concept of *action*, such as produced television, nuclear fission, eye-surgery, etc. For describing this action, we are told, (though the laws of nature have not been broken but only intelligently used) "the word 'miracle' arises naturally to our lips". But although the biblical witness to "the wonderful works of God" – often called in Scripture 'the mighty *acts* of God' – is acknowledged, the analogy between these acts of God and the 'miraculous' human acts referred to is apparently not seen; nor, therefore, is the direct link which, without anachronism, unites our age with that of the Bible through this concept of 'action'. What seems to have happened, rather, is that the 'secular man's' assumption has been accepted – that the mechanistic outlook of science, with its closed continuum of law-bound events, is of universal validity: and since this system cannot admit the intrusion of a supernatural Agent to do mighty acts in nature and history, the possibility of there being any such Agent has been altogether discounted. This means, of course, discarding the possibility of *action* as a basic category for theological understanding (in the old-fashioned sense of 'theology' that makes reference to *God*, and is not content to identify theology with certain aspects of anthropology!). Obviously unnoticed by Geering, also, is the fact stated and illustrated so extensively by M. Polanyi in his book *Personal Knowledge*: that *man* as agent – and with him his acts – are also excluded from the universe of science by the same arguments which are used to exclude the supernatural agency of God; and that only as an automaton, a machine, can man be retained in this world-view.[7] For the 'secular man' cannot consistently account even for human action except in terms which are (on his scientific presuppositions) 'supernaturalist' terms, involving the intrusion of the trans-empirical concept of human *purpose* into the observable, 'objective' world.

We see then that when miracles are rejected today, in the commonly understood sense of 'supernatural events which break laws of nature', they are sometimes redefined in merely naturalistic terms, as by Billings, Geering and the 'secular theologians' generally; which of course constitutes a rejection of biblical Christianity at its very foundations, and the acceptance of a very odd 'mechanical' world-view. As an alternative, however, they may be redefined in terms of *action* by the living, personal God-who-acts; and this constitutes both an advance into a very modern personalist world-view, and at the same time a return to biblical terminology and thought-patterns. The key question today, then, for cutting through the fog of fashionable ambiguity with which many theologians surround their affirmations, is this: Does the theologian regard 'the mighty acts of God' on analogy with human action, as changes purposely made in the world by an Agent, or not?

THE MODERN CONCEPT OF NATURE

Putting this question to Pannenberg's theology, we find ourselves led to interesting indications that really contemporary modern science also, like theology, has turned away from systematic, law-bound determinism as found in the mechanistic science of the nineteenth century, towards an outlook that is much more sympathetic to the possibility of real action in the world. J. M. Robinson who reports, as we have seen, that "Pannenberg rejects the concept of miracle as being in tension with the concept of creation", goes on to say: "In Pannenberg's opinion it would in any case be difficult to argue that an occurrence is to be regarded as miraculous in the common connotation of the term as referring to a breaking of the laws of nature. For with appeal to modern physics he argues: we do not know all the laws of nature; natural law controls only an aspect of events; the validity of natural law is itself contingent. Since the natural scientist can make no definitive judgement, the decision as to whether an unusual event occurred is left to the historian. *Grundzüge der Christologie*, p. 95f. Thus the miraculous as a functional category is eliminated from consideration."[8] Does Pannenberg really dispense with 'miracles' altogether, or is it only the now obviously inadequate 'common' and 'scientific' view of miracles, based on a scientifically superseded concept of nature, that he rejects in order to re-define miracles biblically, and historically, in terms of the acts of God? This possibility is certainly open to him: but we retain the suspicion that he may have chosen to try to bridge the gaps between science, history and theology, as well as between the biblical past and the present, by means of some sort of idealistic concept rather than this concept of 'action', realistically understood.

The *new* scientific concept of 'nature' is important for our theme. Twentieth century science, with its Principles of Relativity, Indeterminacy and the like; with its new understanding of the logic of induction and of statistical procedures; and with its use of the concept of probability[9] no longer thinks that scientific laws of nature 'govern' events. They merely describe, with varying degrees of generality, those patterns of connection or conjunction that have been noted in observed events, thus justifying varying degrees of predictive certainty. The concept of 'nature', once seen as a closed deterministic continuum, is now seen as having many open and ragged edges. And in particular, because of the widespread recognition today of the essential relationship of all 'objective' knowledge of nature to the limited position of the observing 'subject', the concept of 'nature' in contemporary science is wide open towards the 'subject'. Thus terms like 'supernatural' and 'miracle', which in the recent period have had their anchors of definition down in the closed, deterministic concept of nature, are seen to have been tied to drifting sand, and to stand now in need of redefinition from a rationally rigorous point of view.

The relevance of this changed outlook for our late mid-twentieth century understanding is indicated by Meynell in a comment on the definition of miracle offered by Sir Arnold Lunn: "an event above, or contrary to or exceeding nature which is explicable only as a direct act of God". "The trouble with this definition," writes Meynell, "is that it assumes that we have an exact and stable concept of 'nature', and hence of those events which exceed or are contrary to it. But as P. H. Nowell-Smith remarks, there is no conceivable event so bizarre that we can be sure that it will be for ever safe from 'natural' explanation, unless such explanation be defined as that which happens at the present stage of scientific knowledge to be available. It seems that any definition of miracle which depends on an exact account of what is or is not 'natural', and of what is or is not subject to scientific explanation, is vulnerable to Nowell-Smith's argument. But the concept of miracle was coined and theologically elaborated quite independently of the idea of

170

nature as a restricted range of conceivable events, or that of science as a systematic account of it."[10] Indeed, in the Bible the concept which we commonly call 'miracle' is usually described in terms of 'acts of God' (of which Lunn's definition also speaks); but there is certainly no reference to the nature-concept of nineteenth century science!

The Bible speaks of miracles, not in terms of 'events', but of 'acts' – 'the mighty acts of God', including, for example, those things which were done through Jesus Christ by 'the finger of God'. (Luke 11 : 20). And if the idea of 'laws of nature' is alien to the biblical concept of miracle, that of 'event' – in the modern understanding of the word, as an (impersonal) occurrence that must be the 'effect' of an empirical 'cause' – is equally so. We have already considered the very important difference between the concepts of 'event' and 'act' (p. 77f. above). A moment's reflection with this in mind makes clear that to speak of miracles as 'supernatural events' instead of 'acts of God', distorts the biblical concept in a most radical way. This sort of terminology – 'supernatural events' or 'supra-historical events', 'divine events', 'vertical events', etc. – suggests that there is a special quality in certain *events*, the 'holy' events of salvation history. But surely the special quality of miracles, as biblically understood, is to be found in the *Agent* whose acts they are, in God who as Creator *is* supernatural, supra-historical, divine, etc. and not in some aspect or quality of the event itself, considered as distinct from Him. Miracles as spoken of in the Bible are not 'events' that break the 'laws of nature', unique events, contingent events, nor any kind of impersonal occurrence, whose miraculous character can be described apart from God. Miraculous events are essentially *acts*: and the thing that makes them miraculous is that they are the acts of GOD. Modern scientific man may wish to define them differently, more generally, and without specific reference to God and His action: but for the Christian to agree to do so is to part company in a radical way with the Bible, and to 'ask for' and deserve the fate of scepticism, demythologising, and naturalistic re-interpretation which has recently met the 'modern' concept of miracle.

It is on these grounds that we would criticise the otherwise very attractive definition of miracle offered by Alan Richardson in his *Theological Word Book of the Bible*. "A miracle in the biblical sense," he writes, "is an event which happens in a manner contrary to the regularly observed processes of nature. We must not say 'contrary to nature', but 'contrary to what is known of nature'. (St. Augustine, *De Civ. Dei*, Book XXI, Ch. viii) It may happen according to higher laws as yet but dimly discerned by scientists, and therefore must not be thought of as an irrational irruption of divine power into the orderly realm of nature."[11] This is well said, in so far as it partly dissociates miracle from the nineteenth century concept of the closed continuum of nature. But in so far as it fails to acknowledge that a miracle *is* an intervention of divine power, not as an irrational irruptive event, but as a rational, personal act of God, it falls short of what is required both by strict biblical exegesis and also, increasingly, by rigorously exact modern thought – as well as by the common-sense understanding of every age.

It must be added, however – and this might be expected from a leader of what (in our discussion of history) we have called 'the common-sense school of English theology' – that perhaps no other major modern theologian is more faithful to the basic biblical terminology of 'acts of God' than is Richardson, nor more perceptive of the necessity of recognising God's *agency* in any discussion of miracles. "The whole Bible and the Christian preaching which is its climax," he has written, "are concerned chiefly and indeed almost solely with the proclamation of God's action in history; and the New Testament is centred upon God's culminating action in the resurrection of Jesus Christ from the dead."[12] The same emphasis runs throughout his discussion of *The Miracle Stories of the Gospel*.[13] And in the word-study on 'Miracle' already quoted, Richardson goes on to say:

"In the Old Testament the decisive event, which became for the Hebrew mind the symbol and type of all God's deliverances in history, is the miracle of the Red Sea . . . Without the sign of the Red Sea there would have been no Jehovah-religion, no Israel and no Old Testament, just as without the sign of the Empty Tomb there would have been no Christian religion, no Church and no New Testament . . . In these two acts the power of God is revealed supremely as decisive action for our salvation in the concrete events of history. The Hebrew mind dwells not so much upon the *being* of God as upon his activity: God cannot be known to us in his inner being, but only in so far as he reveals himself to us through his acts."[14]

172

BIBLICAL MIRACLES AND CONSERVATIVE THEOLOGY

Understood in a biblical way, then, miracles are 'acts of God'; and this term can be understood only by analogy with the 'acts of men', created by God to be 'agents' like Himself, or 'in His own image'. How are we to understand 'action'?

Action, by definition, involves freedom for a person, an agent, to form a purpose or intention and to initiate a series of events in the world in an attempt to achieve his purpose. By the exercise of his rational freedom as action in the world, man can cause strange 'miracles' to come about in the world – occurrences which without the causality of his purpose and action would have remained unnatural impossibilities, contrary to the formulated regularities of the 'laws of nature'. For men to fly in the air to chosen destinations, (including the moon) faster than the speed of sound and in inanimate objects weighing many tons, is clearly an absurd impossibility in terms of the normal regularities of nature, apart from human purpose and agency. So it is also for men to both hear and see each other almost instantaneously from opposite sides of the earth, by television relay; and many similar examples could be mentioned. These 'miraculous' human actions, however, do not *break* the laws of nature : they intelligently *use* the laws of nature and the forces they reveal; and through the instrumentality of the body, tools, and so on, they achieve results which *appear* to be contrary to nature. We do not usually call these astonishing actions 'miracles', however, because we know the agents to be limited persons like ourselves, free and yet bound by our human nature within limits more or less known. Though we cannot fully explain man and his acts scientifically – for the freedom of all agents lies, as we have seen, essentially beyond the boundaries of science – yet we can largely explain, in terms of man as we know him from both 'objective' observation and 'subjective' experience, how he can use or 'transcend' natural laws to produce such surprising results. Man we know to be integral within the creation, part of nature, despite those aspects of his life which necessarily transcend 'nature' as conceived by objective, nineteenth century science : and therefore we do not describe him as 'supernatural', nor his acts as miraculous.

What are we to say, then, about God and his acts in the world,

173

on analogy with human agency? Unless the biblical terminology of 'acts of God' is to be criticised as essentially erroneous and misleading, we must accept an analogous understanding of God's acts, as the practical expression of personal purposes by an Agent using natural laws and forces intelligently to produce intended consequences in the world. Are such 'acts of God' to be accepted as miracles in the biblical sense: or must we insist that there is no miracle until a law of nature has been broken? What are we to say, for instance, about that great redemptive act of God which laid the foundation for the whole history of the Old Testament People of God – the exodus from Egypt? Was the deliverance of Israel through the Red Sea a miracle? We read of it in Scripture that "the Lord drove the sea back by a strong east wind all night, and made the sea dry land, and the waters were divided." (Exodus 14:21) God used the instrumentality of a wind, a natural force, a 'secondary cause', to achieve His purpose and open a path for His people. Far from asserting the breach of a law of nature, the biblical account seems to go out of its way to say what was known about the natural means God used, in His saving action, to deliver Israel. Do we therefore deny that this was a miracle? Or do we insist that since it *was* a miracle there must have been laws of nature broken, and the walls of water must have stood up in defiance of the laws of gravity, as they are shown to do in so many illustrations? The only ground for insisting thus would seem to be the popular tradition of the Church. May we not, with the Bible, insist simply that God, the living God, the Creator of all things, *acted* here in history and in nature, using nature to achieve His saving purpose: and that as God is not man, so the acts of this Agent are not restricted as human acts are, but can bring and stop winds, empower a human body to walk on the water, and raise the dead to share His eternal life in a spiritual body? Whether in all this He has broken 'the laws of nature' or, being Himself, the Creator, supernatural in His agency, has simply used His perfect knowledge of nature to achieve His purposes, is altogether secondary and irrelevant from a biblical point of view.

It might be thought that this suggested return to the use of the biblical concept and terminology of 'acts of God' for miracles, instead of the 'alien', naturalistic terminology of 'events' involving 'laws of nature', would be eagerly welcomed by theological conservatives: but this is not immediately likely. For the affections of the conservatives, though directed towards the Bible, can easily become conservatively fixed on the terminology to which their own and the immediately preceding generations have become accustomed, as they defended 'biblical theology' against the reductionist attacks of successive generations of 'modernists'. This means that the commonly accepted 'conservative' terminology can be in large measure dictated by the *critics* of orthodox Christianity: for, to be relevant, the defence against an attack must (generally speaking) use the same terminology as was employed in the criticism. Today, for example,[15] the conservative defence against the secular attack on Christian belief in the transcendent otherness of God as Creator must be conducted largely in terms of the 'supernatural' nature of God, because this is the primary terminology being used in the attack. So it can happen that conservative theology becomes crystallised into defensive conceptual and linguistic formations which are specially shaped to repel the barbs that have been used in attacks on the biblical Faith, perhaps in the previous generation, but which are themselves by no means biblical! It would be surprising if this had not in some measure happened in face of the prolonged attack that has been made on 'miracles', formulated in terms of the 'laws of nature' and the supernatural 'events' that are supposed to break these laws. That it has in fact happened is indicated by the recent remarks of the editorial committee of one of today's most effective and influential conservative Christian journals, commenting on an article that spoke of miracles as 'acts of God' which should be understood on analogy with such purposeful acts of men as airplane flights. "Either this weakens the case (for miracles), or it is nonsense," they said. "Because planes do not violate any law of nature. And that is just what the truly miraculous must be supposed to do."[16]

Alan Richardson had apparently not realised the degree to which this defensive crystallisation has taken place when he wrote that Hume defined miracles "in a way in which no theologian from St. Augustine onward would have done; a miracle, he tells us, is 'a violation of the laws of nature'; it is what never happens in the common course of nature . . ."[17] For the fact of the matter seems to be that not only 'ordinary Christians' who make no claim to be theologians, nor yet merely minor modern theologians, but men of the academic stature of Charles Hodge, whose books still exercise an enormous influence among conservatives, have strongly affirmed just this position as essential to the proper definition of 'miracle'; and many, despite the appeal to biblical terminology against it, will probably wish to cling conservatively to this sort of definition.

Hodge defines miracles and their context thus:

"In the first place, there are events ... due to the ordinary operation of second causes, as upheld and guided by God. To this class belong the common processes of nature ... In the second place there are events due to the influence of the Holy Spirit upon the hearts of men, such as regeneration, sanctification, spiritual illumination, etc. *Thirdly there are events ...* whose distinguishing characteristics are, First that they take place in the external world, i.e. in the sphere of the observation of the senses; and Secondly, that they are *produced or caused by the simple volition of God, without the intervention of any subordinate cause.* To this class belongs the original act of creation, in which all co-operation of second causes was impossible. To the same class belong all events truly miraculous. A miracle, therefore, may be defined to be an event, in the external world, brought about by the immediate efficiency or simple volition of God."[18]

Thus miracles are understood as 'events' caused by God, or 'supernatural events' for which no natural ('second') cause can be found. "A supernatural event, therefore," Hodge writes, "is an event which transcends the power of nature, and which is due to the immediate agency of God."[19] He agrees with a quotation from M. Guizot (1861) to the effect that "belief in the supernatural is the special difficulty of our time: that the denial of it is the form taken by all modern assaults on Christian faith: and that acceptance of it lies at the root, not only of Christianity, but of all positive religion whatsoever."[20] There is much here in which we *must* agree with him, if we wish to remain loyal to the faith of the Bible and the historic Church: but in his attribution of supernatural status to 'events' rather than simply to the divine Agent whose acts they are, and also in his insistence that miracles must have *no* natural causes, we cannot follow him: and those who insist on continuing to do so will find themselves led to retreat into an increasingly anti-rational ghetto. It is largely a matter of terminology, but very important!

That miracles are *also* acts of God and that God is creative Agent, Hodge does of course strongly affirm. "The simple and grand truth (is) that the universe is not under the exclusive control of physical forces, but that always and everywhere there is above, separate from and superior to all else, an infinite personal will, not superseding but directing and controlling all physical causes."[21] And he refers to the analogy between human action and the acts of God. "It is utterly impossible to prove ... that every physical effect must have a physical cause. Our own wills are causes in the sphere of nature; and the omnipotent will of God is not tied to any one mode of operation."[22] What Hodge did not realise – and how could he be expected to, for it is only today dawning upon us as we look around desperately from the dead-end alleys into which the secular presupposition has recently led so many aspects of modern thought – was that if 'events' are granted the 'first place' in our world-view, the concepts both of 'action' and 'agent' must be seen in the end as logical monstrosities: taken in this order, 'event' and 'action' are incompatible concepts. Starting with 'agents' and 'purposeful acts' as the primary data of thought, 'events' and 'causes' can be distilled without inconsistency: but not *vice versa*. In the thought-context presupposed by the concept of miracles as *events caused by a supernatural power*, therefore, (rather than as *acts done by God*) the concepts of divine Agent and of God's acts can never emerge without logical inconsistency: and the same is true also of human agency and action. This is why, since Hodge wrote, history has largely broken away from the restrictive company of the natural sciences, with their 'causal-event' world-view, to become a discipline *sui generis*; for history is concerned with agents who act for reasons, and not just with events that are caused.

MIRACLES AS ACTS OF GOD

The only logically consistent end (as we have recently been shown, especially by van Buren) to an intellectual enquiry which starts with 'caused events' as the basic constituents of the universe is a God who is dead and men who are automata – mere machines incapable of action – in a world which is therefore necessarily devoid of 'truth'. The event-structured world-view of the 'secular man' is a self-contradictory conception. "This self-contradiction stems," writes Polanyi, "from a misguided intellectual passion – a passion for achieving absolutely impersonal knowledge which, being unable to recognise any persons, presents us with a picture of the universe in which we ourselves are absent. In such a universe there is no one capable of creating and upholding scientific values; hence there is no science."[23] We find at the end of such an enquiry that "man dominates a world in which he himself does not exist".[24] It is in this doomed context that the debate about miracles, defined as supernatural events that break the laws of nature, will continue if there are still Christians who wish to cling to this definition. The alternative is to accept the biblical terminology, which is also the emergent terminology of modern thought, and to speak of *action* as the primary datum in human understanding of the world, and of the acts of God as the initially given factor, the basic presupposition, of Christian thought.

If the distinctive and essential thing about miracles is not that they are law-breaking events, but that they are 'God's acts', then we must use methods somewhat different from those employed in the past, for distinguishing and confirming true miracles. The methods for an enquiry into miracles will be analogous with those which we use for establishing whether certain situations involve human action or not. We come across an unusual arrangement of stones or flowers. Is it a result of chance, or of design and purpose? If the stones spell out the *word* 'welcome' – and especially if, after you see it, a voice says the same word and your hand is grasped and shaken – then you conclude confidently that purpose and not mere chance was responsible for the arrangement of the stones; that they indicate an *act*, pointing to, and in some measure revealing, an agent. Or again, the dead body on the road – is it there by accident or as a result of purpose; and if so, what purpose? Is it misfortune, manslaughter, or murder? Is it mere biological *event,* or personal *action* that is involved?

It is in such ways that we enquire concerning the purposes and agency of other persons. And the sort of evidence we must seek in any enquiry into the existence of God as Agent must be analogous with that which leads us to a knowledge of other persons. How *do* we come to know the existence of other persons

178

who like ourselves are agents, free to form purposes and to express them as action in the world?

An approach to this sort of enquiry is indicated by I. T. Ramsey in his little book, *Religion and Science*, although he fails to reach the concept of 'action' and of 'agent' here; for being fenced in by the subjective/objective distinction he can reach only as far as the uniqueness of the concept 'I' – the self as Subject. "In the end," he writes, referring to discussions as to how, if at all, persons are to be distinguished from machines, "all these arguments appeal to a first-person *subjectivity* of which each of us is aware in himself and which, as subjectivity, is irreducible to third-person objects, which indeed all presuppose it. In other words, all the stories of cybernetics presuppose at least one subject about whom they are never – logically never – adequate."[25] From this point we shall go on in the next chapter.

The question of definition, with which we opened this chapter, requires some closing comment. It is well known that Karl Barth was so impressed with the *uniqueness* of the Christian gospel that he declared that Christianity is not a religion, not one of a 'class' along with others: it is *sui generis*, alone the revealed Truth in Christ. And the living God of the Bible is not 'a god' – one of a general class: if Christians continue to call Him 'God', this must be understood as His Name, and not as a class-word. The same sort of argument could be applied to the concept 'miracle' as found in biblical Christianity: it is not a general class-concept, including *any* astonishing or even unique event, nor yet all events which have no known natural cause. The Christian concept of miracle is a concept limited to the direct and specific acts of God, the Creator, in nature and history. It is not necessary, on this basis, to deny that there are records of authentic miracles, in garbled versions, in the non-Christian religions or elsewhere: but if they are true miracles it can only be because they are acts of the God and Father of our Lord Jesus Christ, and not by virtue of any other characteristics.

The difficulty here, of course, is that a general class-word is no doubt required for denoting the astonishing happenings, 'unique' occurrences and 'supernaturally caused' events emphasised by all religions and superstitions: and 'miracle' has traditionally been the word used. If we claim the word for the specifically Christian sense, for acts of the One God, then we shall have to insist that all the *claimed* 'miracles' that cannot be accepted as God's acts are not really miracles at all but mere illusion – superstition and magic. The alternative is to abandon the word to these 'debased' meanings and to say that we do not believe in miracles in Christianity, but only in personal acts of the living God in nature and history. Is this, perhaps, what Pannenberg would recommend if, as reported, he really excludes miracles from the Christian Faith? If so, we can understand why, but do not agree. For it would seem that to claim the word 'miracle' for the Christian meaning, and reject demonstrable superstition and illusion as *not* miracle, is much nearer to common usage than this alternative.

Also, to deny miracles in the Christian Faith while affirming the reality of historical acts of the living God in the world is likely only to increase the confusion and ambiguity of theology today, when 'Secular Christians' claim to have a 'religionless Christianity' which does not have a god ('Christian atheism'); in which 'holy worldliness' governs conduct, the 'acts of God' are not acts of any Agent, and so on! No doubt there is a properly biblical and Christian sense in which, with some straining of language, a few of these composite-contrary terms may be understood, if approached in the spirit of Barth. But when interpreted in terms of 'the secular presupposition', in the 'death of God' theology, there seems to many to be in this use of words an element of calculated deception, a deliberate ambiguity that lacks even common integrity, and from which Christian theology must surely try now to escape. We therefore reaffirm the claim of Christianity to the word 'miracle' for 'acts of God'.

CHAPTER 10

Subject, Object, and Action

The God of the Bible is 'God who acts'. But modern man, with his enormous respect for science and 'objectivity' has found it increasingly difficult to understand how God *could* act in our world, and has become increasingly sceptical about this primary affirmation of biblical theology. As we have considered the matter from various points of view – from those of science, existentialist theology, linguistic analysis, and history – it has become obvious that the possibility of action – whether God's or man's – constitutes a problem for thought, and that the subject/object distinction lies right at the heart of this problem, as of the related problems concerning the nature and status of 'mind', 'will', 'purpose', 'freedom', 'personal responsibility', and, indeed, what it means to be a 'person'. If it seems impossible (we have argued) to believe that a supernatural Creator-God has acted in our world as we understand it in this secular age, then it must be agreed also, in logical consistency, that it is equally impossible to believe that men could act in it. From a consistently logical, scientific point of view, men can be seen only as machines, automata.

The ultimate problem of modern theology, therefore, is not really the problem of God and His existence, as is often said. It is the problem (which theology shares with all modern thought) of *action* and its rational possibility: the problem, therefore, of how the existence of *persons* can be rationally acknowledged. Until our thinking is based on presuppositions that acknowledge the reality of action which, more fundamentally than thought, is the *differentia* of persons,[1] the question whether *God* has acted in a personal way cannot rationally be discussed,

181

nor of course the question whether He exists in a personal way, as the Bible affirms.

The obstacle that somehow prevents the rational recognition of action, freedom, persons and the like seems to be in this 'subject/object distinction' and especially in the use made of it by modern science, in which the 'objective' is emphasised to the virtual exclusion of the 'subjective'. The recent escape from the clutches of 'objective science' made by modern historians, whose right to speak of the 'actions of persons' cannot be denied without making nonsense of history, is one indication of the growing awareness of this problem and its importance.

It is *this* change of direction in history, rather than its 'objectification' as a 'science' under Von Ranke and his followers, that is likely to be seen in the future as the truly important revolution in modern historical thought. In other academic disciplines also, expression is increasingly being given to concern about the stultifying effect of the subject/object distinction. Perhaps the most interesting criticism is that coming from the area of science itself, in which the distinction has seemed to be most deeply entrenched; and we shall shortly consider suggestions made by M. Polanyi about this. But first we must examine the claim made by F. Gogarten and R. Bultmann (to which we have made reference already) that in the Existentialist theology of history the subject/object distinction has already been superseded and the attendant problems therefore resolved, at least in principle.

HISTORY AND SUBJECT/OBJECT

After discussing the swing of interest away from the 'static' metaphysical speculations of mediaeval theology to the dynamic and empirical concerns of history in this modern age, Gogarten comments: "No success attended the various attempts to understand history, in its peculiar essential nature, which were undertaken during and after the time of the Enlightenment and of the idealists. Today, however, in the endeavour to achieve an 'existential interpretation', there is being prepared an understanding of history which ... could be characterised by saying that an attempt is being made to extricate history from the subject/object pattern of thought."[2] Bultmann's critics, Gogarten maintains, have failed to grasp that he has really already abandoned the old subjective/objective schema, and they continue to misrepresent his "understanding of self and of existence as a subjectivist phenomenon of consciousness".[3] In fact, however (he declares), the existentialist interpretation "in every assertion it makes is opposed to the old subject/object thinking which has achieved practically unquestioned dominance since the awakening of rationalism in the seventeenth century."[4]

Although Descartes no more originated the subject/object distinction in discursive thinking than Aristotle originated the practice of correct reasoning, yet it is true to say that it was the systematic *development* of his starting point, in the "I think, therefore I am" formula, that brought into increasingly clearer focus the subject/object structure which is essentially inherent in the discursive thought process. The course of this development through the British Empiricists makes a fascinating study – through Locke with his massive and balanced common-sense; Berkeley, whose ruthless logic eliminated the objective pole and left him as a Subjective Idealist in solipsist isolation; and Hume, whose even more single-minded following where Reason led resulted in a sort of Objective Idealism from which the thinking self was virtually eliminated. But it is to the reconciling and systematising genius of the German philosopher Kant that we owe the form in which the subject/object distinction has been taken for granted as a presupposition in virtually all precise thinking from that time until today. "That to us it should seem incredible that men should ever *not* have known that knowledge implies and involves the Subject/Object relation", James Brown remarks in his timely study on *Subject and Object in Modern Theology* "is testimony to the influence of the Critical Philosophy of Immanuel Kant."[5]

The subject/object distinction is properly a logical distinction within thought, not an *ontological* distinction within reality.[6] But it is, within thought, an essential and unavoidable distinction, according to Brown. Thus he takes it to be the mark of a good philosopher "not to forget that there can never be a Subject without an Object, that the two are correlative terms".[7] And he quotes from Coleridge, the enthusiastic populariser in England of Kant's philosophy: "All knowledge rests upon the coincidence of an object with a subject. The sum of all that is merely objective we call nature ... The sum of all that is subjective we may comprehend in the name of the self, of intelligence."[8]

Brown concedes that there must have been once a state in which man was 'together with his world' in a primitive and undivided relationship below the separation of subject and object: but then he could not have *known* it! Essential to his coming to *know* the world and God, by forming concepts and building language, is his own separation from them (the 'objects' of his knowledge) as knowing 'subject'. This, says Brown, "is the natural history of the Subject/Object relation: and according to Buber, it is the story of the Fall. Knowledge, for which the Subject/Object relation is fundamental, is an expulsion from the paradise of primitive relation . . ."[9] The fall of man, therefore, was a fall 'upwards' into discursive conceptual knowledge as well as 'downwards' from the primitive harmonious relationship with God and the world: because the subject/object distinction, and the separation it brings, are essential to all discursive knowledge.[10]

Returning now to Gogarten's claims on behalf of Bultmann and Existentialism, we must ask how they can be substantiated in the face of this contention that formulable knowledge – historical knowledge no less than scientific – is not possible apart from the subject/object distinction? The Existentialists insist that the Self is an existing, thinking and deciding *subject*. Of what, historically, can such a subject think, if not of the 'objects' of his thought; and how can he be distinguished from 'the world', in whose history he is interested, except as subject from object? "Extreme existentialism," as Brown remarks, "has forgotten that a Subject without an Object is nothing at all."[11] If the Existentialists were concerned less with discursive 'truth', and more with real 'action' in the world, there might be some reason to suppose that they could possibly transcend this distinction of subject and object. But in fact Bultmann's is essentially a discursive theology, tied intimately to words and the Word: and in such a context, of language and conceptual thinking, there is no possible escape from the subject/object distinction.

If this contention is challenged, Ian Ramsey can be called to its defence. "All language and all experience presuppose a subject/object distinction . . .", he declares emphatically.[12] The very survival of religion, as well as much else, Ramsey believes, depends upon the retention of this distinction. His view of the world seems to confer a sort of logical priority on the objective, deterministic outlook of science, and relies on the subsequent affirmation of a subjective sphere for the possibility of freedom, purpose, persons and God. Science, being necessarily restricted to 'objectivity' by its presuppositions and its methods of empirical verification, cannot with logical consistency recognise the reality of such things. But, if we were to agree to affirm (as do all those – including the 'Secular Christians' – who accept the exclusive 'secular presupposition') that the objective world-view of science is a fully comprehensive and sufficient one, acknowledging that all reality is "describable without residue" in terms of objective scientific formulations, then we should not only have excluded from our world freedom, purpose and the like, but we should be left, Ramsey writes, with a world in which "the subject/object distinction would be lost. We should indeed have objectified the subject, and the very basis of all our language, of all our talking, the basic presupposition of experience itself would have disappeared."[13] To objectify the subject is to commit, not merely an error of fact, but the ultimate "logical blunder".[14] Thus, although in a sense the 'objective' is accepted by Ramsey as the primary pole in thinking, yet the subjective, he insists, cannot be eliminated.[15]

The formal structure of Ramsey's thought is here very similar to that of theological Existentialism, first granting to science unqualified sway over the objective side of our experience of reality and a sort of normative priority in the structure of thought; but insisting that there is *also* a subjective sphere where persons, freedom, action and religion are at home. And the puzzling question is: how is it possible, with this basic structure of thought held in common that the Existentialist Gogarten can eagerly claim the abolition of the subject/object distinction, whereas Ramsey claims that the loss of this distinction (and therefore of the subjective sphere) would mean the end of persons, religion, and history?

The solution of this puzzle would seem to be given in Gogarten's later book *The Reality of Faith*, with the sub-title *The Problem of Subjectivism in Theology,* published in 1957 (four years after that in which he claimed to have abandoned the subject/object distinction). Here, quietly, Gogarten himself seems to have concluded that in fact, as Ramsey says, the retention of subjectivism and so of the subject/object distinction,

185

is essential to the survival of religion in its existentialist form. "The most appropriate task of faith," he writes, "is to safeguard man's freedom for God and therefore to deprive the world and its laws of religious power. Faith is unable to do this unless it is willing to entrust reason with working out man's independence towards the world and its law. This being the case, faith must not be averse to subjectivism because of its connotation of independence. For faith's own sake it must not. It would contradict itself."[16] It certainly appears that in order to avoid making faith contradict itself, Gogarten has had to contradict himself. Is not the meaning of what he is here saying just what we have maintained concerning the structure of Bultmann's Existentialism: that since, within the closed continuum of causes and effects in the objective world of science, he cannot consistently claim "man's freedom for God" – he has retreated into a subjective/existential world which may be claimed as free from the world's deterministic law, and in which therefore freedom and decision, personal existence and faith may be affirmed? The claim to have superseded the subject/object distinction seems to have been quietly forgotten!

This makes all the more interesting Bultmann's claim on his own behalf in his much-quoted essay on historical method (1957). "One cannot understand the decisions of persons who act in history," he writes, "if one does not understand man and his possibilities for action. In short, historical understanding presupposes an understanding of the subject matter of history itself and of the men who act in history." Having insisted that history cannot be understood by "a neutral, non-participating spectator", but only by one who "participates in it with his whole existence", he continues: "This *existentiell* relation to history is the fundamental presupposition for understanding history. This does not mean that the understanding of history is a 'subjective' one in the sense that it depends on the individual pleasure of the historian, and thereby loses all objective significance. On the contrary, it means that history, precisely in its objective content, can only be understood by a subject who is *existentiell* moved and alive. It means that, for historical understanding, the schema of subject and object that has validity for natural science is invalid."[17]

With the concluding affirmation we must certainly agree, if history is to be about the *purposeful acts* of persons in the past; since these cannot be in any simple way acknowledged as real on the presupposition of the subject/object distinction. We have, moreover, already indicated some streams of modern history, rising in Dilthey, Croce and Collingwood and converging with a stream of English 'common-sense' history which includes Richardson, to which this claim to have avoided the subject/object schema might more reasonably be applied. For these historians have in fact *presupposed* the reality of human action, which occurs at a level of living deeper than the subject/object division of logically precise discursive thought, and unites man-as-Agent with his world-as-Other in a manner simply accepted and understood by common-sense. This they have done, we believe, as compelled by common-sense and *in spite* of their philosophical leanings (Dilthey perhaps as a proto-Existentialist, Croce and Collingwood as Idealists of a sort, and others various), rather than because of them. For it seems clear that neither living language-in-use for ordinary communication nor the simple common-sense understanding of man and his world are troubled about a subject/object distinction: and this is not because they are stupid, but because the subject/object distinction becomes a problem only when the living, moving processes are arrested and frozen for precise analysis and exact examination.[18]

A glance at the terminology and concepts of Bultmann's sentences quoted above, however, indicates that, with regard to the historical outlook of theological Existentialism, his claim to have escaped from the subject/object schema cannot be sustained; for the Existentialist position presupposes the exact analyses and objective emphasis of science in such a way that the subject/object problem cannot be avoided. What Bultmann denies specifically here, and what we must no doubt grant, is that his understanding of history cannot be classed as 'subjective' in a superficial *psychological* way: but the important distinction between subject and object is the *logical* one, and to this he is obviously still deeply committed. Thus the presentation of his case seems inseparable from the *terms* 'subject' and 'object'. We must therefore distinguish the truly modern conception of history, now moving forward apart from science as a discipline *sui generis*, from that concept of 'scientific history' which is still precious to Bultmann and his followers, and which is being left behind in an academic backwater: and we must seek else-

187

where a philosophical justification for the common-sense view of history which simply presupposes persons, freedom and action.

SCIENCE AND SUBJECT/OBJECT

M. Polanyi's massive and scholarly discussion of this matter – under the title *Personal Knowledge*, appears to have as its primary concern the defence of science against what he regards as its worst enemy – itself, in its classical, objectivist form! He seems to be convinced that what we have called 'the Secular Presupposition' *ought* to be true – that all that is really 'knowledge' should be included *within* the boundaries of science. And his concern springs from the conviction that it is absurd to make this sort of exclusive claim for science in its traditional 'objectivist' form, since that excludes great and vital areas of knowledge which we undoubtedly do have, especially in connection with 'persons' and their 'activities'. To remedy this situation Polyani proposes trying to replace or supplement the objectivist criterion of scientific truth with another criterion which will somehow allow the logical inclusion *within* science of our knowledge of persons, purpose, freedom, action, and so on.

He does not appear to consider the possibility of the alternative solution (which we favour) of discarding as wrong the 'secular presupposition', and acknowledging that since scientific knowledge is essentially and properly 'objective', it can therefore comprise only a part – an important but specialised and biased aspect – of our total knowledge; so that other, non-scientific sources, pre-suppositions and criteria must be sought to account for our non-scientific knowledge.

If Polanyi were to succeed in his purpose, it would seem that one consequence would be that history, which has but recently escaped the objectivist shackles of science into a *sui generis* existence, would again be drawn within the boundaries of a modified and enlarged concept of science. If the alternative were adopted, the task would be to find presuppositions which can support and 'explain', in their difference, both scientific and historical knowledge, and presumably also ethical, aesthetic, religious, and any other sort of knowledge there may be.

OBJECTIVITY is the title of the first chapter in Polanyi's book *Personal Knowledge*. "The prevailing conception of science," he writes, "based on the disjunction of subjectivity and objectivity seeks – and must seek at all costs – to eliminate from science . . . passionate, personal, human appraisals of theories . . . For modern man has set up as the ideal of knowledge the conception of natural science as a set of statements which is 'objective' in the sense that its substance is entirely determined by observation."[19] Protesting against this view of science, Polanyi indicates his intention of demonstrating the need to recognise man's "passionate participation in the act of knowing",[20] through which an element of 'subjectivity' is seen to be present in even the most objective knowledge. The exclusive 'objectivist' presuppositions of classical science must be modified, he believes; for they logically necessitate the denial of human freedom, personality and action – the denial, therefore, of man himself in his distinctive nature. The secular ideal of 'objectivity', leading inevitably to self-contradictory conclusions, "has come to threaten the position of science itself", Polanyi writes. "This self-contradiction stems from a misguided intellectual passion – a passion for achieving absolutely impersonal knowledge which, being unable to recognise any persons, presents us with a picture of the universe in which we ourselves are absent." "Objectivism requires a specifiably functioning mindless knower." "Man dominates a world in which he himself does not exist." It is this sort of absurdity which, he fears, "may yet issue in a sweeping reaction against science as a perversion of the truth".[21]

Since these absurd consequences follow with logical necessity from the presuppositions of science, which distinguish subjective and objective and then isolate 'objectivity' as the area, and indeed the criterion, of truth; therefore other presuppositions and another criterion must be found, Polanyi believes. Every act of knowing, he insists, involves a man's "passionate participation": in even the most 'objective' judgements and affirmations the person who knows and affirms is passionately involved. Polanyi now apparently seeks to give this passion form as a selective, truth-finding factor in a largely aesthetic criterion of truth.

It is, he believes, through the perception of a sort of rational beauty, like the apprehension of mathematical harmony, that "passionate, personal, human appraisals of theories" should be made when assessing their truth, and not simply by testing their 'objectivity' experimentally. As an example of the use of this criterion he quotes (amongst other instances) Max Born's salutation of the new Theory of Relativity because it makes the world-picture of science "more beautiful".[22] "These examples could be multiplied," he says. "By them modern physics has demonstrated the power of the human mind to discover and exhibit a rationality which governs nature, before ever approaching the field of experience in which previously discovered mathematical harmonies were to be revealed as empirical facts."[23]

N. R. Campbell writes in similar vein about his reaction on first reading some algebraic formulae by N. Bohr, which were destined to revolutionise electrical theory: "the thrill of a new revelation, such as must have inspired Keats' most famous sonnet" – this is how he describes his apprehension of the new truth. C. A. Coulson, who quotes this comment, then remarks: "Another distinguished professor of mathematics in Britain said in a public lecture not so long ago: 'we can test our theories by this: are they beautiful?'" He then goes on to quote Sir Cyril Hinchelwood as follows:

"Chemistry provides not only a mental discipline but an adventure and an aesthetic experience. Its followers seek to know the hidden causes which underlie the transformations of our changing world ... And to this knowledge they attach an absolute value, that of truth and beauty. The vision of nature yields the secret of power and wealth, and for this it is sought by many. But it is revealed only to those who seek it for itself. Its pursuit has united our predecessors whom we commemorate: it will unite our successors for as long as the spirit of man endures."[24]

Convinced like Polanyi of the self-contradictory inadequacy of traditional science's objectivist criterion, when taken as the sufficient and universal test of truth, it seems that many modern scientists, seeking the necessary universal criterion upon which the common unity of all truth may be established, are looking towards *aesthetic* judgement and the concept of beauty as expressed, for example, in mathematical symmetry or harmony. With this they apparently hope to transcend or bridge over the subject/object distinction and the problems attendant on scientific 'objectivity'. Thus Polanyi, after a discussion of crystallography, with its classes of symmetry and its geometrical space groups, concludes: "We see emerging here a substantial alternative to the normal disjunction of objective and subjective statements, as well as to the disjunction between analytic and synthetic statements. By accrediting our capacity to make valid appraisals of universal bearing within the exact natural sciences, we may yet avoid the sterility and confusion imposed by those traditional categories."[25]

Whilst fully agreeing that sterility and confusion follow from the exclusive use of objectivity as the criterion of truth, in conjunction with the experimental methods of the natural sciences, we cannot see how this intensely *subjective* criterion – the perception of symmetrical beauty – can significantly help matters, either as replacing or as supplementing the objectivity criterion. It does not really transcend or under-pass the subject/object distinction, but seems rather to inject a subjective element as such into the area of objectivist thinking. It injects "passion" or *feeling* into the realm of thought, but it does not yet reach down into a rational acceptance of the reality of *action*. It confines the search for truth still to the level of theory – of 'I think' and 'I feel', or 'I think with feeling'; but it does not fully embrace the level of practice – of 'I act'. The experimental activity of the scientist himself, purposefully manipulating and changing the world in the action of his experiments, must still present insoluble problems for science, even with a passionate factor admitted into judgements of truth. And no matter how 'passionate' his thinking may be, it must still be the thinking of a Subject about the world as Object. Man as agent, as person, as *man* in living transforming contact-through-action with his world, is still as far as ever beyond the reach of science. Thus although the aesthetic criterion for truth, of which scientists and poets speak, may well be a very important and necessary supplement to objective criteria within the boundaries of objective science, yet it cannot save science from absurdity when it aspires to include *all* knowledge within its boundaries, denying that there is any other sort of knowledge from other sources, dependent on other criteria.

Man's knowledge includes not only objects and objective events in patterns of relation, whether harmonious and beautiful or not, but also dynamic movement, freedom, action and persons, which objective science cannot consistently recognise. H. Bergson argued many years ago that this is because of the way in which Kant's ubiquitous Critical Philosophy deals with the concepts of time and space in their relation to subject and object, and that until the presuppositions of the Critical Philosophy are replaced with action-acknowledging ones, this situation cannot change. "Science cannot deal with time and motion," he wrote, "except on condition of first eliminating the essential and qualitative element – of time, duration, and of motion, mobility."[26] At some of his comments on these matters we shall now glance.

BERGSON ON TIME AND SPACE, FREEDOM AND SCIENCE

Our deepest perception of ourselves, Bergson maintains, is dynamic; we intuitively know ourselves to be free in the ordinary acts which take place every day in the 'flowing time' of real living. But when we want to *think* about ourselves and our actions, we have to break up time and our continuous experience into bits, into discrete sensations and objects which we can freeze into static concepts, and to which we can give names in language, so that we may continue to think and speak about them clearly. The result is that when, instead of simply going on living and exercising our freedom, we stop to think about ourselves and what we are doing in an exact, analytical way, what we find is a stuck-together-from-objective-bits self, and acts of the same sort. We cannot *think* the dynamic, active, free self that we nevertheless *know* we really are! The 'objective' self, which is the only one accessible to exact thinking, cannot consistently be thought of as free, because in 'objectifying' it thought has made of it (paradoxically) a static 'subject who thinks'. "We shall see," writes Bergson, "that the contradictions implied in the problems of causality, freedom, personality, spring from no other source, and that, if we wish to get rid of them, we have only to go back to the real and concrete self and give up its symbolic substitute."[27]

Another way of expressing this is to say that thought tends to conceive everything in a basically spatial way, including even the real, flowing *time*, in which we live and act. When trying to think in an exact way about time, we usually draw a mental line (or perhaps a real line like Cullmann's famous time line) and put marks along it which are meant to represent in space – along the extended line – events in the flowing movement of time. But of course this is not what time is really like, as we live and act in it – spread out in space and broken up into bits, which we then relate together in our thinking in patterns of 'cause and effect'.

These matters of time and space and how they are related to all our experience were among the most important questions dealt with by Immanuel Kant when formulating his brilliant systematic 'solution' of the problems posed by Descartes and the British Empiricists: and the subject/object structure of his answer is intimately intertwined with his views on space and time. Indeed, according to Bergson, it was the way in which Kant dealt with time and space together, as 'Forms of Intuition', that has brought these problems to such sharp focus for us today. Kant was concerned to show us how we 'see' time rationally, how we *think* time. But, says Bergson, at the deepest level "time does not require to be seen, but to be lived".[28] And when we 'live' time and act in it, we find it to be very different from the 'thought' time with which Kant's Critical Philosophy presents us, which can reasonably be represented by a spatial line. "To sum up," Bergson writes, "every demand for explanation in regard to freedom comes back, without our suspecting it, to the following question: 'Can time be represented by space?' To which we answer: 'Yes, if you are dealing with time flown; No, if you speak of time flowing.' Now the free act takes place in time which is flowing and not in time which has already flown. Freedom is therefore a fact, and among the facts which we observe there is none clearer. All the difficulties of the problem, and the problem itself, arise from the desire to endow duration with the same attributes as extensity, to interpret a succession by a simultaneity, and to express the idea of freedom in a language into which it is obviously untranslatable."[29] We cannot *live* in the past, which we remember and think about; and therefore we cannot be free in the remembered past, and we can quite properly represent it by a line in space, and relate the events there in terms of cause and effect if we wish, for it is already 'determined'. But when that time, now remembered as past, was present time and we were living and acting in it, it was altogether unlike space and in it we were free. If, with Kant, we assume that all time, like time remembered and thought about, can be properly represented by space, as conceptually fixed and frozen in event-bits, then freedom, action and persons are rational problems or impossibilities, precluded by determinism.

N

"All determinism," as Bergson says, "will be refuted by experience : but every attempt to *define* freedom will open the way to determinism."[30] Time, or movement in time, as *seen* by the scientific observer, the thinking subject who seeks to analyse and define, will always be objectified time, and will always yield deterministic answers in terms of events, not acts. Real time and action, when 'captured' in precise thought and logically analysed in language, become piece-meal, divided and immobilised, like the individual pictures in a cine film. And although living communication can project the dynamic, living reality into the mind of a hearer, logical analysis of the language again breaks up this picture of reality into discrete events and objects which can be understood only as 'determined', and not as free. Since such were the basic constituents for his thought, Bergson says, "Kant preferred to put freedom outside time and to raise an impassable barrier between the world of phenomena, which he hands over root and branch to our understanding, and the world of things in themselves, which he forbids us to enter."[31] Though we must somehow be *really* free in the world of 'things in themselves', he agrees, we can never begin to understand, or to 'experience', that freedom : we must accept it only by faith. The modern Existentialists, however, though basically accepting Kant's Critical structure, claim to have burst open the gates of "the world of things in themselves", and to have discovered there real, existing subject-selves in a world of decision. But the timeless, 'punctual' nature of the freedom-in-decision to which they have there found themselves confined, and the logical impossibility that these 'decisions' should ever alter the observable world in the manner in which we well know that our actions do alter it, make this 'solution' of the problem of freedom altogether unsatisfactory. Action remains logically impossible for the self as subject, observing critically, thinking linguistically, and existing subjectively over against the world : and of course the possibility that God as Subject should act is excluded equally with human action.

If we are to escape from this impasse, a new foundation for rational thought must be found, with new presuppositions upon which we may think of man not as subject-self distinguished from the world-as-object, but as agent, acting in the world-as-other; as a psychosomatic unity, united in himself, and in action united also with his world at a level of being more fundamental than that on which the intellect sharply distinguishes mind (or soul) from body, subject from object, real time from remembered time, and so makes possible discursive thought. This does not imply that such thinking – objective, scientific, logically precise – is either wrong or unnecessary. In conjunction with the technological ability of modern man, scientific thinking has opened up undreamed of possibilities for action and for the future life of man as a person. But it nevertheless yields limited, specialised and biased knowledge, and is altogether unsuited to provide the overall foundation of all that man knows and can know. The foundation we need for modern thought must *start with our knowledge of persons and of agents,* with our knowledge of action and of freedom, and on this basis build a systematic account of the different sorts of knowledge we have – intuitive knowledge; knowledge by personal revelation through acts and words (whether of man or of God); objective, scientific knowledge; and so on.

The subject/object presuppositions of the age of Descartes and Kant have run out now into conclusions which are obviously absurd : in science, man (the scientist) does not exist in his own world-picture; in language, even verbs cannot express life and action but only relations; and in theology, God is dead. We need new presuppositions for a new age of thinking; we must enter a New World of understanding and 'see' man, action, language, God and the world in a new way, or else hand over the academic world to cynical nihilism and unfathomable frustration.

The blessing of the revolutionary time in which we live is that the gate of such a New World has, I believe, been opened by modern personalist philosophy, especially that of John Macmurray, whose Gifford Lectures in 1953-54 under the overall title "The Form of the Personal", have been published in two volumes – *The Self as Agent* and *Persons in Relation*. "The complete work," commented *The Church of England Newspaper*, "promises to be the most important philosophical study of our time". And *The Times Literary Supplement* declared : "It is certainly a work of major importance; it is to be commended in the strongest possible terms to philosophers, to theologians and to psychologists. It is not improbable that, a century hence, they will still be arguing its propositions."

We do not propose at this stage to attempt to give any

account of the argument of these books, but only to indicate with a few quotations the direction of the road that leads forward from this 'gateway to the future' before drawing, in our final chapters, a few conclusions concerning its implications for theology tomorrow.

JOHN MACMURRAY AND THE FORM OF THE PERSONAL

Macmurray offers "a double criticism of our philosophical tradition. The traditional point of view is both theoretical and egocentric. It is theoretical in that it proceeds as though the self were a pure *subject* for whom the world is *object*. This means that the point of view adopted by our philosophy is that of the Self in its moment of reflection, when its activity is directed towards the acquirement of knowledge. Since the Self in reflection is withdrawn from action, withdrawn into itself, withdrawn from participation in the life of the world into contemplation, this point of view is also egocentric ... This theoretical and egocentric character of our philosophy is not doctrinal. It is a presupposition, generally unconscious, implicit in philosophical procedures ... Against the assumption that the Self is, at least primarily, a 'knowing subject', I have maintained that its subjecthood is a derivative and negative aspect of its agency. This corresponds to the fact that most of our knowledge, and all our primary knowledge, arises as an aspect of activities which have practical, not theoretical objectives, and that it is this knowledge, itself an aspect of action, to which all reflective theory must refer. Against the assumption that the Self is an isolated individual, I have set the view that the Self is a *person*, and that personal existence is *constituted* by the relation of persons."[32]

That what Macmurray is offering is both revolutionary and of the utmost importance there can be no doubt. He denies any intention to erect a philosophical system, comparing what he is trying to do not so much with the systematisers like Kant or Aristotle as with the originators of new directions in philosophy and human thought, like Pythagoras and Descartes. "The present work," he writes, "is a pioneering venture. It seeks to establish a point of view. Its purpose, therefore, is formal and logical – to construct and illustrate in application the form of the personal ... The function of a philosophical form is to exhibit the unity of human experience as a whole, in all its general aspects, both theoretical and practical. To verify it is to show that it is capable of doing so."[33] Here we may hope to find, therefore, – assuming that these 'action presuppositions' are indeed the proper and necessary ones for a modern understanding of truth – common ground upon which the distinct methods of empirical science and of history can be seen and understood together as in harmony; on which linguistic analysis and the theology of God as Agent may find common links with the rest of human thought in its wholeness – a wholeness which well might find its best rational foundation in the concept of the Living Creator God who acts.

Macmurray's writing is philosophical and not theological: but he realises that in their common concern to know the truth about persons and action, the two disciplines run here very close together. "The long argument which Descartes initiated has moved decisively in the direction of atheism," he writes: and, on the basis of the Cartesian 'subject/object' presuppositions, "the more closely modern philosophy keeps to its programme, the more purely objective its procedure becomes, the more inevitable is the atheism of its conclusion. Within the limits of its assumptions no other result is permissible. Yet ... quite apart from all specifically theological questions, I believe that the emergent problem of contemporary philosophy necessitates a revision of traditional assumptions; and that when this revision has been made the direction of the argument will be so altered that it will tend thereafter to a theistic conclusion."[34]

The sort of consequences for 'secular theology' which follow from the development of these new presuppositions may be illustrated with reference to Bonhoeffer's famous description – so precious to the 'Secular Christians' – of secular man as 'man come of age' because he has outgrown his dependence on God and is now willing to stand on his own feet and be independent as an autonomous individual. An analysis of human nature which presupposes the primacy of action rather than of reflection shows that this secular concept of man could hardly be further from the truth. Individual independence of this sort may be a proper goal for some kinds of animals within the organic world of nature, Macmurray concedes, when considering this matter in a discussion of the dependence of a human child upon its mother; but it is not appropriate for *persons*. "If the *terminus a quo* of the personal life is a helpless total dependence on the Other, the *terminus ad quem* is not independence, but the mutual interdependence of equals. In comparing human and animal development it is not enough to say that the human infant is dependent upon its parents for a much longer period. This tends to suggest that the difference is one of time: and that the child at length reaches a stage when he can provide for his own needs as an animal can from a much earlier age. But this is not the case. The boy who has reached maturity in dependence on his parents does not then find himself fitted to wander off into the wilds and find food and shelter for himself in animal isolation. He finds employment in which he can earn money with which to buy what he needs. He exchanges a direct and personal dependence upon his family for a dependence on a wider society, a dependence which is impersonal and indirect."[35]

When he discusses Freud's view of religion in relation to these facts about the life-long and essential dependence of persons on other persons, without which they cannot be fully personal, Macmurray agrees that Freud's primary assertion – that religion is a development of the child's experience of family life – must be accepted. But the conclusion that religion is therefore illusory, so that the acknowledgement of continuing dependence on God as Father should be outgrown by 'man come of age', is quite false. "We have seen that the form of the child's experience is dependence on a personal Other, and that this form of experience is never outgrown," he writes, "but provides the ground plan of all personal experience, which is constituted from start to finish by the relation to the Other and communication with the Other. It is this form which finds expression in religion, no doubt, but there is nothing illusory about this. The adult who endeavours to create or discover, in the context of mature experience, the form of positive personal relationship which he experienced as a child, is not indulging in phantasy, but seeking to realise his own nature as a person. Phantasy, as Freud recognises, is the result of a failure to grow up properly . . . the wish to destroy the father and take his place is one of the common phantasies of childhood. Would it not be as good an argument as Freud's, then, if we were to conclude that adult atheism was the projection upon the universe of *this* childish phantasy?"[36] Man who claims to have 'come of age' with the assertion (as in *Secular Christianity*) that he no longer believes in, and no longer needs, the living Personal God of biblical theology, is perhaps indulging a negative and destructive childish phantasy : and in adopting his secular attitude of autonomy and independence he is demonstrating his deluded immaturity! Man, as *person*, is essentially dependent on the personal Other. Whether this personal Other consists merely of other human persons, or includes supremely the living and personal Creator-God of biblical faith – our Father in Heaven – is the primary theological question. This question cannot even be rationally considered on the basis of the secular outlook's narrowly exclusive presuppositions, as we have seen : for the evidence relevant to a decision about God is excluded *a priori* by 'secularity', together with all evidence that relates centrally to the concepts of human action and of persons as agents.

The main source of evidence in this area of persons and action, of course, is *revelation*, as distinguished from discovery through experimentation, scientific investigation, and so on. And those who promote 'secularity' and affirm the objective methods of science as the sole source of knowledge in 'the new world', as the 'Secular Christians' do, cannot consistently admit personal revelation, whether from God or man, as valid data for knowledge. Thus one of them (as we have already seen), indicating the scientific method as 'The New Source of Knowledge', goes on (consistently enough) to declare that "theology cannot be defined as the study of the revealed knowledge of God, for there is none".[37] But the same outlook precludes the admission (as data for knowledge) of all the personal revelations upon which we are so dependent in our personal life. "The form of religious reflection is necessarily determined by its data;" Macmurray writes, "and these are our practical experiences of our relations with one another" – and, we would add, with the living God. "How then do we know one another, and what form does this knowledge take? ... It is not and cannot be objective and scientific. A purely objective attitude to another person precludes personal knowledge, because it excludes direct personal relationship. We can know a great deal about other people, both in particular and in general, without knowing them ... To know another person we must be in communication with him, and communication is a two-way process ... *All knowledge of persons is by revelation*. My knowledge of you depends not merely on what I do, but upon what you do; and if you refuse to reveal

199

yourself to me, I cannot know you, however much I may wish to do so . . . This puts the scientific form of knowledge out of court in this field . . ."[38] To exclude the possibility of revelation from God because it cannot be dealt with by the methods of science requires also the exclusion of the sort of data by which alone we can come to know and live with other people as *persons*.

The problem with which we left I. T. Ramsey grappling at the end of the last chapter, as to how we can know other persons, is insoluble on the basis of the objectivist presuppositions of science and secularity; and even the invocation of the subjective 'something more' of my knowledge of my 'self' cannot provide an adequate basis or model for my knowledge of other persons. We must *start* with personal data as 'initially given', the data of action and communication, of revelation and speech; data which is neither objective nor subjective, but more ultimate in human experience, more profoundly 'known', than the data of discursive thinking for which the subject/object distinction is essential. It is simply not possible to speak rationally of 'persons', as known to be 'agents', nor to consider rationally the biblical claims about God, unless we will take the epoch-changing step from Descartes' foundation-formula for rational thought – 'I *think*, therefore I am' – to Macmurray's formula – 'I *act,* therefore I am agent; and through action I know that the world is, and that other personal agents are also'.

We have already considered briefly the way in which Macmurray outlines the form and logic of the personal, of a new world-view that sees man primarily as personal agent. And all the evidence of our study confirms his conviction that this is the direction in which human interest must now turn in order to find rational answers to the questions which have been thrown up by many branches of contemporary thinking. In the various academic disciplines, the immediate effects of entering this new world of thought will differ. It will of course necessitate the rejection of the exclusive 'secular presupposition', and science will have to accept a limited place, along with other kinds of knowledge, within the whole body of truth. Modern *sui generis* history will find rational philosophical support for its methodology and its assumption about man and his past. One of the most interesting results, however, is surely the new light that is thrown on the theological scene.

The God who has been declared 'dead' by some of the most

rigorously logical of modern theologians is seen to be the Subject God of the Cartesian-Kantian stream of thought, the God who, we are told, must never be 'objectified', the God who cannot conceivably *act* since such a possibility is logically incompatible with the ultimate presuppositions of this whole system of thought. But *this* God is not and never has been the Agent God of the Bible – "God who acts"! Although in their efforts to be academically respectable in this era of Critical Philosophy – and indeed in their sincere and dedicated search for truth – many who really believed in, knew and loved this Living God have spoken of Him in the fashionable 'subject/object' terminology, true Christians must now agree that the Subject/Object God of the philosophers *is* dead and never was alive! The 'Secular Christians' of the 'God is Dead' school are quite correct – their conclusion is the only possible logically consistent one, granted their presuppositions: their God is dead. But of course the God believed in, loved and worshipped by simple Christians through the centuries of the Church has always been the Bible's Creator-God who acts, who sent Jesus Christ and raised Him from the dead – not this dead philosophical abstraction. Now it is becoming increasingly clear to thinking men today that the period of the Critical Philosophy and the secular outlook have led man's thinking out into conclusions of the utmost absurdity in various disciplines, and that, therefore, new personalist presuppositions must be accepted for modern thought. Those who accept this modern necessity, – realising that the world-view of Copernicus and Galileo, of Descartes and Kant is *not* the 'new world' for today and tomorrow, but the old world of yesterday – and who accept new presuppositions such as can rationally acknowledge man to be person and agent, will find the Living God still 'there', still alive and waiting for 'the wise men of the world' to return to Him, still ready and able to act, to save and to bless. The truly New Theology must concern itself with God as Agent, the God of the Bible – the God who was largely lost from sight in the philosophical speculations of 'static' mediaeval theology as also in the critical secularism of more recent theology. As we prepare to enter a post-Critical age of human thought,[39] wonderful prospects stretch out before Christian theology – for the God of the New World is the Living God who acts, the God of the Bible.

CHAPTER 11

Time, Eternity, and God Who Acts – Some Modern Views

A new world for theology and for thought in our Western society seems bound to open increasingly to our view as we understand better the implications of adopting new basic presuppositions which recognise persons as *primarily Agents*, with their status as thinking Subjects derived and subordinate. It seems clear that questions about the relation of action and of persons to various concepts of *time* are certain to be of great importance in the theological discussions of this new thought-world; and indeed not only in philosophy but also on the frontiers of contemporary theology there has already been a growing focus of interest on questions concerning time, some expressions of which we shall now briefly consider.

CULLMANN ON TIME AND ETERNITY

Oscar Cullmann's book *Christ and Time* attracted widespread attention to this subject, and particularly to his contention that the New Testament knows nothing of any timeless eternity, or of a God who is beyond or outside time and not within it. "Between what we call eternity and what we call time, that is, between everlastingly continuing time and limited time, the New Testament makes absolutely no difference in terminology," he wrote.[1] "We shall establish the fact that Primitive Christianity places both the divine creation 'in the beginning' and the divine goal of all becoming 'at the end of the days' in precisely the same Christocentric perspective of Biblical history, that is, in precisely the same temporal Christ-line which it uses to view the historical events in which figure the people of Israel and the activity of Jesus and the apostles and the Primitive

Church ... *All Christian theology in its innermost essence is Biblical history*: on a straight line of an ordinary process in time God here reveals himself, and from that line he controls not only the whole of history, but also that which happens in nature! There is here no room for speculations concerning God that ignore time and history ... Nowhere is God's action more concretely revealed than in the history which, to speak theologically, presents in its innermost nature the revelation of God to men."[2]

Cullmann is emphatic that all philosophical speculation about time must be excluded from theology, as foreign to the Bible; and he specifically declares that "the distinction which has such fundamental significance for H. Bergson has no relevance for biblical thought about time."[3] He claims that his linear view of time is in no sense philosophical, but is merely an exposition of the simple, unspeculative realism of the Bible. We must affirm to the contrary that time 'seen' as extended in space in linear form is already an objectification – and thus a limiting distortion – of real time as we *know* it in life and action (and of which I believe we often *think* and *speak* with uncritical common-sense, though I am not concerned to argue that here). Time conceived as a straight line is already a sophisticated philosophical concept, no less so than a cyclic conception of time as in Greek Philosophy. This spatialised concept of time is indeed very closely related to a concept of timeless space, and this in turn to the idea of a timeless eternity in which all points of time may be made equally visible – equally 'present' – at once. Time conceived as linear is 'objective' time as reflected on by a thinking Subject. In such time, as we have seen, freedom and the possibility of action become problems, irrational impossibilities. Cullmann declares that "None of the New Testament expressions for time has as its object time as an abstraction."[4] But if he is correct in saying that the New Testament always conceives time as a line in space (how else could a line be conceived?) then precisely the opposite is true, and the New Testament always and only sees time as an objective abstraction. In that case the concept of action is as irrational in the Bible as it is in classical, objective science, and the biblical presuppositions are as inconsistent as those of science with the concept of God as Agent. We prefer to think that Cullmann is in error in saying that the Bible always and only understands time as linear.

Cullmann is no doubt correct, however, in his insistence that the Bible knows nothing of a timeless eternity, or of a God outside time. And although these concepts from Greek philosophy might appear to have some value in Christian theology for 'explaining' the omniscience of God, predestination, and so on, yet with reference to a God who *acts* these concepts raise far more problems than they 'solve'. Action cannot possibly be conceived apart from movement, and movement requires time – real, flowing duration. If God is to be believed in as Agent, in the sense of biblical faith, then we *must* conceive of Him as in time, the sort of time in which action is possible, similar to if not identical with the sort of present time which we know directly and with uncritical immediacy as qualitatively different from the spatially extended, linear time of discursive thought. Must we not say that for the Bible, with the acts of God and the freedom of God as Agent everywhere presupposed, the 'eternity' which characterises God's being must be understood as temporal, but *not* linear? A line may well represent past and future, time remembered and time imagined, but not present time, the time of action and of living. As the Living God, the Creator, our God must be understood as the source and centre of the time in which we live and move and have our being. "I AM WHO I AM", which was the Name of God revealed to Moses, suggests the nature of God's time, somehow extending the *present time* of life and action which *we* know only as NOW, back beyond all creation and forward beyond the end of our history, as an eternal, dynamic and moving present. As Lord of time through the power of controlling action, by which He will shape all things to conform in the end with His eternal purposes, this may equally mean "I WILL BE WHAT I WILL BE" : but only because this future will become present reality through the creative action of God.

MOLTMANN ON TIME

It is, of course, with this temporal aspect of modern theological enquiry, and especially with the future, that Jürgen Moltmann's book, *The Theology of Hope,* is concerned. But instead of distinguishing the living present, that time in which alone actions can be done, from the remembered past and the imagined future which can both be represented as linear time, he links present and past together as historically determined time, and isolates the future as the realm of freedom and action. He seems to assume that Bultmann's wish to transcend the subject/object distinction in 'historical time' has somehow fathered the reality, and that it is now possible to 'think' the linear time of the as yet unreal future, the 'promised future', in a way that is 'concrete' or whole and able to sustain action, rather than as objectively limited, and futuristically unreal, thought-time. Of this promised future he writes: "What is here regarded as 'time' is then concrete time as seen in the process of historic and expected changes. To that extent the sense of time and the ideas of time also change along with the expectations. The abstract scientific concept of time, which has categorically determined modern thinking since Kant, must not be applied here until we have tested its eschatological scope – which in Kant's sense means its transcendental scope."[5] Moltmann projects the flowing quality of time, which we know only NOW in life and action, into the promised future. "The conditions of possible experience which were understood by Kant in a transcendental sense must be understood instead as historically flowing conditions. It is not that time at a standstill is the category of history, but the history which is experienced from the eschatological future of the truth is the category of time."[6]

It is not easy to understand how the future can properly be called more concrete and less abstract than scientific time which has actually determined the past, when *as future* it is not and never can be real; when it can achieve reality only by becoming determined in the present and moving into the already determined past. For as Macmurray has written: "The past is that which exists, the future that which does not exist. It is not that which will exist, for the action may not be completed, or it may complete itself in an unanticipated manner; in that case the future never comes. When what is now future comes to existence, it is no longer future but past."[7]

The God of the theology of Hope, "a God with 'future as his essential nature'... the God whom we therefore cannot really have in us or over us but always only before us":[8] this God who cannot be 'behind' us as One who has already acted, nor *with* us in the living present, is not the God we need today, nor the God of the Bible. To base on such a future non-reality, as Moltmann invites us to do, the solution of modern theological problems such as what Christians should do now that the Subject-God is judged dead, or how to transcend the historical impossibility of the Resurrection of Jesus (scientifically understood), is to try to build the Christian Faith not even on a sand foundation, but on a vacuum. Christian hope builds, not on a promised future in which we hope we may find God, but on the faithfulness of the Living God who in the past has acted in Jesus Christ to bring us into fellowship with Himself NOW in the living present, and opened for us a way into His future-shaping eternity.

PANNENBERG ON TIME

That temporal concepts are of real importance for the themes of Pannenberg's theology also seems to be evident from the fact that almost all the contributors to the American discussion of his views in *Theology as History* give some attention to questions of time, and one contributor heads his chapter "Past, Present and Future".[9] "I am disturbed by Pannenberg's position," J. B. Cobb writes, "because it subordinates the present too much to the future and the past."[10] "The problem of Lessing assumes that there is a real gulf between the past and the present", Hamilton comments about Pannenberg's views on time; and he indicates his impression that Pannenberg believes "a careful examination of history reveals no such gulf".[11] Pannenberg himself, discussing Grobel's suggestion that "the resurrection of Jesus qualifies as an event in time, but that as an event in space it either does not qualify or does so only as an historically incredible event",[12] asks: "Do not space and time belong indissolubly together in reality?"[13] Surely they do! But he elaborates his views on time in a way which seems to confirm the correctness of Cobb's view that he sees past, present and future as a homogeneous continuity in space, presumably in a linear conception of time. "I see the present as laid open by the future and connected with the heritage of the past, which for its part refers again towards the future. These connections seem to me to be constitutive of the present itself. A present isolated from the past and future would be empty, at least for a finite being. The present always receives its tension-filled content from the interaction with the heritage of the past in the light of a perspective towards the future."[14]

The 'visual' form of Pannenberg's statement on time is perhaps significant in an indirect way – "I *see* the present . . ." – for, as Bergson remarked, time 'seen' is time already spatially represented, already transformed from the known reality and 'wholeness' of the present as experienced in action into an objective abstraction for the purposes of discursive thinking. J. M. Robinson quotes G. Klein as believing that Pannenberg over-emphasises the visual as against the auditory aspects of revelation, with consequent distortion. Discussing Pannenberg's emphasis on the seen acts of God rather than the heard word of God (in a critical review of his introduction to *Revelation as History*) Klein comments, (according to Robinson) that this "presupposes the model of sight rather than hearing, and hence misses the dialectic of God's call . . ."[15]

In an earlier consideration of hearing and seeing (p. 58f. above) we found both Torrance and Bultmann in agreement that the emphasis of the prophets, and indeed of the whole Bible, is upon the primacy of hearing over vision with respect to God's revelation of Himself to man. "Hearing is the means by which God is apprehended," Bultmann declares.[16] Indeed, we may say generally that hearing is the primary means by which we recognise, and hold personal communion with, other persons. For, in a manner which is not true of things seen, sounds are present (spatially) with the hearer in the continuing dynamic present (of time), where space and time intersect in the reality of personal life and activity. Sounds are essentially temporal, held in the continuing present: time, we might say, is the 'form' of sound. On the level of personal life, words spoken in communication unite the hearer with the speaker in a shared and continuing mutuality of activity such as cannot be paralleled in visual experience, which tends rather to emphasise the difference, the separating space, between the 'object' seen and the viewing 'subject' or spectator. In our experience of movement, which is essential to our knowledge of action and of personal life, "time is the form of action; while space is the form of reflection, and . . . time is prior to space because action is prior to reflection," John Macmurray writes. "We might almost say that the space-factor is simply the time-factor objectified, or thought, either in anticipation or in retrospect. For in retrospect all the successiveness in the actual movement disappears and all its moments are apprehended simultaneously.

From the point of view of the Subject, therefore, time is spatialised, and is represented by a 'line', or 'path' or 'track'. We can only distinguish space from time by saying that in space all the elements are simultaneous; not, as in time, successive; and simultaneity is itself a determination of time. This indicates that time is logically prior to space; and if we remember that all reflection is included in action as its negative component, the relativity of space and time is accounted for, since the reflective discrimination of space from time must be relative to the action of moving."[17]

Pannenberg, however, seems to be restricted by his Idealism to a concept of homogeneous time-as-thought, on the level of reflection, and he sees the 'present' as little more than the junction of past and future, the mathematical point where they meet. One suspects that he might accept the 'movement' of dialectical logic, with its thesis, antithesis and synthesis, as almost an adequate substitute for real action, and that the 'tension' of which he speaks as giving content to the present is conceived as a logical tension between thesis and antithesis which yields a sort of synthetic 'action' on the level of ideas and reflection, out of which history and theology are constructed by Idealism.

He rightly insists that without the correct logical presuppositions the Christian truth cannot be accepted and Christian faith cannot emerge: "To be able to have Christian faith one must at least presuppose that the message about Jesus Christ is true. This includes primarily the affirmations that Jesus really proclaimed the coming of God's reign and that he really rose from the dead. It may very well be that one cannot always comprehend the truth of this message, but one must be able to *presuppose* that it is correct, and that, at least in principle, its truth is intelligible. In the sense of a logical presupposition (though not always a psychological antecedent) the knowledge of Jesus' history, including his resurrection from the dead, is the basis of faith."[18] But surely this goes too far and begs the question at issue. What must be said is that unless we presuppose that the message about Jesus Christ *could* be true – His coming among us through an act of God, His loving actions 'with the finger of God', His resurrection by the act of God – we cannot come to have Christian faith. The predicament of modern theology is that the thinking-Subject/experienced-Object structure presupposed by modern thought (since Descartes and Kant) precludes the possibility of rationally acknowledging the truth of the claim that God has acted to change the world – as it precludes, for the logically consistent, the recognition of any real action whatsoever. What is needed is not to presuppose the truth of faith's foundational beliefs as 'given', but to presuppose them as rationally *possible* : and this requires the radical change of our Western Culture's basic presupposition which is indicated by Macmurray, from "I (presupposed as Subject) think..." to "I (presupposed as Agent) act..." Then the acts of God as Personal Creator God become rationally possible if not fully intelligible or 'thinkable'. Man, therefore, *knowing* in his presuppositions that personal action is possible and can change the world in surprising ways, is left to consider the historical and other evidence and decide whether all or any of these reported events in biblical history were indeed *acts* of an Agent who is super-human, super-natural.[19] If he comes to believe (without at this discursive level 'knowing') the basic account of "Jesus' history, including his resurrection from the dead", he may make the personal approach of faith to the Agent-God whom he can come to *know* personally through Jesus Christ the Risen Lord, in the continuing present time of life and action. This change of ultimate presuppositions, involving acceptance of a real, enduring, action-filled present-time, from which past and future are derived by our experience and on a different level, is what Pannenberg apparently has not made – and cannot make within the context of philosophical Idealism : and his presupposition of the historicity of the acts of God as "known" remains therefore essentially irrational if not anti-rational.

KARL BARTH ON TIME AND ETERNITY

Oscar Cullmann criticises Barth for rejecting the linear concept for God's eternity while agreeing that it is not timeless but essentially temporal. "Karl Barth," he writes, "in contrast to his earlier publications, lays very strong emphasis in his *Dogmatik* on the temporal quality of eternity. But...here still, in spite of everything, he takes as his starting point a fundamental distinction between time and eternity, and refuses to regard eternity as 'time stretching endlessly forward and backward'. The time-marked character of eternity, which Karl Barth strives so urgently to bring out in this section of his book, is understood

o

in the biblical sense only when the symbol of the straight line is applied to both, to time and to eternity, so that the very time during which creation exists appears as a limited portion of the same line, and not as something essentially different."[20] If this were so, then the problem of the possibility of God's acting in timeless eternity would simply be replaced by the problem, which we have already discussed, of how He could act in objectively determined linear time. But Barth has a different view about the biblical concept of time.

Karl Barth's discussion of the eternity of God and time gives no indication of having been written with the logical problems of action, with which we have been concerned, in mind. But it is very relevant to this subject.[21]

"Eternity," he writes, "is just the duration which is lacking to time, as can be seen clearly at the middle point of time, in the temporal present and in its relationship to the past and future ... In this duration God is free ... Only God is eternal: only His love ... except that in the act of His love God exalts something else to share in His eternity, so that there is now and for this reason an eternal life of which even we may live in hope and an eternal fire which even we have to fear. Yet even in God's fellowship with His creature, this eternity still belongs exclusively to God ... Being does not include eternity, but eternity includes being. The genuineness of being is examined and weighed and measured by eternity ... As the eternal One *it is He who surrounds our time and rules it with all that it contains*. How can He be and do all this if as the eternal One He does not Himself have his own time, superior to ours, undisturbed by the fleetingness and separations of our time, simultaneous with all our time, but in this way and for this reason absolutely real time?"[22]

God – the living God who acts – comes in His eternal time to meet us in our NOW, where the time of man's life, created in the image of God, gives us freedom for action and for love and personal communion – for these things which we know to be real and primary though they cannot be captured without distortion in the static concepts of words or in visual images, nor be the object of exact thinking without self-contradiction. Here is the root of Christian paradox, and the glory of Christian truth!

These static concepts enshrined in words, however, *can* and do in fact convey in living use an understanding of the dynamic

210

meaning of personal communication, even through the visual symbols of written language or in word-pictures like that of the living God 'surrounding' our time with His eternal present, acting in and ruling the world from above as well as from within. Similarly, visual symbols in diagrammatic form, understood in the same sort of way, can help to create and sustain in modern man a living faith in the God who acts. Theological thinking, not only in its profoundest and most creative moments, but also if it is to be communicated effectively on a popular level, must work with such symbols and models in a positive way, as science does. We must overcome our fear of precision in theology, and use the courage needed to clarify our thinking on such matters by working *analogically* with visual representations such as those used above on pages 46 and 61.

To a consideration of the consequences that follow from the radical theological differences between these two 'models' which we have presented – that of 'Secular Christianity' and that of the Biblical world-view – we shall return shortly. We must first note, however, another implication of the relationship between God and time, which is so important for theology in the 'personalist' world of tomorrow's thinking.

It is always in the here and now that we meet the Living God, where our created time touches the eternity of His time on which it was modelled. And God here and now we call the Holy Spirit – God at work in the world today, changing society in personal ways by changing the lives of men, and working out His eternal purposes in time and space.

Within the mystery of the Trinity, when we think of *God at all times and all places,* the root and source of God from whom have been sent to us the Son and the Holy Spirit, we speak of God the *Father. God as made known to us there and then,* expressing the fulness of the Godhead bodily in our world at a particular place and time – in Jesus Christ in Palestine almost 2000 years ago – we call God the *Son.* And *God here and now,* God acting in the continuing present of our world-time, God in His fulness as we meet Him today, we call God the *Holy Spirit,* who brings Christ to us and brings us to the Father through Him.[23]

In a post-Critical, personalist world-view, therefore, Christian theology must be basically a theology of the Holy Spirit. And the modern 'Pentecostal movement', sweeping through the denominations of the world Church, even with its off-centre emphasis on 'tongues' and other oddities, and its excessive emotionalism, is surely the voice of a forerunner crying in the wilderness of the modern secular outlook: "God is not dead – He is very much alive! 'Prepare the way of the Lord'."

"Now the Lord is the Spirit, and where the Spirit of the Lord is, there is freedom. And we all, with unveiled face, beholding the glory of the Lord, are being changed into His likeness from one degree of glory to another: for this comes from the Lord who is the Spirit." (II Corinthians 3:17, 18)

CONCLUSION

A CALL FOR INTEGRITY

Conclusion

A Call for Integrity

Although the proliferation and relativity of objective, scientific world-views is a mark of our age, and no one such view is ever again likely to be accepted as *the* scientific world-view, yet we have seen that all of them share a common form, as closed objective, deterministic systems of nature. As 'objective', however, they are all essentially limited and partial views, and all can be contained without formal or logical conflict within the wider, more comprehensive world-view of modern personalist philosophy; or within the even wider personalist world-view of biblical Christianity, founded on faith in the supernatural Creator-God who acts. This biblical world-view, as diagrammatically represented on page 61, is therefore in principle fully compatible with the world-views of modern science. Only when it is claimed for science that the objective form of its world-views gives a fully comprehensive and adequate picture of the world does logical conflict with the biblical world-view become inevitable.

It is, of course, just such a claim that distinguishes the 'secular outlook'; and this means that the 'secular world-view' becomes an alternative or rival to the biblical world-view in a way that no scientific world-view as such can ever be. The secular world-view and the biblical world-view, each claiming to give a comprehensive, overall picture of the 'form' of the world, cannot both be true together. If one is true, the other must be false.

It is surely therefore one of the most surprising things in this strange age that inside the Church today we find that we are offered both of these incompatible alternatives at once, with some people claiming to have combined them successfully in 'Secular Christianity'!

Only by means of word-twisting, logic-flouting mental acrobatics could this claim be given any appearance of rationality, however; and the process of attempting it cannot but issue in crippling confusion in the Church, with a drastic loss of integrity in the use of theological words. If we attempt to accommodate these contrary views together in the Church, we will have to accept fluid definitions for even the most basic Christian terms. Every theologian will then be able to express in conventional Christian terminology even secular views which are quite contrary to biblical Christianity, if he wishes, without danger of being judged to be 'in error'.

When this becomes known in the Church, is not a loss of confidence in all statements of Christian 'truth' inevitable? And in the wider academic world, surely this situation must quickly bring about an almost total loss of respect for theology and for those who practise it.

TRUTH AND ERROR

"Every kingdom divided against itself goes to ruin," Jesus said (Luke 11 : 17 N.E.B.), "and a divided household falls." The Church cannot, without disaster, continue trying to give allegiance both to the living, supernatural Agent-God of the biblical world-view and also to the merely natural and essentially immanent Subject-God (the 'Ground of Being', 'depth of existence', etc.) of the 'Secular Christian' world-view – the God whose only possible end, logically considered, (because of the ultimate presuppositions of the whole system) is denial or 'death'.

The predicament of many Christian theologians during the past century and more, in the increasingly secular climate of the Age of Criticism, has been that to choose the biblical 'God who acts' has seemed to them to require a denial of Reason: a choice of 'faith' *instead* of truth, rather than a choice of 'the Faith' *because* it is believed to be true. It has recently become increasingly clear, however, that the secularism of the Critical outlook is essentially self-contradictory when developed with logical consistency, and issues in conclusions that are manifestly absurd. The balance of 'reason', we may now claim, is to be found today in a post-Critical personalist outlook which is at least compatible with the personalist foundation of biblical faith and which accepts, as valid and relevant, historical evidence that was formerly excluded (as irrational) from serious consideration, by 'objectivist' Critical prejudice, though always claimed by Christians as important support for their belief in a personal and supernatural Creator-God.

It appears that the time is now right, therefore, for the Church to act in a positive way for the recovery of the lost integrity of her theology. Taking the broken remains of her courage, battered by the pressures of the modern world, let the Church now affirm unambiguously and with confidence – to a lost and sinful world which desperately needs to hear it – that the Christian Gospel of the living God who acts, the God of the Bible who raised Jesus Christ from the dead, is TRUE.

A bare affirmation of the truth, however, no matter how apparently unambiguous it may be, cannot by itself remove all doubts about meaning, especially in these days of fluid theological definitions. It is impossible today to be sure just what a theological affirmation does mean, until it has been made clear what it does *not* mean, by the exclusion of possible 'interpretations' which are incompatible with the positive meaning. This sort of 'definition of the positive by indication of the negative' has, in fact, always been found necessary by the Church with respect to doctrinal truth; though perhaps the necessity is now more obvious than ever before.

Thus we find the close conjunction of affirmation and denial at the very heart of the Gospel in the New Testament. "By grace you have been saved through faith", St. Paul declares positively: but he immediately goes on to exclude errors of 'interpretation' which some in that day were inclined to favour. By grace – therefore "this is *not* your own doing, it is the gift of God"; through faith – therefore "*not* of works, lest any man should boast." The meaning of the affirmation is clearly defined and made unambiguous only by means of the exclusion of erroneous interpretations which were likely to be put on it in that day.

Another example of the same principle is to be found in the Nicene Creed. Some leaders in the Church, before A.D. 325, had interpreted the New Testament to the effect that as 'Son of God', Jesus Christ had been created by God, and was therefore part of the creation along with us, and not truly within the Trinity of the Creator-God. The Church, therefore, when framing in the Creed the scriptural truth that God the Son, who was incarnate in Jesus Christ, was "begotten of His Father before all worlds, . . . Very God of Very God", went on to exclude specifically the fashionable theological error of that day: "Begotten, *not* made." It was realised that the statement of the negative was required in order to render unambiguous the positive affirmation.

The same principle can be seen working in virtually all the major Creeds, Confessions and Catechisms of the Church down the years since then. Whenever there has been a period of acute theological questioning, a time of crisis for the Faith, the Church has found herself forced to go beyond the simple affirmation of her beliefs, and has had to muster her reserves of energy and courage to deny the prevalent theological misconceptions of the day.

A striking recent example of this is *The Theological Declaration of Barmen*, drawn up by an Evangelical Synod of the Christian Church in Germany when political pressures from Adolf Hitler's government had caused many Church leaders to swerve from the path of Christian truth. The fact of its inclusion, alongside other great documents of the Church's history, in the new *Book of Confessions* recently adopted by The United Presbyterian Church in the U.S.A., gives an indication of the high esteem in which this Declaration is rightly to be held. "In view of the errors of the 'German Christians' in the present Reich Government," the Declaration states, "we confess the following evangelical truths." After each affirmation of an endangered truth there appears the formula, "We reject the false doctrine . . .", and the errors of 'interpretation' prevalent in that situation are specifically excluded as false. The concluding paragraph states: "The Confessional Synod of the German Evangelical Church declares that it sees in the acknowledgment of these truths and *in the rejection of these errors* the indispensable theological basis of the German Evangelical Church as a federation of Confessional Churches." (My italics)

Throughout the whole range of human thought, the way of intellectual integrity, by which alone man's understanding and knowledge have been able to advance through the centuries, has involved, together with the affirmation of what is believed to be true, the rejection of what must therefore be considered as false. The road of scientific advance, for example, as is made clear by Polanyi's book, *Personal Knowledge*, and by all text-books on the history of science, is strewn with the 'wrecks' of theories once sincerely believed by some, but now seen to be incompatible with truth as more fully known. How hypocritical it must sound to men of simple integrity when theologians, who claim that Christianity is concerned with the truth, extol the scientific method and the integrity of scientists, whilst refusing to apply in theology the simple integrity that is willing to define and reject error so that truth may be clearly seen and accepted!

HERESY AND HERETICS

We have already noted the view, advanced so forcefully by Francis Schaeffer, that the reluctance of modern man (including modern Christians) to deny error so that truth may be affirmed in an unambiguous way, is a consequence of the adoption of a dialectical, 'triangular' logic of synthesis, which reconciles a thesis with its antithesis instead of excluding one or other as false, in the manner of the 'straight-line' traditional logic of simple antithesis. As a result of accepting the dialectical form of logic, Schaeffer argues, modern man has actually begun to think in a new way, different from the way of thinking characteristic of man through all former ages. He has become logically incapable of distinguishing between truth and error as mutually exclusive opposites, and 'relativity' now determines all his thinking. Only those who refuse to become 'modern men', and who remain logical straight-liners (as none but the faithful among evangelical conservatives have done, Schaeffer seems to suggest), are still capable of recognising clearly the truth/error distinction.[1] And before the mass of modern Christians in the Church could possibly comply, therefore, with the call we are now making for the sort of theological integrity which would attempt to banish ambiguity, it would be necessary for not only the content of their basic presuppositions, but also the entire logical manner of their thinking, to be radically transformed.

Against Schaeffer's view that dialectical logic has changed the actual thought-processes of humanity, we have argued that no matter how many and various are the logical descriptions given of man's thinking, the basic manner of valid thinking continues always the same, and no new form of logic can change it. And against his view that modern man is reluctant, and indeed unable, to distinguish adequately between truth and error be-

219

cause of a chronic failure of logical consistency and rationality, we can set the main flow of the argument of our whole study. We maintain that, in so far as there are logical as well as psychological roots to modern man's present reluctance to deal with 'error' in a significant way, they are to be found, not in a failure of logical consistency, but rather in the unswerving courage and tenacity with which he has followed, to their absurd and self-contradictory conclusions, the implications of pre-suppositions bequeathed to him as 'rational' by his predecessors, having been passed down the generations since Descartes' time. 'Secular Christianity', 'Christian Atheism', 'Holy Worldliness', and so on – these self-contradictory modern theological terms express well the sort of logical conclusions that follow inevitably from a ruthless application of Schaeffer's 'straight-line logic' to the exposition of the concept of 'God as thinking Subject' – which is the best concept of God available on the Cartesian premise. It has happened only in this present period, however, that a few Christian thinkers have had the perception, consistency and courage to draw out these conclusions clearly.

It is hardly surprising that confusion and uncertainty have settled on Christian theologians today, when they see their best logical thinking ending up in self-contradiction and absurdity. And it is not to be wondered at that so few of them seem willing to speak with any confidence about the truth or error of any specific theological view.

It might prove impossible to restore confidence here until it is seen that the self-contradictory confusion of modern theology has resulted, not from a failure of logic or of human reasoning, nor because (as some suppose) these matters are inherently incapable of being thought through to clear conclusions; but because of a basic misconception about the nature of reality which has been enshrined at the very foundation of all modern thought, and not just of theology. 'Man' has been wrongly conceived during the whole modern period, as basically a 'thinking subject' instead of as a 'living agent' : and the 'God' of post-Cartesian, modern theology has been 'created' by man in the image of that inadequate concept, instead of being simply 'received', from the revelation recorded in the Bible, as the living and acting Creator-God. It now appears that the simple, common-sense and Bible-based judgements of ordinary Christians about theological truth and error have been better-founded rationally (though of course not better argued), than all the deliverances of the great theological thinkers of recent centuries who have built their thought-systems on the shifting sands of the Cartesian dualism. Realisation of this fact may help to restore to modern Christians, it may be hoped, the courage to aim once more at avoiding ambiguity and affirming truth clearly.

Erroneous beliefs are not merely logical abstractions, however. And therefore to these *logical* reasons for modern man's reluctance to define and exclude errors in theology we must add the *psychological* reasons derived from the fact that such errors usually become relevant and important only when they are beliefs sincerely held, or likely to be held, by *people*. Inevitably, this being so, the process of discarding errors so that the truth may be affirmed without ambiguity is likely to hurt people. Many, in fact, have in the past been left behind by the historical wayside, bruised and perhaps broken in spirit, when what they had sincerely believed to be true was rejected by their community as error.

The Christian rightly recoils from the prospect of hurting others in this way. On the surface it appears to contravene the great, primary imperative of the Christian life, the 'law of Love'. And looking back down the way she has come through the years, the twentieth century Church is appalled to see the extent to which, in former ages, this principle has been infringed, so that people have sometimes been not only broken in spirit, when their beliefs were declared to be false, but broken also in body – tortured, racked, burned at the stake – and all in the name of truth and the exclusion of error. The churchman of today, therefore, who after formulating and affirming the truth is reluctant to go on and attempt to exclude errors also, has good reasons for his attitude. He knows how indefensibly wrong, both in attitude and belief, many of the dogmatic opponents of supposed 'heresy' were in the past, when they tried to eliminate error.

When added together, these reasons – logical and psychological – constitute a formidable obstacle in the mind of the modern theologian, often obstructing all consideration of suggestions (like those we have made) that truth should be affirmed in such an unambiguous way as to involve the exclusion of specific errors of doctrine.

The modern mood is well indicated in the issue of *TIME* magazine dated May 23rd, 1969, where an article headed *Is Heresy Dead* notes the increase in the Churches of beliefs which by all traditional Christian standards must be classified as 'false', but which pass unchallenged today because of a general reluctance to declare them false. "For many Christian thinkers, Catholic and Protestant alike," the article states, "the whole notion of heresy has become a treacherous one. In fact heresy may be as dead as God was supposed to be. Except for extremely conservative denominations, most Protestant bodies have abandoned the idea that a communicant can be expelled or punished for denying an article of faith. After an abortive attempt to condemn the Rt. Rev. James A. Pike for heresy by the Episcopal House of Bishops, a committee of prelates concluded that moral suasion and intellectual arguments were the only means the church had to keep dissidents in line.

"One of the problems with heresy," the article continues, "is that its very existence depends upon an outdated concept of what faith is – adherence to a particular body of doctrine rather than an inner spiritual commitment. According to Lutheran theologian Joseph Sittler of the University of Chicago: 'Heresy is a workable notion when faith is identified with propositions, but it becomes a flexible notion when a distinction is made between the reality of faith and statements made about it.' Catholic theologian Eugene C. Bianchi of Emory University suggests that the whole notion of heresy rests on the presumption that doctrine is static rather than dynamic and subject to change . . . Jesuit Joseph Fichter of Harvard Divinity School, proposes that the question of whether a man is a heretic or not 'should be left in the hands of God'."

No one today, surely, could fail to agree that rather than have any more *heretics* die, killed by the ignorant bigotry of the Church, it would be better to let *heresy* die. Certainly, in view of the tragic history linked with the term, it would be wise to kill and bury the *word* 'heresy' at once, if possible. But, we must pause to ask, does the swinging reaction in our day away from the awful heresy-hunting past of the Church mean, as seems to be suggested here, that we must also allow to die the possibility of recognising, and of denying as false, radical doctrinal errors that are contrary to the Christian Faith? For if we agree to this we announce thereby the funeral of the concept

222

of Christian *truth*; since truth and error are inseparably united and complementary concepts. Dispose of one, and both are lost. If this is indeed what we have come to today, then the demise of the Christian Church is inevitably close : for throughout her history the Church has always claimed to be, and has always been generally believed to be, essentially concerned with truth as well as with grace, concerned with love and other 'attitudes' only as related to truth.

Summarising the argument now, we see that persons and 'personalities' inevitably enter into situations where truth is affirmed and error denied. For the denial of error becomes relevant and important only when persons are committed to, or are likely to become committed to, the errors in question. And it is at the point where this is realised that, with the history of 'heresy' in view, the straight-thinking of the Church begins to bend, and Christian courage often fails. Is not the exclusion of doctrinal errors from the Christian Faith inseparable, it is asked, from the exclusion from the Church of those people who believe these errors? And how can this be justified in face of the command to love, especially at a time like this when the whole field of theology is in a state of unparalleled confusion?

It is most important here to be clear about two vital distinctions which seem to have been lost from view by the 'modern mood'.

(1) There is a very important distinction between faith as a personal relationship and 'the Faith' as a body of doctrine; but recognising the reality of the one does not abolish the other.

(2) Judging that a *belief* is unchristian is a very different thing from judging that the *person* who holds that belief is unchristian.

FAITH AND 'THE FAITH'

The difference between faith (as an attitude within a relationship) and 'the Faith' (as a body of doctrines) has been often underlined in the theological debates of recent years, and yet many men of intelligence seem deliberately to ignore it. This distinction is written deep into the Constitution of the particular Church to which I belong, the Presbyterian Church : and in order to avoid vague generalities I propose to illustrate from this Church the points I have to make, hoping that readers will mentally adapt them as necessary to fit their own situations.

Our Church does not demand of communicant members that they give direct assent to any statements of belief or formulations of doctrine, however simple. All that is asked of them, at the time of their reception into communicant membership by adult Baptism or by Confirmation, is that they declare their faith (as relationship) in God as their Heavenly Father, Jesus Christ as their Saviour and Lord, and the Holy Spirit as their Helper and Guide; and that they make some simple promises about their life and relationship to the Church in the days ahead. (An alternative form in our Book of Order asks that they confess their faith in the Apostles' Creed, but its use is optional.) It seems fairly obvious that important beliefs which are basic to the Faith are *implied* in these affirmations of faith-relationship; but specific acceptance of them is not required at this time.

The idea referred to in the *TIME* article above, therefore, that a *communicant member* could be expelled or punished for denying an article of faith, has had no constitutional place in our Church for many years now, for assent to such articles has not been included in the essentials of membership.

The case is very different, however, with regard to ministers and elders. Included in the responsibilities of their 'office' is the guarding of 'the Faith', the safe-keeping of the Church's doctrines. In their Ordination and Induction Vows, therefore, both ministers and elders are required to state specifically that they "believe the fundamental doctrines of the Christian Faith" as stated with final authority in the Bible, and that they will "uphold the doctrine of this Church". For them, as also for theological professors, induction to their office can take place only after they actually subscribe assent to the *doctrines* which, in the view of the Church, are fundamental to the biblical Faith.

This being so, continuing tenure of office must surely depend, in honour, upon a sincere and continuing acceptance of these biblical doctrines. The minister or elder who has made such Vows and who later finds that he can no longer accept doctrines which the Church believes to be 'fundamental', as measured by the standard of the Scriptures, is surely in honour bound to relinquish his office – though not, of course, his membership in the Church, nor in an increasingly secular world, the regard of the community. Instances of the honouring of similar 'obligations of honour' and of integrity are not uncommon among – for example – Cabinet Ministers in a political government, who come to disagree with basic policies of their government; or business executives and salesmen who have lost faith in the value of what their firm is producing. Should not ministers of the Church be expected to conform with at least an equivalent standard of integrity? And when an ordained minister of the Church, who has vowed that he will defend the doctrines of the Church, finds that he can no longer accept even the *primary presupposition* of all biblical theology – that God acts in the world, and as living, personal Agent meets with His people in fellowship – how can it be right that he should cling to office, especially if he publicly denies the doctrines he is pledged to defend, and causes distress and controversy in the Church?

This issue has nothing at all to do with 'academic freedom'. That conscientious criticism of the Church and any other institution in a society, however venerated, should be not only permitted but encouraged, seems clear to me: and no doubt men in academic positions should be especially privileged in this respect. Inevitably also, in our divided Christian Church, theologians in one denomination will sometimes criticise doctrines held as basic in another denomination; and it should be so. But this does not make it honourably correct for a minister who has voluntarily accepted the authority of a particular Church, and has vowed acceptance and defence of its basic doctrines, to publicly deny these doctrines, especially if he does it in a controversial manner and hides behind a screen of re-defined basic terms and verbal ambiguity.

To do this seems almost to have become a fashion among certain groups of theologians in several denominations of the Church in recent days. And in doing it they usually maintain, firstly, that it is doubtful today if any Christian doctrines remain which can be affirmed as *true* with the degree of conviction that would justify their earnest defence: and secondly, if there should still happen to be some such doctrines, then the fluid ambiguity of modern theological terms is such that no one could possibly be shown to be in obvious and radical *error*. 'The Faith', as a body of beliefs containing true and essential Christian doctrines, has been washed away in the floodwaters of modern scepticism and ambiguity: only 'faith', as an attitude or commitment, remains.

The drastic consequences which must surely follow if this view is generally accepted by the Church have already been

P

stated. And surely it has now become clear that, if what we have said about 'Secular Christianity' is true, urgent action must be taken in those Christian Churches in which a majority of members and ministers continues to believe that there *are* still some fundamental biblical truths to defend. What sort of action? The Church must be prepared, firstly, not only to affirm biblical truth as she sees it, but also, as in former ages, to exercise the courage and self-discipline required to isolate, and to deny in a specific and unambiguous way, the theological errors which are fashionable today. Any attempt to formulate a comprehensive new Creed or Confession of Faith today is foredoomed, I believe, to failure or confused mediocrity: but if we will use language with integrity in our piecemeal dealings with truth and error, under the Standard of the Bible and with the guidance of the Holy Spirit, much more can be achieved. And secondly, the Church must make clear to her ministers to whom has been entrusted especially her biblical heritage of doctrine, that she expects from them a degree of intellectual integrity and a standard of honour at least equal to that found elsewhere in the community.[2]

EXCLUDING ERRORS AND EXCLUDING PERSONS

It should now be abundantly clear that what we are discussing has nothing to do with 'excommunication': there is no suggestion that those who dissent from any of the Church's doctrines should be severed from membership in the Church. It should be made even more clear that if we say that certain current formulations of doctrine are not Christian, or are even anti-Christian, *we are not denying that those who hold these beliefs are, by personal faith, real Christians,* nor are we saying that *they* are anti-Christian.

It is a theological commonplace that everyone who has faith is accepted by God through sheer grace, and despite the fact that he is still certainly involved in sin in some measure. It seems to be less well recognised, however, that every 'believer' (a term traditionally synonymous with 'Christian') is also accepted by God through sheer grace, despite the fact that he is still involved in some degree of error, greater or less, in his doctrinal beliefs. There is not one of us in the Church who, in matters of doctrine, is in a position to declare any other person unacceptable to God by reason of error. If freedom from error were demanded of us by God, we should all fail together. Jesus' words, "Judge not, that you be not judged", are at least as applicable here as in matters of moral conduct. (Matthew 7:1) Also the words of Paul, who wrote to some servants of God who were over-critical of their fellow-Christians, and declared that if a person has faith, "God has welcomed him. Who are you to pass judgement on the servant of another? It is before his own Master that he stands or falls." (Romans 14:3, 4) If a man claims to have faith in God – and especially if he is willing to affirm his faith in a trinitarian formula such as we ask communicants to use – then no matter what his sins or errors may be, none of us is in a position to declare that he is not a Christian, or that God does not accept him by grace and through faith.

It is a very different matter, however, to declare that certain formulations of belief are false and unchristian; and the Christians of New Testament times were constantly urged to make clear judgements concerning the truth or error of doctrinal statements. A proper acknowledgement of the primacy for salvation of personal faith over correct belief, and of the fact that all Christians are in some measure of error, cannot free us from the obligation to "struggle in defence of the faith, the faith which God entrusted to His people once and for all." (Jude 3 N.E.B.) Nor may it be assumed to establish the possibility of a genuine personal faith which has no foundation in correct belief. The New Testament frequently states, to the contrary, that faith in God through Jesus Christ is impossible except on a basis of certain essential beliefs. Thus Paul, the great champion of faith (in the sense of personal attitude and relationship), insists that it is essential for Christians to accept 'the Faith', at least on certain points. "Do you still hold fast the Gospel as I preached it to you?" he asked the Corinthian Christians, for example. "If not, your conversion was in vain." (I Corinthians 15:1, 2, N.E.B.) The very 'terms' in which he preached the Gospel to them were important, he insists. And referring especially to the Resurrection of the Lord Jesus, he goes on to detail what he meant by 'the Gospel' in terms that are clearly incompatible, for instance, with the so-called 're-interpretation of the Resurrection' as subjective experience of the disciples, which 'Secular Christianity' offers.

227

The Pastoral Epistles are full of exhortations to maintain and guard sound doctrine. We read, for example, that "a bishop (*episkopon*), as God's steward, ... must hold firm to the sure word as taught, so that he may be able to give instruction in sound doctrine and also to confute those who contradict it." (Titus 1 : 7a, 9) In Churches in which the *episkope* or over-sight is exercised corporately rather than by selected individuals, these 'courts' are obviously enjoined not only to affirm and declare the truth doctrinally, but also to identify, and exclude from the Faith, doctrinal errors. It is by no means implied that the verbal formulation of the truth must always be the same, static : but it is required that the Church make sure that it is the same truth—and not just the same 'attitude' or 'outlook'—which continues to find affirmation in the changing patterns of word and concept through the passing ages.

The urgent question which must be decided in our time, then, is whether 'Secular Christianity' constitutes a genuine reformulation of the truth of 'the Faith' as stated in the New Testament, or whether it contradicts and is incompatible with biblical truth. To me it seems now to have been clearly established that 'Secular Christianity' and biblical theology are mutually exclusive incompatibles; and that therefore the Churches, if they wish to retain with integrity the right to call themselves 'Christian' Churches, must now act with free and rational responsibility under God to exclude, as false and unchristian doctrine, this popular error of modern secular man who wants to be a secular Christian. Failure now to clearly affirm the Gospel and to repudiate these contrary errors could be due only, I believe, to a failure of intellectual nerve or of moral integrity, and would constitute a betrayal of Christ and His Church. For though we have no right to judge individuals as to their personal relationship to God and His willingness to accept them, we have as Christians an inescapable obligation to judge concerning the apostolicity and catholicity of formulations of belief which are put forward as 'Christian' beliefs.

'SECULAR CHRISTIANITY' AND THE BIBLICAL FAITH

In these days of large and amiable tolerance, when all sorts of odd and radical innovations are accepted in our society with hardly a comment, it is unfashionable and unpopular to speak

in urgent protest about 'serious doctrinal errors', or to declare
that they threaten the very life of the Church and must be
rejected. But must it not in honesty be agreed, when we examine
this modern phenomenon called 'Secular Christianity', that never
before in the history of the Church has such a vast departure
from the basic beliefs of the Bible and the historic Faith been
claimed as a proper interpretation of Christianity by influential
people in the Church? The errors of Marcion, Arius, Pelagius
and others, who were judged by the Church to have led their
followers away from Christian truth in days gone by, are all
minor errors compared with the vast, compounded error of this
movement in the Church today. All the classical 'heresies' could
be fully plotted on our diagrammatic representation of the form
of the biblical, supernaturalist world-view of historic Christianity
through the centuries (p. 61). For they all retained the biblical
belief in a living and acting, personal Creator-God, with all
that this implies for the status and context of the 'natural world'.
'Secular Christianity', however, requires (as we have seen,
p. 46) an altogether different diagram of its own: it cannot
be placed in proper continuity with all the varied forms of
Christianity and even Christian 'heresy' thrown up by the
centuries. Indeed, this contemporary movement in the Church,
though using still most of the traditional biblical terminology
(in radically redefined senses), rejects the whole structure of the
biblical world-view – its foundation on the living, acting God
and its setting within His supernatural reality, as well as most of
its essential contents – and constructs on a different foundation
(scientific method) a wholly naturalistic world-view which it
calls 'Christian', although its 'God' is conceived as fully contained within nature, and a complete new set of concepts is
required to fit (under the old names) with this new situation.
The extent of the difference seems too much to believe – this
staggers the imagination! And so the relatively orthodox theological ostriches of the Church (of whom there seem today to
be many), after a startled glance at those who suggest that this
is what has happened, classify them quickly as narrow-minded
reactionary bigots, mumble something about the need to accept
the new insights of modern science, and bury their heads again
under the fashionable sands of easy tolerance. How *could* these
things be true about the nature of 'Secular Christianity', which

finds support today from such brilliant theologians, such fine leaders!

Yet . . . are they not true, in fact? Is the analysis that emerges from our study of the concept of 'action' entirely false? He will be a bigoted dogmatist (for all his talk about toleration and academic freedom) who quickly assumes that there is nothing in it, without first undertaking the discipline of careful study and thought.

We maintain that 'Secular Christianity' is a whole system of radical doctrinal error. It is not just that it needs some correction and revision, but that it is radically false as a whole, even though in places it may contain important glimpses of truth: for it is based on the acceptance of a modern secular attitude which is simply incompatible with the primary presupposition and total structure of the biblical outlook. An increasing number of influential voices today can be heard in agreement with this estimate.

H. Gollwitzer, after a masterly analysis – in his book on God's existence – of some of these problems with which we have been concerned, writes: "No less is at stake here than the unity of the Church among other things. The cleavage in the understanding of the Gospel can be so deep as to drive us to Luther's words about 'two churches', the Church of God and the church of anti-Christ."[3]

J. M. Morrison in *Honesty and God* refers to J. A. T. Robinson's view (expressed in *The Honest to God Debate*) that, among other things, the questions of the supernatural and of demythologising need further discussion. "On both these questions there is a very deep and fundamental cleavage of opinion," Morrison writes, "but the way to an answer becomes doubly difficult when many of the self-styled 'radical' writers keep on using the words Christian and Christianity for something completely unrecognisable as Christian in any sense."[4]

In his foreword to this book of Morrison's, E. P. Dickie hails it as "a timely exposure of the 'heretical theology' and the 'elastic morality' which have gained of late an unpleasant notoriety and an unwarranted attention."[5]

T. F. Torrance writes: "The Church is suffering from a very serious malady: it has become so obsessed with itself and its own consciousness that it is unable to distinguish the objective reality of the truth and action of God from its own subjective states . . . Thus I find it scientifically and theologically impossible to see in the so-called 'new theology' of Protestantism anything like a new Reformation, but rather the reverse, something revealing a deep-seated traumatic disturbance in modern Protestantism, in fact a diseased understanding of the Gospel."[6]

Writing about van Buren's book on 'Secular Christianity', E. L. Mascall states: "He provides a *soi disant* 'Christianity' in which there is no such being as God, nobody survives bodily death, nobody hears us when we pray, there is no risen Saviour and nothing for us when we are dead: but only, while we are in this life, an undefined 'freedom' which is alleged to be contagious and to give us the same 'perspective' on the world as was possessed by a Galilean peasant who no longer exists." And he declares: "The conclusion to which I have found myself forced is that what we are being offered is not a re-interpretation of the Christian religion, but a substitute for it."[7]

Coming to expression in what I believe to be the self-contradictory, dying years of the great Cartesian-Kantian period of modern thought – a period of three brilliant and earth-changing centuries of civilisation based on Descartes' primary principle, 'I think therefore I am', and structured by Kant's Critical Philosophy – 'Secular Christianity' has tried to force the Christian Faith to conform with the increasingly naturalistic and godless pattern of modern secular man's outlook. But Christian Faith and the secular outlook are incompatible alternatives, and they cannot be forced together without shattering the integrity of language. Because it *is* secular, 'Secular Christianity' cannot be Christian.

It is my conviction that we have reached NOW in the Christian Churches a time of decision, like that in which Joshua long ago challenged the Israelites to decide and to act. "Choose this day whom you will serve . . . But as for me and my house, we will serve the Lord." (Joshua 24:15) And I believe that Christians may choose the biblical God-Who-Acts with confidence today, and with clear intellectual integrity, for there seems every reason to think that these coming years will show with increasing clarity the self-contradictory nature of the secular outlook, and the deep rationality of the personalist-theism of the biblical-Christian outlook.

We must act in the Churches, in whatever ways are the most

effective, to reject 'Secular Christianity' as radical and dangerous error. The alternative is a betrayal of Christ and the Christian Faith. Here is the negative requirement of our situation today, and it seems sadly inevitable that it will bring into the life of the Church a good deal of distress, since errors of doctrine involve people. Every possible care must be taken, therefore, for Christ's sake and for love's sake, to ensure that those *persons* who have been swept away in this mistaken modern attempt to meet 'the world' on its own ground, are *not* rejected by, or excluded from, the Church, but are cherished and nourished and drawn back onto the rock-firm foundation of the Bible and its God.

In contrast with this negative aspect of our situation, an exciting positive prospect confronts theology today, I believe. A new world for thought, to which the concept of 'action' seems likely to be the key, is opening before man at this time. In this the chronic dualism of classical Western thought can be transcended, the 'subjective' and 'objective' worlds being known as one world in and through action. The living and acting personal God of the Bible, the story of whose mighty acts in history has been so roughly handled in terms of the subject/object split of the Critical outlook and the unbalanced objectivism of the secular outlook, will again be rationally seen (or heard) as the One who has given ultimate unity to all reality and all knowledge by His acts in Creation, Redemption and Revelation.

We may expect, then, to come on wonder upon wonder in new dimensions of truth as we are led forward into the new world by God the Holy Spirit, God who is personally with us in the living time of the present, as God Who Acts.

Notes

Preface

1 Stuart Hampshire's scholarly book, *Thought and Action* (Chatto and Windus, 1960) is helpful, but still presupposes the logical primacy of 'thought'.

Introductory

1 Carl F. H. Henry in *Christianity Today*, March 1st, 1968.
2 In the *Bulletin* of the Department of Theology of the World Presbyterian Alliance, 1968 Spring issue.
3 Ibid., pp. 2, 3.
4 *Christianity Today*, June 21st, 1968.
5 David Jenkins, *Guide to the Debate About God* (Lutterworth, 1966), p. 32.
6 *Encyclopaedia Britannica*, article on Kierkegaard.
7 John Macquarrie, *God and Secularity* (Lutterworth, 1968), p. 33.
8 James Denney, *Studies in Theology*, p. 2f.
9 John Macmurray, *The Self as Agent* (Faber and Faber, 195/).
10 H. H. Rex, *Did Jesus Rise from the Dead?* (Blackwood and Janet Paul, 1967), p. 75.
11 Lloyd Geering, *God in the New World* (Hodder and Stoughton, 1968).
12 E. M. Blaiklock, *Layman's Answer* (Hodder and Stoughton, 1968).
13 G. S. Hendry, *The Holy Spirit in Christian Theology* (S.C.M. Press, 1957), p. 12.
14 *Proceedings of the General Assembly of the Presbyterian Church of New Zealand*, 1966, p. 406a.
15 Ibid.
16 Ibid.
17 Article on "Priesthood of all Believers" in Fontana's *A Handbook of Christian Theology*.
18 James Barr, *Biblical Words for Time* (S.C.M. Press, 1962), p. 162.
19 He might well join us in agreement with A. Flew's comment on R. M. Hare's 'blik' concept: "If Hare's religion really is a *blik*, involving no cosmological assertions about the nature and activities of a supposed personal creator, then surely he is not a Christian at all?" *New Essays in Philosophical Theology* (S.C.M. Press, 1955), p. 107.
20 *God and Secularity*, p. 20.

21 "Faith without works is dead", James 2:17. "In Christ Jesus nothing
counts but faith working through love", Gal. 5:6. "If anyone has
the world's goods and sees his brother in need, yet closes his heart
against him, how does God's love abide in him?" I John 3:17; etc.

Chapter 1: The Secular Presupposition

1 *Guide to the Debate About God,* pp. 13, 14.
2 Alan Richardson, *History Sacred and Profane* (S.C.M. Press, 1964),
p. 110.
3 Lesslie Newbigin, *Honest Religion for Secular Man* (S.C.M. Press,
1966), p. 8.
4 Paul van Buren, *The Secular Meaning of the Gospel* (S.C.M. Press,
1963), p. 83.
5 Ibid., p. 102. My italics.
6 Ibid., p. 85.
7 H. Cox, *The Secular City* (S.C.M. Press, 1965), pp. 20, 21.
8 *Time* magazine, March 11th, 1966.
9 Ibid.
10 *Guide to the Debate About God,* p. 56.
11 *God in the New World,* p. 70.
12 C. A. Coulson, *Science and Christian Belief* (1955; Fontana, 1958),
p. 57.
13 Ibid., p. 40.
14 R. E. D. Clark, *The Christian Stake in Science* (The Paternoster
Press, 1967), p. 45f.
15 C. S. Lewis, *Miracles* (Fontana, 1947), p. 75.
16 M. Polanyi, *Personal Knowledge* (Routledge and Kegan Paul, 1958),
p. 15f.
17 H. Meynell, *Sense, Nonsense and Christianity* (Sheed and Ward,
1964), p. 18.

Chapter 2: The Biblical Presupposition

1 J. M. Morrison, *Honesty and God* (St. Andrew Press, 1966), p. 42.
2 G. E. Wright, *God Who Acts* (S.C.M. Press, 1952), p. 11.
3 *History Sacred and Profane,* p. 134f.
4 G. E. Ladd, *The New Testament and Criticism* (Eerdmans, 1967),
p. 26.
5 *Jesus of Nazareth, Saviour and Lord,* edited by Carl F. H. Henry
(Eerdmans,1966), p. 246.
6 John Baillie, *The Idea of Revelation in Recent Thought* (O.U.P.),
p. 50.
7 *Theology as History* edited by J. M. Robinson (Harper and Row,
1967), p. 232.
8 T. F. Torrance, *Theology in Reconstruction* (S.C.M. Press, 1965),
p. 64.

9   R. Bultmann, *Primitive Christianity* (Fontana, 1956), p. 17, 18.

10 Ibid., p. 113.

11 John Baillie, *Natural Science and the Spiritual Life* (Oxford University Press, 1951), p. 20.

12 *Theology in Reconstruction*, pp. 272, 273.

13 J. B. Phillips, *Ring of Truth* (Hodder and Stoughton, 1967), p. 42.

14 Ibid., p. 43.

15 R. S. Barbour, *Scottish Journal of Theology*, September, 1967, p. 258.

16 Ibid., p. 263.

17 *Primitive Christianity*, p. 25. This contrast can be overstated, of course, as James Barr has pointed out in *The Semantics of Biblical Language* (Oxford University Press, 1961), p. 8f., and as is indicated by the opening words of the Book of Amos: "The words of Amos, which he *saw* concerning Israel ..." But it is basically valid.

18 *Theology in Reconstruction*, p. 19.

19 *Studies in Theology*, p. 2.

20 Wolfhart Pannenberg's comment on the concept of God as Creator of the world is interesting: "With C. F. von Weizsäcker, I accept not only the explanation of the red shift (Hubble effect) by reference to a finite beginning of our universe, but also the general validity of the law of entropy." *Theology as History*, p. 141f. note.

Chapter 3: The Acts of God in 'Secular Christianity' and Biblical Theology

1   A. E. Loen, *Secularisation* (S.C.M. Press, 1967), p. 8. Translated from German, 1965.

2   *The Secular Meaning of the Gospel*, p. 5.

3   Ibid., p. 44.

4   Ibid., p. 11.

5   Ibid., p. 100.

6   Ibid., p. 110.

7   Ibid., p. 148.

8   Ibid., p. 149.

9   Ibid., p. 177.

10 *The Secular City*, p. 73.

11 Ibid., p. 266.

12 Ibid., p. 256.

13 Ibid., p. 256f.

14 Ibid., p. 105.

15 Ibid., p. 126.

16 Ibid., p. 255.

17 R. Gregor Smith, *Secular Christianity* (Collins, 1966), p. 26.

18 Gerhard Ebeling, *The Nature of Faith* (1959), p. 90. Eng. trans. (Collins, 1961).

19 Gregor Smith, op. cit., p. 26.

20 Ibid., p. 117ff.

21 Ibid., p. 47.

22 Ibid., p. 82.
23 Ibid., p. 86.
24 Ibid., p. 83.
25 Ibid., p. 122.
26 Ibid., p. 124
27 Ibid., p. 119.
28 Ibid., p. 111.
29 Thomas J. J. Altizer, *The Gospel of Christian Atheism* (Collins, 1967), pp. 18, 26, 27, etc.
30 Ibid., p. 25.
31 Ibid., p. 23.
32 Ibid., p. 68.
33 Ibid., p. 89f.
34 *Guide to the Debate about God,* p. 93.
35 Ibid., p. 93.
36 Ibid., p. 94.
37 Helmut Gollwitzer, *The Existence of God as Confessed by Faith* (S.C.M. Press, 1965), trans. from German, 1964, p. 152.
38 cf. John Macmurray, *The Self as Agent,* p. 116. "All human knowledge is necessarily anthropomorphic for the simple reason that we are human beings."
39 *The Existence of God as Confessed by Faith,* p. 151.
40 Ibid., p. 163.
41 Quoted by Gollwitzer.
42 Martin Buber, *Kampf um Israel* (1933), p. 181f., quoted by Gollwitzer, op. cit., p. 161.

Chapter 4: Science and Human Action

1 J. Macmurray, *The Boundaries of Science* (Faber, 1939), p. 144f.
2 Ian T. Ramsey, *Religion and Science – Conflict and Synthesis* (S.P.C.K., 1964), p. 37f.
3 Ibid., p. 37.
4 Teilhard de Chardin, *The Phenomenon of Man* (Collins, 1959), pp. 56, 57.
5 *Personal Knowledge,* p. 9.
6 Ibid., p. 9.
7 Ibid., p. 142; see also pp. 77 (f/note), 153, 214, 262, 335 (f/note), 340, 380, etc.
8 Ibid., p. 340.
9 Reported by I. T. Ramsey, op cit., pp. 49-52.
10 *The Secular Meaning of the Gospel,* p. 194.
11 *Science and Christian Belief,* p. 93f.
12 Ibid., p. 138.
13 Ibid., pp. 95, 96.
14 Ibid., pp. 96, 97.

15 Ibid., p. 48f.
16 This same logical confusion is surprisingly prominent in I. G. Barbour's otherwise masterly book, *Issues in Science and Religion*. The approach using "complementary languages", he writes, "provides a way of acknowledging both the special characteristics of man and the findings of science, without reverting to dualism. Here *mind* and *brain* are not two separate entities, but the same set of events viewed from two perspectives – from within and from without." And he clearly assumes the unification of the subjective-objective distinction of mind-brain to be logically (or methodologically) analogous to the wholly objective dichotomy of living-nonliving entities. (*Issues in Science and Religion*, S.C.M. Press, 1966, p. 7 and 358f.) Prentice-Hall copyright 1966.

Chapter 5: Existentialist Theology and Action

1 John MacQuarrie, *An Existentialist Theology* (S.C.M. Press, 1955), p. 5. In the Foreword to MacQuarrie's book Bultmann himself writes: "I have seldom found so unprejudiced and penetrating an understanding of my intentions and my work as in this book." It can therefore be quoted with more confidence than can usually be given to such a commentary.
2 This matter is further discussed in Chapter 10.
3 *Guide to the Debate About God*, pp. 56, 57.
4 Ibid., p. 59.
5 *An Existentialist Theology*, p. 168.
6 D. Jenkins, *Guide to the Debate About God*, p. 60.
7 *An Existentialist Theology*, p. 181.
8 *Guide to the Debate About God*, p. 62.
9 R. Bultmann, "Is Exegesis Without Presuppositions Possible?" in *Existence and Faith* edited by S. M. Ogden (Meridan Books, 1960), p. 291f.
10 *History Sacred and Profane*, p. 143. My italics.

Chapter 6: Linguistic Theology and Action

1 *Sense, Nonsense and Christianity*, p. 265.
2 Ibid., p. 1.
3 *The Secular Meaning of the Gospel*, p. 87.
4 Ronald Hepburn, *Christianity and Paradox* (Watts, 1958), p. 17.
5 *Proceedings of the Aristotelian Society*, Supt. Vol. 17, 1938.
6 The degree of violence done to language and to reason by talking of 'acts without an agent' – as so many theologians seem willing to do today – is apparent from these considerations.
7 I. T. Ramsey, "Miracles, an Exercise in Logical Mapwork", a lecture given in 1951 and included in the S.P.C.K. volume, *The Miracles and the Resurrection* (1964).

8   Ibid., p. 8.
9   Ibid., p. 16.
10 Ibid., p. 16.
11 Ibid., p. 17.
12 Ibid., p. 18.
13 Ibid., p. 19.
14 *Religion and Science,* p. 39f.
15 *The Miracles and the Resurrection,* p. 21.
16 Ibid., p. 25.
17 Ibid., p. 26.
18 I. T. Ramsey, *Religious Language* (S.C.M. Press, 1957).
19 Ibid., p. 38.
20 Ibid., p. 144.
21 Ibid., p. 145.
22 Ibid., pp. 147 and 150.
23 Ibid., p. 146.
24 John Locke, *An Essay Concerning Human Understanding* (1690), Book LV, xvii, 4.
25 Francis Schaeffer, *Escape From Reason* (Inter-Varsity Fellowship, 1968), p. 64.
26 Ibid., p. 21.
27 Francis Schaeffer, *The God Who is There* (Hodder and Stoughton, 1968), p. 21.
28 Ibid., p. 21.
29 Ibid., p. 20.
30 Ibid., p. 20.
31 *Escape from Reason,* p. 35. My italics.
32 Ibid., p. 44.
33 *The God Who is There,* p. 44.
34 Ibid., p. 47
35 Ibid., p. 80.
36 *The Self as Agent,* p. 32.
37 Ibid., p. 33.
38 Ibid., p. 33.
39 Ibid., p. 34.
40 Ibid., p. 37.
41 Ibid., p. 86f.

Chapter 7: History and Action – on a Secular Base

1   *History Sacred and Profane,* p. 57.
2   *Existence and Faith,* p. 291.
3   Ibid., p. 127.
4   Daniel Fuller, *Easter Faith and History* (Eerdmans, 1965 and Tyndale Press, 1968), p. 69.
5   Ibid., p. 68.

6 Martin Kähler, *Der sogenannte historische Jesus und der geschicht-liche, biblische Christus* 2nd edition (1898) edited by Wolf (1956), quoted by D. Fuller, ibid., p. 71.
7 F. Gogarten, *Demythologising and History* German Edn. (1953), Eng. Trans. (S.C.M. Press, 1955).
8 Ibid., p. 64.
9 Broadcast talk on the B.B.C. published in *The Listener,* December, 1965. Dr. Mascall makes the same point in his book *The Secularisa-tion of Christianity* (Darton, Longman and Todd, 1964), p. 84f.
10 Carl Henry, *Frontiers in Modern Theology* (1964); (Moody Press Forum Books, 1966), p. 50.
11 G. W. H. Lampe and D. M. McKinnon, *The Resurrection* (Mowbrays, 1966).
12 Ibid., p. 29.
13 *The New Testament and Criticism,* p. 15.
14 Ibid., p. 183. My italics.
15 Ibid., p. 191.
16 Ibid., p. 186.
17 J. Moltmann, *Theology of Hope,* German Edn. (1965), Eng. Trans. S.C.M. Press, 1967).
18 cf. *Theology of Hope,* p. 226, for example.
19 Ibid., pp. 172-182.
20 Ibid., p. 172ff.
21 Ibid., p. 102.
22 Ibid., p. 103.
23 Ibid., p. 103.
24 Ibid., p. 103.
25 Ibid., p. 103.
26 Ibid., p. 83, my italics; cf. also pp. 21 and 172.
27 Ibid., p. 22.
28 Ibid., p. 16, my italics.
29 Ibid., p. 112.
30 Ibid., p. 109.
31 Ibid., p. 16.
32 H. Berkhof, *Christ the Meaning of History* (1962); (S.C.M. Press, 1966), p. 32.
33 Some may think it strange that the name of Karl Barth should in this way be linked together with those of Bultmann and the others here. Carl Henry, from a slightly different angle, supports the propriety of this. "So many and so great are the differences among the dialectical and existential theologians of our generation that should any effort be made to combine them into a single formula, one might expect an immediate disclaimer from almost all quarters. When one notes the variance between Barth and Bultmann, for example, and Barth's increasing inclusion through the years of more and more 'objectifying' elements to escape an existentialised 'Gospel', it might seem inaccurate indeed to view the whole dia-lectical-existential development as a theological monstrosity that rejects objective revelation. But a simple test will justify classifying

239

both the dialectical and the existential schemes in this way. However much theology stresses 'objectifying' elements, the determinative question is whether or not it views divine revelation as objectively given in historical events and in intelligible concepts and words. While the dialectical-existential theologians differ from one another at many secondary levels, they all agree in respect to this ruling notion of the non-objectivity of divine revelation." cf. Carl Henry, op. cit., p. 82.

34 *History Sacred and Profane,* p. 134.
35 A. D. Ritchie, *Civilisation, Science and Religion* (Pelican Books, 1945), p. 27.
36 *The Secular Meaning of the Gospel,* p. 194.
37 Ibid., p. 110.

Chapter 8: History and Action – Towards a Better Foundation

1   In *Encyclopaedia Britannica.*
2   Ibid.
3   *History Sacred and Profane,* p. 160ff.
4   Ibid., p. 172.
5   *Honest Religion for Secular Man,* p. 103.
6   From the commentary written for a film-strip series on "The Spread of Christianity".
7   Alan Richardson, *History Sacred and Profane,* p. 193, quoting from Carl Becker.
8   Ibid., p. 208.
9   Oscar Cullmann, *Christ and Time,* German Edn. (1946), Eng. trans. (S.C.M. Press, 1951).
10 Ibid., Foreword.
11 Oscar Cullmann, *Salvation in History,* German Edn. (1965), Eng. trans. (S.C.M. Press, 1967), pp. 44-47.
12 Ibid., p. 16.
13 Ibid., p. 277 and cf. p. 16.
14 Ibid., p. 16.
15 Ibid., p. 96.
16 Ibid., pp. 94, 96.
17 Ibid., p. 16.
18 Ibid., p. 24, my italics.
19 Ibid., pp. 70, 134, 142, 322.
20 Ibid., p. 166.
21 Ibid., pp. 21, 42, 51-53, 59, 65-74, 114-122, 192, 211, 321-327.
22 Ibid., p. 65.
23 *Christ and Time,* p. 21.
24 *Salvation in History,* p. 148.
25 Ibid., p. 151.
26 Ibid., p. 153.
27 Ibid., p. 78.

28 Ibid., p. 155.
29 Ibid., p. 154.
30 Ibid., p. 166.
31 *Theology as History.*
32 *Salvation in History,* p. 57f.
33 *Theology as History,* p. 220.
34 D. P. Fuller, *Scottish Journal of Theology,* June, 1966, "A New German Theological Movement", p. 169.
35 Op. cit., p. 242.
36 Ibid., p. 126f.
37 Ibid., pp. 247, 248, note.
38 cf. ibid., pp. 226, 231 note, 236, 239, etc.
39 Ibid., p. 253.
40 *Scottish Journal of Theology,* June, 1966, "A New German Theological Movement", p. 171.
41 *Theology as History,* p. 262, note.
42 Ibid., p. 239.
43 Ibid., p. 131.
44 Ibid., p. 272.
45 Ibid., p. 161.
46 Ibid., p. 238.

Chapter 9: The Supernatural and Action – 'Miracles'

1 *Theology as History,* p. 32 note.
2 Ibid., p. 32 note, my italics.
3 Max Lerner, article on "Liberalism" in *Encyclopaedia Britannica.*
4 See the article, "The Supernatural in Reformed Theology" by the present writer in *Scottish Journal of Theology,* June, 1967, also "Reformed Theology and the Supernatural" in *Colloquium – The Australian and New Zealand Theological Review,* May, 1967.
5 *Learning for Living* – November, 1966.
6 *God in the New World,* p. 63f.
7 *Personal Knowledge,* pp. 142, 159, 214, 262, 263, 340, 380, etc.
8 *Theology as History,* p. 32 note.
9 "From the middle of the 19th century, probability gradually gained ground as a part of physical theory," writes G. H. von Wright. "It first appeared in the theory of heat. J. C. Maxwell in 1860 deduced the familiar gas laws from underlying probabilities for the distributions of positions and velocities over the molecules. Ludwig Boltzmann (1877) interpreted the irreversibility of thermal processes as a tendency toward a most probable distribution of the energies of the molecules. The rise of quantum mechanics saw the theory of radiation put on a probability basis by Max Planck (1900). With the further development of quantum physics, probability invaded atomic theory. By the middle of the twentieth century the deterministic view of nature was thought in some quarters to be in process

Q

of being replaced by a probabilistic view. The concept of probability had become one of the fundamental notions of a modern science and philosophy of nature." Article on 'Probability' in *Encycl. Brit.*

10 *Sense, Nonsense and Christianity,* p. 203f.
11 Alan Richardson, *A Theological Word Book of the Bible* (S.C.M. Press, 1950), article on "Miracle".
12 *The Bible in the Age of Science,* p. 127.
13 Alan Richardson, *The Miracle Stories of the Gospel* (S.C.M. Press, 1941).
14 Op. cit., article on "Miracles".
15 As I have argued elsewhere – *Scottish Journal of Theology,* op. cit.
16 *Christianity Today,* in a letter (1967) to the present writer.
17 *History Sacred and Profane,* p. 188.
18 Charles Hodge, *Systematic Theology,* Vol. I (Thos. Nelson, 1883). My italics.
19 Ibid., p. 623.
20 Ibid., p. 623.
21 Ibid., p. 621.
22 Ibid., p. 624.
23 *Personal Knowledge,* p. 142.
24 Ibid., p. 380.
25 *Religion and Science,* p. 36.

Chapter 10: Subject, Object and Action

1 "The human *differentia* we have decided is not the capacity to think, but the capacity to act." John Macmurray, *Persons in Relation* (Faber and Faber, 1961), p. 26.
2 *Demythologising and History,* p. 57.
3 Ibid., p. 56.
4 Ibid., p. 58.
5 James Brown, *Subject and Object in Modern Theology* (S.C.M. Press, 1953), p. 59.
6 This remains true despite the fact that this distinction, which, says Brown, "we have seen is properly at home ... as epistemology, is elevated ... into an ontology" by Karl Barth. Ibid., p. 190.
7 Ibid., p. 59.
8 Ibid., p. 20, quoting from *Biographia Literaria.*
9 Ibid., p. 117.
10 The separation from God and others that comes through moral disobedience is of course another thing.
11 Ibid., p. 120.
12 *Religion and Science,* p. 60.
13 Ibid., p. 40.
14 Ibid., p. 57.
15 The structure of Ramsey's thought here presents an 'ontological' parallel with what he has said in his analysis of religious language

(which we have already criticised) where he speaks of religious language as *"object* language and more", rather than regarding scientific, objective language as "the language of living communication *less* something" – language minus its normal subjective reference. In *Religion and Science,* he insists that the fact that man is not only object but also subject presents us with a situation "whose understanding demands everything that any and every scientific account can give, yet which *also goes further* and demands a distinctive concept of the human personality." (p. 43). Again, "man is his scientific observable behaviour *and more."* (p. 64, his italics).

If we accept the point of view from which it is expressed, this is very true and important. The subjective 'something more' about man, which science cannot deal with (and which the consistent secular man therefore rejects) is indicated by Ramsey in terms of "acts of will". An act of will, he says, is "an ontological peculiar which, while displaying itself in spatio-temporal behaviour is not limited to the behaviour it displays in this way." (p. 57). Just how, as subjective act, it can become or cause an objective event, he does not try to tell. But what cannot be denied, he insists, (unless we blunder into objectifying the subject) is that "in certain cases of decision, at the moment of decision, *we know ourselves active* in a way which transcends all that a scientific story, however complex, might talk of." (p. 57, my italics). Now the crucial question is whether it is not necessary for us in the light of this, to challenge the 'given primacy' of science, which must regard action – the immediately known and undeniably real *differentia* of man-as-person – as an "ontological peculiar" whose reality cannot be consistently acknowledged: as we have already challenged the primacy of "object language", to which "something more" must be added to make possible any adequate reference to action, or to persons who act? Does not this evidence indicate a need to go back to the foundations of our thinking, to find presuppositions that freely acknowledge the reality of purposeful, personal action; and then to declare 'science' and 'object language' – though very important – to be essentially limited and biased aspects of a wider and deeper range of human knowledge than can be encompassed by 'objectivity' alone?

16   Ibid., p. 105.

17   *Existence and Faith,* "Is Exegesis with presuppositions possible?", p. 193. For Moltmann also this matter is of importance. "This cleavage into objectification and subjectivity," he writes, "is not to be escaped – nor can theology escape it in bringing the gospel to the modern world, by declaring one side of this kind of thinking to be vain, deficient, corrupt and decadent. Rather theology will have to take the hardened antitheses and make them fluid once more, to mediate in the contradiction between them and reconcile them. That, however, is only possible when the category of history, which drops out in this dualism, is rediscovered in such a way that it does not deny the antithesis in question, but spans it and understands it as an element in an advancing process." (*The Theology of Hope,*

p. 50). Very true – but only by *action,* and therefore only in 'real time', or duration lived and not thought, can this spanning be done – (see below p. 192f.). It is certainly not logically possible in 'the future', which is the time of history as Moltmann conceives it, and which we have already briefly discussed.

18 John Macmurray touches on this question of language and objectivity when discussing the genesis of thought in infants (from which analogical application may be made with regard both to its origins in the human race and its structure in the life of mature adults today). "So soon as the infant can perceive at all," he writes, "its perception is a perception of the Other and therefore knowledge, however minimal. There is no problem of how an originally subjective experience becomes objective. If there were it would be insoluble. The idea that there is such a problem arises from the assumption that language is essential to knowledge. What is essential to knowledge is *communication,* of which language is the most important but not the only medium ... Communication is for all human beings a fact before it becomes an act, before explicit perception and the formation of intention is possible for us. The reference to the Other, of which the objectivity of thought is a particular case, is present from the beginning." *Persons in Relation,* p. 76.

19 *Personal Knowledge,* p. 15f.

20 Ibid., p. 17.

21 Ibid., pp. 141, 142, 264, 380.

22 Ibid., p. 14.

23 Ibid., p. 15.

24 Quoted by C. A. Coulson, *Science and Christian Belief,* p. 67f.

25 *Personal Knowledge,* p. 48.

26 Henri Bergson, *Time and Free Will,* French edn. (1889), Eng. Trans. (George Allen and Unwin, 1910), p. 115.

27 Ibid., p. 139.

28 Ibid., p. 191.

29 Ibid., p. 221.

30 Ibid., p. 230.

31 Ibid., p. 235.

32 *The Self as Agent,* Introductory, p. 11f.

33 Ibid., p. 13.

34 Ibid., pp. 19, 20.

35 *Persons in Relation,* p. 66f.

36 Ibid., p. 154f.

37 L. G. Geering in *God in the New World,* Chapter 1 and p. 70.

38 *Persons in Relation,* p. 169, my italics.

39 The sub-title of Polanyi's book *Personal Knowledge,* "Towards a Post-Critical Philosophy". This points to a much more adequate name for the age we are entering, from the Christian point of view, than the name 'post-Christian age' which has already become dear to the 'Secular Christians' and others.

Notes

Chapter 11: Time, Eternity and God who Acts _ Some Modern Views

1 *Christ and Time*, p. 62.
2 Ibid., pp. 23, 24, his italics.
3 Ibid., p. 69, note.
4 Ibid., p. 49.
5 *The Theology of Hope*, p. 126.
6 Ibid., p. 50.
7 *The Self as Agent*, p. 131f. and especially p. 133.
8 Ibid., p. 16.
9 *Theology as History*, J. M. Buss, pp. 137, 138; K. Grobel, pp. 173-75; Wm. Hamilton, pp. 190-92; J. B. Cobb, pp. 197-220.
10 Ibid., p. 219.
11 Ibid., p. 191f.
12 Ibid., p. 175.
13 Ibid., p. 266.
14 Ibid., p. 267, note.
15 *Theology as History*, p. 74.
16 *Primitive Christianity*, p. 25.
17 *The Self as Agent*, pp. 131, 132. Both time and space are, of course, necessary for movement, and so for real actions and events. (Grobel's concept of an event in time but not in space seems therefore quite irrational, unless he means a purely 'subjective event', whatever sort of abstraction that may be). Also, both the past (as the source of reflective concepts for purposeful thought) and the future (as the locus of the purposes or intentions which are integral to action) are necessary for the reality of action in the dynamic enduring present which is 'real time', so different from the objectified, spatialised time which thought builds out of the concepts derived from visual experience. Similarly *faith*, rooted in God's acts in the past, and *hope*, anticipating the shape of God's future, are essential to the Christian life of *love*. But love belongs essentially in the living present of action; only here can we meet the Agent-God who *is* love, and in this living, moving present our time joins the eternity of God's time. 'Heaven' is action, movement, personal communion in a life free from the restrictions of space as we know it.
18 *Theology as History*, p. 128f.
19 Thus, for example, when William Hamilton, one of the 'Death of God' theologians, writes in *The New Essence of Christianity* (p. 116 note): "The empty tomb tradition, at least, seems to me to contain historical material of a high degree of probability"; or when J. A. T. Robinson, in *But That I Can't Believe* declares, "I myself find the evidence for the empty tomb very compelling: I find it difficult to get away from the fact that the tomb was found empty" – (p. 13) – we may then ask what better historical explanation they can give for this fact than that God acted to empty the tomb in the miraculous

way affirmed in the New Testament? And in the absence of some better explanation, which can account more adequately for all the known facts, must not the denial of the biblical explanation be classed not only as 'unbelief' but as dogmatic and prejudiced irrationality, based on a blind faith in the truth of the 'secular presupposition'?

20 *Christ and Time*, pp. 62, 63.

21 *Church Dogmatics*, Vol II, Part 1 (Eng. Trans. T. & T. Clark, 1957), p. 608f.

22 Ibid., p. 608f. my italics.

23 cf. Donald Baillie, *God Was in Christ*, Chap. 6, "The Meaning of the Doctrine of the Trinity". Former students of his will recognise here echoes of his teaching.

Conclusion: A Call for Integrity

1 Although *psychologically*, the primary emphasis of Schaeffer's 'Fundamentalist' faith is undoubtedly the reality of the dynamic, personal God-who-acts, yet *logically* his basic presupposition is the truth of the Bible, conceived as an error-free propositional revelation. "God has spoken," he writes, "in a linguistic propositional form, truth concerning Himself and truth concerning man, history and the universe. Here is an adequate basis for the unity of knowledge." (*The God Who Is There*, p. 93). Rational thinking, Schaeffer believes, involves the simple application of the logic of antithesis upon this basis, and therefore requires the unambiguous exclusion, as error, of whatever conflicts with any of the propositions of Scripture. He considers that the failure of modern theologians to use logic in this way and on this basis is proof of their dialectically warped irrationality, and that the 'Fundamentalist' position is the truly rational one.

Our criticism of this approach to truth, in the light of our study of the concepts of 'action' and 'agent' in theology, would be that it is in fact foredoomed to irrationality! For the static, propositional form of the base which it presupposes and on which it builds, together with the abstract, mathematical form of the logic to which it is self-restricted, make it logically impossible that it should ever be able to include rationally within its 'world-view' the dynamic, personal reality of God or His acts in history (which form the base and main contents of the world-view we have outlined). From such a starting point, and using only such thought-patterns, God and action must always remain inevitably as 'surds' beyond the rational limits of that system of truth. It is therefore logically impossible that a comprehensive "unity of knowledge" should ever be constructed on the base-presupposition and thought-forms of the 'Fundamentalist' position, as advocated by Schaeffer.

One recalls the words of Jesus to the Jews: "You search the

scriptures, because you think that in them you have eternal life; and it is they that bear witness to me; yet you refuse to come to *me,* that you may have life." (John 5:39, 40). Only by presupposing (or accepting by faith) the living, personal Agent-God Himself, rather than the error-free truth of the Bible, can we provide an adequate base on which to build a comprehensive and rational unity of all knowledge: and only by using a concrete dialectical logic, patterned to 'the form of the personal', can this project be rationally executed.

Such a logical form, as has already been pointed out, (pp. 87-89) contains within itself and continues to employ the simpler logical forms such as these dialectical patterns used for thinking 'biologically', and also the basic mathematical, 'straight-line' forms appropriate to thought about 'things' and to formal relations between propositions.

Speech, of course, is a specialised form of personal action: and propositions are a deposit of speech. Within a logical system that can rationally recognise the possibility of a Speaker, as a personal Agent (which of course requires a logic of personal dialectic), there is no great logical problem about accepting and assessing (with the logic of antithesis) the rationality and truth of a deposit of fixed propositions. But the logical direction cannot be reversed here without running into irrationality.

We must agree, I believe, that *psychologically,* in terms of our learning processes, etc., the Bible both has and must be recognised as having first place. Only through the Bible, ultimately, can we today come to learn about and believe in the living God. Within a world-view, therefore, that has already presupposed and is founded upon the reality of the Agent-God of biblical faith, and in which the logical forms of the personal are accepted for thought, the Bible must be accorded primary importance – 'Sola Scriptura!' Thus in the constitutional definitions of many Churches the Bible is properly named as "the Supreme Standard of Faith and life". But it can be properly accepted and interpreted as such only in terms of the Living Word, who said "I *am* the Truth", and who today is mediated to us through the Holy Spirit, as God active now in the world.

2 Let me confess here that I am very conscious, while writing thus of the need for the Church to think clearly and with integrity, and to deny and exclude error as well as affirming the truth, that I myself am at present unable to accept the doctrine of the omniscience of God with regard to the future actions of human persons, as individuals. It seems to me that by creating man 'in His own image', God conferred upon man a sort of freedom and a responsibility for action which necessarily preclude the possibility that He should foreknow with certainty what any man in his freedom will in fact choose to do. In the creation of man, therefore, as in the Incarnation, God in some measure 'emptied' Himself and accepted certain self-limitations, which are the necessary complement of the personal powers given to man. As omnipotent, God could of course eliminate man and again

know all things: but the existence of other 'personal agents' is impossible without His self-limitation in this matter. It is the rejection of the concept of timeless eternity that has closed to me the escape-route normally taken by theologians when faced with the problem as to how God's foreknowledge is compatible with man's freedom. It therefore happens that as a consequence of my intense conviction that the fundamental presupposition of the Bible is simply and supremely true – God, as living personal Agent created man in His own image for fellowship with Himself – I am unable to accept the traditional doctrine of the omniscience of God with respect to my own and any other particular man's actions in the future. In this I am trying to be faithful to the Bible as I understand it. But if my Church were to declare (perhaps at someone's request for a decision in the matter) that in this respect the doctrine of God's omniscience is to be regarded as 'fundamental doctrine' in terms of the Ordina-tion Vows I took, then I sincerely believe I would have the integrity to resign my office as a minister, and would honour the Church all the more highly for fulfilling her God-given responsibility and speaking up for truth as she sees it.

3 *The Existence of God as Confessed by Faith,* p. 225.
4 *Honesty and God,* p. 16.
5 Ibid., p. 5.
6 *Theology in Reconstruction,* p. 271.
7 *The Secularisation of Christianity,* pp. 7, 282.

Subject Index

Action, Passim, especially, 13f, 18f, 23f, 30, 33f, 44, 48f, 58, 69, 72f, 77f, 82f, 88, 93f, 98f, 101f, 105f, 114f, 120, 133, 140f, 146f, 152, 154f, 159f, 168f, 173, 178, 181, 193, 195f, 202f, 243;
  as neutral common ground between secular and biblical views, 163;
  as differentia of persons, 15, 72, 120, 181, 242;
  as key to rational world-view, 15, 33, 232;
  as thinking, decision, 21, 94f, 243;
  as purposeful, intentional, 20, 22, 30, 44, 48, 51, 77, 82, 86, 97, 114, 140, 150;
  as 'state' of relation, 69

Acts, 'I act, therefore I am (agent)'; Macmurray's formula, 20, 22, 120, 200, 209;
  of God, 13–16, 24, 28, 48f, 62, 63f, 94f, 100, 110, 114f, 129, 146, 150;
    in history, 20, 25, 49f, 94f, 121, 123ff, 146f, 157f, 162ff, 180, 202, 209, 245f, 246f;
    in nature and history, 45f, 49f, 60, 63f, 78, 81, 96, 110, 123, 136, 162, 164f, 174;
    as miracles (see 'miracles'), 20, 51, 60, 61, 168ff;
    as social change (see 'social change'), 14f, 65f;

  acts and events—see 'events and acts';
  of Man, 13f, 18f, 33, 65, 73, 77ff, 96f, 114f, 139ff, 150;
  as basic units of world-view, 14, 33, 63, 78, 96, 148, 154, 156, 177, 178, 194f
Agent, God as, 14, 15, 19, 25, 30, 48, 49, 62, 63, 67, 70ff, 114, 133, 148, 157, 168f, 171, 177, 201, 203, 209, 247;
  Man as, 15, 18, 19, 21, 25, 72, 80, 83, 85, 118, 120f, 173, 186f, 191, 194f;
  Personal, 62, 70f, 110, 120, 140, 163, 194f
Ambiguity, 29, 30f, 61f, 64, 107, 126ff, 165f, 169, 179f, 215f, 219f, 229f
Analogy, 14, 18, 20, 43, 71, 113, 124, 146, 169, 211, 244
Anthropomorphism, 71f
Ascension, 56f
Atheism, 52, 70, 133, 197, 220

Biblical criticism, 26f, 68, 123ff, 134, 142, 150, 160f
Biology, 85, 119, 246f
Blik, 32, 105, 233

Christianity (Christian),
  biblicak, 15, 31, 54f, 57f, 78, 97, 126, 202f, 215, 231, 246f;
  conservative, 18, 29, 64, 117, 128f, 130, 133, 162, 174f, 222, 246f;

evangelical, 13, 115, 130, 218;
liberal, 18, 60, 92, 124f, 128, 142, 160;
secular, 18, 30f, 37ff, 61ff, 78, 89, 102, 126, 128f, 132, 146, 166, 201, 215f, 226, 228f
Church, 15, 25f, 31f, 38, 64, 68, 126, 131, 174, 202f, 230f
Common-sense, 17, 18, 19, 21, 24, 29, 33, 87, 97, 99, 101, 110, 114, 126, 141, 142, 146, 148, 155, 156, 161, 172, 187, 203, 220
Complementarity, Principle of, 84ff, 237
Cosmology, cosmos, 23f, 33, 39f, 50ff, 63, 79, 104, 113f; (see also 'Diagrams', 'World-views')
Creation, 30, 33, 48, 51f, 59f, 65f, 72f, 105, 125, 162, 169, 173, 176f, 204, (see also 'God—as Creator')
Creeds, 142, 217f, 226
Apostles' Creed, 224
Nicene Creed, 217
Critical Philosophy, 15, 18, 20f, 26, 27, 133, 201, 203f, 217;
Post-critical, 203, 211, 216, 244

Determinism, Passim, especially, 22, 44f, 77ff, 90, 93ff, 114, 123f, 130f, 170, 185, 241
Diagrams of 'world-views';
scientific, 40;
'secular Christian', 46;
primitive biblical, 55;
modern biblical, 61;
references in text, 43, 53ff, 211, 215, 229
Disclosures, 113f
Dualism, 19, 21, 28, 45, 65, 70, 85, 111, 115, 122f, 148f, 160, 163

Eternity (eternal), 14, 25, 147, 202ff, 211
Events (and Acts), 23, 44, 46, 49, 63, 66, 69, 77, 84, 86, 95, 99f, 129, 140, 147ff, 155ff, 162f, 176f, 194;

supernatural events, 165f, 171, 178f;
'vertical' events, 150f;
contingent events, 155f;
events as basic units of world-view, 44, 63, 77, 88f, 113, 154, 155f, 176f
Existentialism, 17, 50, 67f, 89ff, 103, 113, 128, 130, 140, 141, 145, 147, 150ff, 182ff, 194, 239f
Exodus, 174
Red Sea Crossing, 172, 174

Faith, 26, 29, 33, 61, 71, 103, 114, 131, 134, 215, 217, 222f;
biblical, 19, 31f, 48f, 59, 150f, 157, 161, 216f, 229f, 246f;
the Christ of, 68, 96, 98, 124;
leap of, 85;
secular, 22, 38, 45, 61f, 245;
The Faith, 30, 32, 56, 60, 90, 128, 130, 134, 135, 160, 206, 216, 218, 222f
Fall, the story of the, 184
Freedom, 17, 19, 21f, 24, 52, 70f, 77f, 81f, 93f, 100, 104, 108, 113f, 135f, 140, 156, 173, 181f, 203, 204, 210, 212;
for decision, 90f, 94f, 96f
Fundamentalism, 45, 60, 246f

Gap, 82, 97, 149
God, Passim: 'God who acts', 25, 28, 32, 33, 49, 53, 64, 66, 69, 70, 134, 147, 163f, 197, 201, 204, 232, 246f;
and Being, 32, 67ff, 104, 148, 172, 181f;
as Creator, 22, 23, 25, 30, 32, 33, 45, 48, 51, 52f, 59ff, 114, 125, 162f, 171, 181, 197, 220, 229;
as Object, 71, 104, 113, 148;
as Personal, 15, 18, 30, 32, 45, 48f, 54, 63, 64, 71f, 114, 129, 162, 163, 181, 209, 231f;
as Process, 14, 66f, 70;
as Redeemer, 25, 129;
as Saviour, 57;

Subject Index

as Subject, 16, 18, 25, 157, 206, 216, 220;
as Supernatural (see 'Supernatural'), 33, 45, 50, 54, 56, 60, 65, 67, 94, 125, 157f, 163ff, 167f, 171, 181, 209, 216, 217, 241;
as Trinity, 25, 30, 211, 246;
and time, 202ff, 247f;
and the world, 31f, 45, 50ff, 71f, 162ff;
death of, 13–26 passim, 45, 133, 177, 180, 222;
(see also 'Agent, God as')
Greek thought-forms, 28, 50ff, 58f, 130, 147, 156, 203

Hearing, 58f, 207
Heaven, 31, 32, 45, 47, 53, 54, 57, 60, 64, 245
Hebrew thought-forms, 28, 50f, 58f, 147, 172
Heresies, 31, 60, 219ff, 222, 229, 230
Historiography, 99f, 122f, 127ff, 139f, 145
History, Passim, especially, 14, 20, 64f, 94ff, 110f, 121, 122ff, 181ff;
and action, 19, 95, 100f, 121, 135f, 146, 154, 160, 163, 181f;
biblical, 147f, 152, 202f, 209;
as closed system, 99f, 122f, 131
Communist, 145;
Existentialism and, 67f, 94ff, 145, 182f;
God and, (see 'Acts of God in history');
Jesus of, 67ff, 95f, 124f;
modern concept of, 139f, 145, 182
and promise, 130, 132f;
and process, 39, 156;
and revelation, 48f, 51, 60, 123, 129, 153f, 157f, 203, 207, 239f;
salvation history (Heilsgeschichte), 126, 134, 148, 152f;
secular, 64f, 129, 132, 135, 144, 145, 153;

and subject-object, 98f, 112f, 140ff, 151f, 182ff;
supra-history, 123ff, 130, 134, 160
Holy Spirit, 25, 26, 27, 28, 30, 176, 211, 232, 247
Hope, 245
theology of, 130ff, 204

Idealism, 69, 115, 118, 119, 130, 141, 145, 155f, 182, 183, 187, 208, 209
Images (Imagination), 25, 41ff, 53ff, 71f, 210f
Incarnation, 25, 46, 70, 95, 247
Indeterminacy, Principle of, 170
Integrity, 15, 20, 31, 83, 180, 215ff, 231

Jesus Christ, 25, 26, 27, 30, 46, 48, 49, 54, 65, 67, 68, 71, 95f, 123, 125f, 127f, 131, 146, 208, 209, 234

Knowledge, 14, 37f, 41ff, 82f, 91f, 97f, 101f, 105f, 141, 182f, 187, 188f, 208f, 220;
intuitive, 21f, 108f, 141f, 192, 195;
personal, 23f, 49, 51f, 57, 98, 119f, 199f;
scientific, empirical, 16f, 22, 37, 41f, 78f, 82f, 89ff, 97f, 118f, 189ff, 195;
theological, 18, 20, 26f, 33f, 57f, 71f, 94f, 110f, 197, 199f, 208f

Language, etc., 21, 28, 58f, 64, 78, 102, 103ff, 110, 123f, 129f, 147f, 151, 163, 174f, 184, 192f, 195, 216;
anthropomorphic, 71f;
different 'levels' of, 108f;
living, 106, 113, 187, 210;
objectifying, 64, 71, 106, 108, 112f, 184;
scientific, 78f, 106, 112f;
theological, 14f, 58f, 65, 66f, 71f, 91f, 108ff, 129f, 151, 162, 163, 179, 217f, 246f
Layman, 26, 28

251

Logic, 19, 33, 88, 93, 98, 101, 103ff, 114, 135, 151, 156, 163, 183, 185, 187, 196, 219f, 246;
boundaries of, 108, 110;
dialectical, 115, 117f, 208, 219f, 246f;
observational, 109f;
relational, mathematical, 107, 118f, 246;
traditional (of antithesis), 107, 114ff, 141, 219, 246f

Logical Positivists, 103

Love, 45f, 210, 234

Man, human, 46, 69, 77, 187, 220;
as 'machine', 24, 30, 80, 81f, 135, 168, 177, 181;
as object, observed, 77f, 81f, 140;
as person, 18, 23, 44, 83, 87, 173 (see also 'Personal, impersonal');
secular, 22, 37f, 43, 44, 50, 78, 80;
death of, 19, 22, 24, 47

Metaphysics, 17, 39, 67, 78, 86, 125, 131, 150, 157, 182

Mind, 20f, 80ff, 115, 181

Miracles, 15, 20, 46, 51, 60, 61, 81, 100, 101. 105, 108, 110f, 161, 162ff (see also 'Acts of God —as miracles')

Missions, 144

Nature (natural), 22, 32, 37, 45, 49, 51f, 78f, 101, 124, 158, 160, 162ff;
biblical view of, 49, 51, 59, 60, 166;
as closed continuum, 41, 165f, 172;
Laws of, 41, 45, 50, 77, 92, 139, 162ff;
mechanistic view of, 164f, 168;
mediaeval view of, 49, 52f, 164f;
modern view of, 51f, 60f, 165f, 169f;
Reformation view of, 49, 52, 165;
secular view of, 45f;
Thomist view of, 165

'New Theology', 18, 26, 55

Object (objective, objectify), 17ff, 44f, 50, 58, 63f, 69, 71f, 77ff, 90ff, 106f, 115, 126f, 140f, 148, 151f, 159f, 181ff, 197f, 210, 215, 217, 239

Omniscience, 204, 247f

Ontology (ontological), 32, 38, 48, 79, 102, 104, 125f, 160, 242f

Organism, 119

Pantheism, 163

Paradox, 104, 210

Pentecostalists, 26, 211f

Personal, impersonal, 15, 23, 30, 51, 59, 63, 72, 80f, 87, 93f, 112ff, 139f, 146, 150f, 156, 172, 178f, 181ff, 196ff, 217

Positivism, 37, 100, 122f, 131, 134, 145, 152, 157

Presuppositions, 20, 50, 92, 115, 144, 146, 147, 148, 151, 163, 188, 208f, 219, 246;
action,-accepting, 24, 30, 33, 101, 111, 114, 136, 139f, 146, 196f, 201, 202f, 209;
biblical, 28, 33, 48, 49, 55, 63, 69, 73, 111, 146, 148, 151, 203, 247;
Critical, 18, 201, 208;
Existentialist, 91, 92, 98, 102, 128;
historical, 99, 136;
positivist, 136, 139, 142, 145f, 149, 157;
scientific, 19, 30, 73, 78f, 109, 166, 185, 188, 200;
secular, 22, 37, 38, 43f, 45, 63, 69, 71, 80, 83, 87, 104, 111, 114, 128, 135, 139f, 145, 146, 180, 185, 189, 200

Priesthood, 26f;
of all believers, 28f

Probability, Theory of, 170, 241f

Process, 70, 156f

Psychology, psychological, 47, 51, 77f, 81f, 120, 166, 198f, 208, 221, 246f

Quantum Physics, 43, 241

Reconciliation, 65f, 109

Reformation, 26, 27, 28, 49, 52

Relativity, Principle of, 42f, 170

Resurrection, 45, 51f
    of Jesus, 13, 25, 30, 47, 56, 57,
        64, 70, 95, 127f, 130f, 145,
        172, 206, 208, 245f;
    Empty Tomb, 172, 245

Revelation, 13, 16, 25, 28, 32, 33, 41,
        45f, 48f, 51, 60, 67f, 71f, 129,
        146ff, 150, 154f, 159, 172,
        199, 200, 204, 246

Revolution, 14, 15, 20
    historical, 122, 131, 182;
    scientific, 164

Science (scientific), Passim, especially,
        14, 16f, 22, 29, 32, 38, 41f,
        44f, 60, 73, 77ff, 89ff, 93,
        117, 122, 124, 131, 133, 139,
        164, 169f, 171, 188ff, 215,
        218, 241f
    boundaries of, 32, 77f, 82, 86f,
        97, 97f, 101, 110, 173, 188;
    empirical methods of, 16, 37ff,
        46, 63, 64, 77ff, 91f, 97, 103,
        109, 122, 125, 135, 200;
    imagination in, 41f, 139f, 189ff,
        211;
    objectivity of, 16ff, 21, 23, 30,
        44, 50, 77ff, 87, 90, 93, 113,
        118, 136, 139f, 173, 181, 185,
        188ff;
    origins of, 51, 218f

Scientist, 22, 37, 40f, 44, 143, 165,
        169

Secular, Passim, especially, 16, 29f,
        37ff, 64, 83, 87, 111, 135,
        215;
    age, 24, 37;
    attitude, outlook, 18, 22, 32, 37f,
        39, 43f, 44f, 65f, 78, 80f, 89,
        102, 105, 140, 143f, 166f,
        197f

Secularisation, 38, 39, 63

Secularism (secularist), 16, 38, 39,
        143, 216
    (see also, 'Christianity', 'Man',
        'Presupposition', etc.)

Secularity, 32f, 38

Seeing, 20f, 58f, 97, 207, 235

Self, as Object, 81f, 192;
    as Thinking Subject, 17ff, 30, 94,
        99, 119f, 152, 159, 163, 170,
        183, 194, 200, 203, 220;
    'I think, therefore I am (thinking
        subject)' — Descartes'
        formula, 16, 20, 116, 120,
        149, 183, 200, 209

Social Change, 14, 15, 29f, 66, 211;
    sociology, 120

Space, 40f, 43, 56f, 83, 192f, 206, 211;
    time, 20, 42, 57, 60, 193f, 206ff

Speech, as action, 66, 94f, 247

Subject/Object distinction, 16ff, 28, 44,
        50, 52, 63, 77f, 85ff, 90ff, 97f,
        102, 106, 108f, 111, 113, 118f,
        125, 140, 151f, 160, 179,
        181ff, 192f, 200f, 208f, 242,
        244
    (see also 'God—as Subject')

Subjectivity (subjective), 17f, 21, 68,
        77, 90ff, 105, 110, 113, 126ff,
        131

Substance, 118

Supernatural, 33, 45, 50, 65, 80, 94,
        100, 101, 114, 124f, 131, 157f,
        160, 162ff, 181, 209, 230, 241
    (see also 'God—as Supernatural')

Theological Education, 26, 127

Thinking (thought), 16, 18f, 21f, 38,
        42ff, 50ff, 53, 56, 59, 109,
        114, 115f, 116ff, 157, 192ff,
        219f, 246f
    as action, 21, 98;
    as negative activity, 120;
    and imagination, 42ff, 53f, 56;
    'primitive', 50ff, 111, 117, 184;
    (see also 'Logic', and 'Know-
        ledge')

Time, 42, 119, 131ff, 147f, 158f,
        192ff, 202ff, 231f;
    duration (real time), 192ff, 210;
    linear time (spatialised), 192ff,
        202ff

Truth and Error, 28, 30f, 50, 80, 82f,
        87, 103ff, 111, 116f, 126f,

135, 136, 145f, 151f, 179f,
184, 203, 208f, 211, 215ff,
243f, 246f

World-Views,
  biblical (primitive), 54f;
  biblical (modern), 15, 30, 31, 32,
    49, 53f, 57ff, 63, 163f, 202f,
    210f, 215, 246f, 229, 232,
    245;
  closed, 39, 41, 44, 58, 91f, 92, 99f,
    164f, 215;
  comprehensive, 13, 18, 29, 87,
    102, 215;
  fundamentalist, 246f;
  Greek, 51, 58, 156;
  Hebrew, 51f, 130, 207;
  historical, 99, 123, 125f, 131f,
    139f, 145, 205;
  linguistic, 107f, 110, 114, 118ff;

  mechanical, 164f, 168;
  metaphysical, 17, 39, 125f;
  mythological, 23, 55, 64, 92, 131;
  New World, 29f, 199, 200, 201,
    202, 231f;
  personalist, 20, 113, 119f, 169,
    181f, 187, 192, 200, 211,
    215, 229, 232, 246f;
  scientific, 20, 22, 23, 29, 33, 39ff,
    56, 59, 80, 91f, 131, 215;
  secular, 18, 22, 23f, 30, 37, 80, 87,
    135, 185;
  'Secular Christian', 30, 32, 46f,
    60f, 63ff, 87, 163, 167f, 215,
    229, 231;
  relativity of world-views, 39, 60,
    215;
  unity of world-views, 20, 39, 41,
    51, 111, 125f, 156f, 160f, 231

Index of Names

Acton, Lord J. E. E. D., 142
Altizer, T. J. J., 69f
Apostles' Creed, 224
Aquinas, Thomas, 165
Aristotle, 112, 114, 117, 141, 183,
  195, 196
Arius, 229
Augustine, 172, 175
Ayer, A. J., 103

Baillie, D. M., 170
Baillie, John, 49, 51
Barbour, I. G., 237n
Barbour, R. S., 57
Barmen, The Theological Declaration of, 218
Barr, James, 28, 235n
Barth, Karl, 60, 123, 134, 141, 142,
  150, 154, 179, 180, 209f, 239f,
  242n

Becker, Carl, 145 (240n)
Beethoven, L. von, 81
Berdyaev, N., 17
Bergson, H., 191f, 203
Berkeley, Bishop G., 183
Berkhoff, H., 134
Bevan, E., 43
Bianchi, E. C., 222
Billings, A. R., 165f, 169
Blaikie, R. J., 165n, 175n
Blaiklock, E. M., 23, 29
Bohr, N., 84, 190
Boltzmann, L., 241f, n
Bonhoeffer, D., 197
Born, Max, 189
Braithwaite, R. B., 105
Brown, James, 183f, 242n
Brunner, E., 123, 134, 141, 154
Buber, Martin, 73, 151, 184
Bultmann, R., 50f, 54, 58, 64, 68,

90f, 103, 123, 134, 141, 142, 147f, 165, 182, 184f, 207, 237n, 239f, n
Buren, P. van, 38, 64f, 83, 102, 104, 105, 108, 127, 135, 177, 231
Burke, E., 142
Buss, M. J., 245n

Campbell, N. R., 190
Camus, A., 66
Christianity Today, 14, 130, 175, 233
Clark, R. E. D., 43 (234n)
Cobb, J. B., 155, 206, 245n
Coleridge, S. T., 142, 183
Collingwood, R. G., 139, 144, 151, 187
Comte, A., 119
Copernicus, 11, 56, 57, 201
Coulson, C. A., 42f, 84f, 190
Cox, Harvey, 39, 41, 66f
Croce, B., 139, 151, 187
Cullmann, O., 147ff, 155, 157f, 161, 202f, 209

Darwin, C. R., 57, 81
de Broglie, Prince, 84
Denney, James, 18, 59
Descartes, R., 16, 20, 22, 23, 24, 116, 120, 149, 151, 183, 193, 196, 197, 200, 201, 208, 220f, 231
Dickie, E. P., 230
Dilthey, W., 139, 151, 187
Dorling, J., 81

Ebeling, G., 67
Einstein, A., 11, 43

Fichter, J., 222
Flew, A. G. N., 32n, 104
Foster, John, 144
Freud, S., 198
Fuller, D., 123f, 156, 158

Galileo, 11, 57, 201
Gardiner, P. L. G., 139
Geering, L. G., 11, 23, 29, 41, 54, 166f, 169, 199n
Geneva Conference on Social Revolution, 13
German Evangelical Church, 218

Gill, T. A., 27
Gogarten, F., 50, 91, 125, 141, 151, 152, 165, 182, 184f
Gollwitzer, H., 71f, 230
Goster, T. H., 55
Grobel, K., 159, 206, 245n
Guizot, M., 176

Hamilton, Wm., 206, 245n
Hampshire, S., 11
Hare, R. M., 32n (233), 105
Hegel, G. W. F., 69, 112, 116f, 130, 133
Heidegger, M., 92, 125, 151
Hendry, G. S., 25
Henry, Carl F. H., 13, 29, 127, 234n, 239f, n
Hepburn, R., 104
Hinchelwood, Sir Cyril, 190
Hodge, Charles, 176f
Hort, F. J. A., 142
Hume, David, 80, 149, 162, 175, 183

International Missionary Council, 37

Jacobi, H., 73
Jenkins, David, 17, 37, 41, 70, 91f

Kähler, M., 123, 160f
Kant, Immanuel, 16, 17, 20, 22, 45, 73, 87, 116, 149, 157, 183, 191, 193f, 195, 196, 201, 205, 208, 231
Kantzer, K. S., 49
Keats, J., 190
Kepler, J., 81
Kierkegaard, S., 17, 116, 119
Klein, G., 207

Ladd, G. E., 49, 128f, 134
Lampe, G. W. H., 127
Lerner, Max, 164n, 165
Lessing, G. E., 206
Lewis, C. S., 43
Lightfoot, J. B., 142
Locke, John, 80, 114, 116, 149, 183
Loen, A. E., 63
Lorenz, K. Z., 81
Lunn, Sir Arnold, 170f

Macaulay, Lord T. B., 142
McCulloch-Pitts theory, 81
McKinnon, D. M., 239
Macmurray, John, 19, 77, 106f, 115, 118f, 141, 195ff, 205, 209, 236n, 242n, 244n
Macquarrie, J., 17, 32, 89f
Marcion, 150, 229
Mascall, E. L., 127, 231
Maxwell, J. C., 241f,n
Mead, Margaret, 29
Meynell, Hugo, 45 (n234), 103f, 170
Michelangelo, 23
Molière, 141
Moltmann, J., 129f, 158, 204f, 243f,n
Morrison, J. M., 48, 230
Munby, Denys, 14

Napoleon (Bonaparte), 144
Neitzsche, F., 133
Newbigin, L., 37, 144
Newton, Sir Isaac, 11, 57, 164
Nicene Creed, 217
Nowell-Smith, P. H., 170

Ogden, S., 64, 237n
Ounsted, C., 77

Pannenberg, W., 49, 115, 147, 154ff, 162, 169, 180, 206f, 235n
Pelagius, 229
Phillips, J. B., 56
Pike, J. A., 222
Planck, Max, 84, 241f,n
Plato, 23, 73, 117
Polanyi, M., 44, 80f, 87, 98, 168, 178, 182, 188f, 244
Presbyterian Church of New Zealand, 26, 223f
Pythagoras, 196

Ramsey, Ian T., 7 184f, 200, 242f,n

Ramsey, Paul, 15
Ranke, L. von, 122, 182
Rex, H. H., 22
Richardson, Alan, 13, 37, 49, 100, 122f, 134, 136, 140, 142, 145, 161, 171f, 187
Ritchie, A. D., 135
Ritschl, A., 18, 142
Robinson, J. A. T., 27, 53f, 59, 230, 245f,n
Robinson, J. M., 154, 162, 169, 207, 234n, 241n
Russell, Bertrand, 112
Ryle, Gilbert, 84

Sadducees, 51
Scaer, D. P., 130
Schaeffer, F. A., 115f, 219f, 246f,n
Schleiermacher, F., 17, 91
Scottish Journal of Theology, 234, 241, 242
Shakespeare, W., 81
Shinn, R. L., 13
Sittler, J., 222
Smith, R. Gregor, 67f, 89

Teilhard de Chardin, P., 79, 156
Tillich, Paul, 17, 70f, 123, 134
Time Magazine, 39n, 40, 222
Torrance, T. F., 49, 52, 59, 207, 231

U.N.E.S.C.O., 144
United Presbyterian Church in the U.S.A., 218
Uppsala, W. C. C. Meeting 1968, 14, 29

Weiss, J., 124
Weizsäcker, C. F. von, 235n
Westcott, B. F., 142

, 241f,n